THE EVERYTHING® TRAVEL GUIDE TO IRELAND

Dear Reader,

We are truly grateful for the honor to have put together one of the best, clearest, and most fun travel guides covering the Republic of Ireland and Northern Ireland. We believe the material presented, covering all the best cities, ancient sites, hidden havens, and pastoral domains, will help you put together an unforgettable itinerary. Moreover, the tips, insights, and up-to-date travel information throughout will make you a true Ireland travel expert.

For us, Ireland has always had a magnetic draw. It is a nation of raw beauty and extraordinarily gracious people. Having visited routinely and traveled extensively, we have come to know the country on an intimate level that we hope shines through as you peruse each chapter. This text has been written to be more than *just* a guidebook; we aspire for it to be the perfect resource as you journey through one of the world's most amazing destinations.

"May good luck be with you wherever you go, and your blessings outnumber the shamrocks that grow"   's
Irish Blessing

Happy Travels,

Thomas Hollowe

and Katie Kelly E

Welcome to the EVERYTHING Series!

These handy, accessible books give you all you need to tackle a difficult project, gain a new hobby, or even brush up on something you learned back in school but have since forgotten. You can choose to read from cover to cover or just pick out information from our four useful boxes.

 Alerts

Urgent warnings

 Facts

Important snippets of information

 **Essentials**

Quick handy tips

 **Questions**

Answers to common questions

When you're done reading, you can finally say you know **EVERYTHING®**!

PUBLISHER Karen Cooper

DIRECTOR OF ACQUISITIONS AND INNOVATION Paula Munier

MANAGING EDITOR, EVERYTHING® SERIES Lisa Laing

COPY CHIEF Casey Ebert

ACQUISITIONS EDITOR Lisa Laing

DEVELOPMENT EDITOR Brett Palana-Shanahan

EDITORIAL ASSISTANT Hillary Thompson

EVERYTHING® SERIES COVER DESIGNER Erin Alexander

LAYOUT DESIGNERS Colleen Cunningham, Elisabeth Lariviere, Ashley Vierra, Denise Wallace

Visit the entire Everything® series at *www.everything.com*

THE
EVERYTHING®
TRAVEL GUIDE
TO IRELAND

From Dublin to Galway and
Cork to Donegal—a complete
guide to the Emerald Isle

Thomas Hollowell
and Katie Kelly Bell

Avon, Massachusetts

This travel guide is dedicated to all those discovering
for the first time or rediscovering again the
enchanting allure of the Emerald Isle.
—TH

To David, who knows the way.
—KKB

An Everything® Series Book.
Everything® and everything.com® are registered trademarks of F+W Media, Inc.

Published by Adams Media, a division of F+W Media, Inc.
57 Littlefield Street, Avon, MA 02322 U.S.A.

www.adamsmedia.com

ISBN 10: 1-60550-167-0
ISBN 13: 978-1-60550-167-3

Printed in the United States of America.

10 9 8 7 6

Library of Congress Cataloging-in-Publication Data
is available from the publisher.

This publication is designed to provide accurate and authoritative information
with regard to the subject matter covered. It is sold with the understanding that
the publisher is not engaged in rendering legal, accounting, or other professional
advice. If legal advice or other expert assistance is required, the services of a com-
petent professional person should be sought.

—From a *Declaration of Principles* jointly adopted by a Committee of the
American Bar Association and a Committee of Publishers and Associations

Many of the designations used by manufacturers and sellers to distinguish their
products are claimed as trademarks. Where those designations appear in this
book and Adams Media was aware of a trademark claim, the designations have
been printed with initial capital letters.

Maps created by Map Resources

This book is available at quantity discounts for bulk purchases.
For information, please call 1-800-289-0963.

Acknowledgments

We would like to wholeheartedly thank all of those involved in putting together this extensive guidebook. Thank you to our agent Mr. Bob Diforio for your resourceful and responsive manner, along with your willingness to let us bounce ideas your way. Thank you Ms. Lisa Laing, the Managing Editor of the Everything Series, for your communication and editing prowess throughout the writing process. And, thanks to the team at Adams Media for all your work throughout. Without such astute professionals, quality publications would never materialize.

Thanks to my loved ones for their support and reading through the manuscript in its initial stages.

—TH

Grá mor to my Irish aunties and uncles and Papa Doc for making Ireland my home.

—KKB

Top Ten Ways
to Pass as Irish

1. Wait approximately two minutes before sipping a Guinness, allowing it to settle completely.

2. Before enjoying a refreshing beverage with friendly pubbers, say slainte (pronounced "slawn-cha"), which means "to your health."

3. Venture to the local pub for some real trad (traditional/folk music) and craic (good times)!

4. Play golf in the rain. In fact, do anything in the rain.

5. Ramble about hill walking, especially on a sunny day.

6. Enjoy every morsel of a full Irish breakfast.

7. Ensure a potato-based food item accompanies every meal.

8. Handle the curvy roads like a racing pro.

9. Quote Joyce, Yeats, or take a risk and go Wilde!

10. Have a good joke and a good story to tell.

Contents

Introduction

The Irish will say they are closer to Boston than Brussels; their history is forever linked to North America and their dedicated interest in the happenings abroad show it. Likewise, Americans are closely connected to the people, history, and culture of Ireland. This bond dates back more than 150 years. Their having contributed directly to our own history and we to theirs, Ireland is more than an inspiring place to visit, it is a destination in which to revel, feel wholeheartedly welcome, and to hold dear.

Since more tourists visit the country than there are inhabitants, vacationers to the isle help support a certain portion of the livelihoods on the island. And, in no other European country will you find a people more welcoming and brimming with the warmest hospitality imaginable.

Like a Guinness that needs time to settle, so should you travel unhurriedly through Ireland. Give yourself occasions to absorb the unique world around. Enjoy a lovely walk about the countryside to discover moments no guidebook could muster. It might happen while meandering along a green pasture lit by the last mist-filled ray of the day, while talking with locals in a bustling pub, or witnessing country folk whispering into each other's ears. More than the monuments of yore and the awe-inspiring sea cliffs will these memories be etched into your mind.

The Everything® Travel Guide to Ireland is designed as a handy reference that can be enjoyed before, during, and after your travels. It is geared for seasoned and nonseasoned travelers, offering advice that is insightful, accessible, and chock-full of indispensable expertise that will be much like having a friendly local showing you around. Additionally, it is an invaluable travel resource for independent travelers, couples, honeymooners, families, small groups, golfers, outdoor enthusiasts, luxury seekers, and everyone in between.

One central goal of this guidebook has been to construct a vade mecum of sorts, containing a broad range of things to see and activities to do. Because of the diligent research and easy-to-use setup of this guide, each reader will discover her own momentous experiences that will make her travels personal and unique.

The opening chapters offer insightful details about traveling in Ireland, such as what to bring and what itinerary might work best for your interests. Following, specific counties are expanded upon, making it effortless to find information about particular spots or regions. Within these sections, not only are sites discussed in full, but also well-priced, quality restaurants and accommodations are thoughtfully reviewed. Finally, because Ireland lends itself to so much to see and do outdoors, this guide delves into a wide range of activities travelers can do alfresco. This includes an array of places to play golf, to go fishing, and to bird watch, along with an analysis of the best places to walk in the entire country.

Included in the guide is up-to-date information outlining the location, hours of operation, and prices of monuments and sites throughout Ireland. At the end of each chapter, meticulous detail is given on the best, quaintest, most affordable, and even most luxurious bed-and-breakfasts, guesthouses, self-catering lodges, and castles in each region. Additional details are highlighted throughout the book's whole; warnings to keep you safe, fascinating historical tidbits to keep you aware, and spotlighted activities not to miss are underlying elements that add substantially to the guide's polished feel and look.

Ireland is a small country with an abundance of rich history, proud culture, sublime natural wonders, and happening cities to keep any traveler satisfied. This book will assist you greatly whether you plan your entire route beforehand or wait until the plane lands to begin your adventure. Welcome to the Emerald Isle, a country of fairy tales where story and song enchant the land!

Ireland Counties

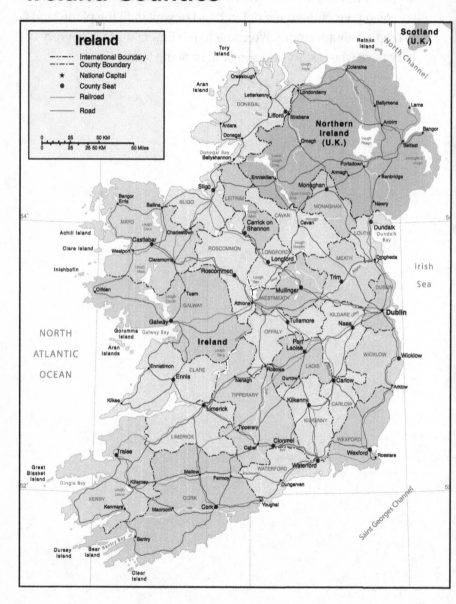

CHAPTER 1

Everything Ireland: An Overview

Encompassing all that makes the Emerald Isle exceptional is difficult to do in one book. By outlining and describing the various sites, both well known and hidden, travelers will have an array of choices to determine what they most want to see and do. As an introduction, this chapter is an overview deciphering Ireland's regions, environment, terrain, flora and fauna, weather, the best times to travel, holidays and festivals, its eco-friendly side, and the country's premier highlights.

Understanding Ireland's Counties and Regions

At first glance, Ireland's makeup might seem overly complicated; however, after perusing a map, taking in the suggestions outlined in this book, and ultimately getting your feet wet in country, you will begin to distinguish the smorgasbord that is Ireland.

Politically, the Republic of Ireland and Northern Ireland are two separate entities. The Republic was partitioned in 1921 with the signing of the Anglo-Irish Treaty in London. This agreement came into full effect by royal decree the next year amidst the short-lived Irish Civil War. Northern Ireland remains a part of the United Kingdom, which is also made up of England, Wales, and

Scotland. The Republic of Ireland is always referred to as "Ireland" in conversation and sometimes in writing as "the Republic" (or ROI). In Gaelic, it is known as "Éire."

Jointly, the Republic of Ireland and Northern Ireland have thirty-two counties; the Republic has twenty-six, while Northern Ireland has six. Dublin is the capital of Ireland, while Belfast is the capital of Northern Ireland. Nearly 4.5 million reside in Ireland and 2 million in Northern Ireland.

Provincially speaking, Ireland is composed of four Gaelic-derived, cardinal regions. Those are Leinster (the east), Munster (the south), Connaught (the west), and Ulster (the north).

The counties of Ireland and their respective regions are:

- **Leinster is made up of twelve counties including:** Louth, Meath, Westmeath, Longford, Dublin, Kildare, Laois, Offaly, Carlow, Kilkenny, Wicklow, and Wexford.
- **Munster is constituted of six counties including:** Waterford, Cork, Kerry, Limerick, Tipperary, and Clare.
- **Connaught includes five counties:** Leitrum, Roscommon, Galway, Mayo, and Sligo.
- **Ulster includes:** Donegal, Monaghan, and Cavan in Ireland and all six counties in Northern Ireland, which are Derry, Fermanagh, Tyrone, Antrim, Armagh, and Down.

Ireland's Most Popular Regions

The most popular regions of the country are its hip cities, rugged outer edges, and inspirational isles. Since a greater part of the Republic's population is concentrated in and around Dublin, a lot of space remains to be explored. A drive one-hour south to Wicklow, west into Kildare, or north to the Mourne Mountains, for example, is a pastoral treat.

The South and Southwest

Everlasting is the popularity that Ireland's southern regions have earned with travelers. The medieval delight of Kilkenny and the quaintness of Kinsale and Kildare are the reveries of historic-city lovers. Unmatched ruggedness and natural wonders attract millions each year to the Ring of Kerry (Iveragh Peninsula) and Killarney National Park. Remote and awe-inspiring are the Beara and Dingle peninsulas, along with the Skellig and Blasket Islands.

 Alert

Those looking to get off the beaten path certainly will be able to do so. However, careful research should be done beforehand. The middle regions of Ireland are composed mostly of heath and bog land. This mushy terrain with bog pits (akin to quicksand), accompanied by extreme temperature variations, can ruin any outing for the underprepared.

The West

Easily entered via the Shannon Airport, this region of Ireland is as diverse and stunning as any other. The Gaelic tongue enchants while pure Irish hospitality delights. The most popular urban area is Galway City, filled with historical sites, as well as hip and young crowds. Not far away is the rolling, stark beauty of Connemara National Park and the peaceful stone walls lining the Aran Islands. Up the coast is County Mayo, where picturesque towns such as Cong and Clifden await discovery, while Achill Island's (accessible by car) rustic seascapes beckon exploration.

Moving North

Counties Sligo and Roscommon inspire poetry and art; just ask the Yeats brothers. Indelible are the moments journeying through a land that shaped their livelihoods. Along the coast are beaches with top surf spots, followed by Ireland's most-removed county, Donegal. With the Slieve League cliffs, Glenveagh National Park, Mount Errigal, and the timeless Inishowen Peninsula, Donegal is worth days of peregrination.

Northern Ireland

Historical walled-in Derry (or Londonderry) opens up a doorway into Northern Ireland's tumultuous past. The city presents a firsthand view of how far the entire north has evolved in peace. Northern Ireland proffers the Fermanagh Lakelands, the Giant's Causeway, the Glens of Antrim, Belfast, and the spectacular Mourne Mountains. Towns such as Enniskillen, Ballycastle, Cushedum, and Newcastle make perfect bases with the friendliest of folks.

Ireland's Environment

Ireland is a country whose environment is a part of its soul. Glaciers have cut its valleys and rain gives way to sunshine, bringing verdant pastures and sprouting forests. Torrentially swept cliffsides are witness to the apathetic currents of both wind and ocean. Ireland's environment is what makes the country appealing, diverse, and magnificent.

 Fact

About 300 million years ago, Ireland was not in its current position. The island was actually a desertlike mass in line with North Africa. With the shifting and movement of Earth's tectonic masses, Ireland drifted north. Over the subsequent 250 million years, it settled in its current position on the globe.

Measuring roughly 500km (310 miles) in length and 300km (185 miles) in width, Ireland is an astonishingly multifarious land where one lush valley is replaced with craggy landscape. Nowhere is this more apparent than in County Clare and the lunar landscape of the Burren. The area looks barren to the untrained eye, but a myriad of plants found nowhere else in Europe call the place home. Equally noted for their sublime perilousness are the nearby Cliffs of Moher, and to the north, the Slieve League of Donegal, followed by the gargantuan columns of the Giant's Causeway.

Geologically speaking, Ireland is a relatively flat island surrounded by a ring of mountains, the most prominent formations being in the southwest. Ranges vary from granite, limestone, and basalt, among other elements. A good portion of the plains is made up of swaths of bog, an acidic wetland of peat.

 Fact

Trees are not as abundant as they once were in Ireland; birch, beach, and oak once covered the rolling hills. The Killarney National Park is home to a wonderful oak forest. The Avondale Forest Park in Wicklow or the Castlewellan Forest Park in Down are both fine examples of working arboretums. In Cork City, Fota Island offers wonderful nature-based adventures.

Ireland's Mountains

Impressive in their own right, hiking Ireland's mountains is a worthwhile adventure. The highest peak is County Kerry's 1039m (3,409 feet) Carrantuohill, located in the Macgillycuddy's Reeks range. Other ranges of note are the Twelve Bens in the Maumturks range of Connemara, the Derryveagh Mountains and Bluestack Mountains of County Donegal, the Wicklow Mountains south of Dublin, and the Sperrin and Mourne Mountains in Northern Ireland.

Ireland's Bog Lands

Ireland's umber-colored quagmire regions make up over 20 percent of the country's landmass. The bog is viewable in the midlands and also in the hinterlands of Counties Kildare, Cork, and especially Counties Mayo and Donegal. In various regions, the peat is cut, dried, and burned in fires.

Ireland's Wildlife

Surprisingly, Ireland has an array of flora and fauna that makes it a true anomaly in Europe. Ireland's position makes it favorable for all sorts of plant varieties to exist, including the cliff-topping sea campion and the bog-loving water lobelia and bogbean that sprout lovely white flowers. Alpine, Arctic, and Mediterranean varieties thrive in the Burren.

Gardens throughout the country display the island's diversity to visitors. The most impressive are Mount Stewart House in Northern Ireland, National Botanic Gardens in Dublin, and the Mount Usher Gardens and Powerscourt Gardens, both in County Wicklow. Another impressive collection can be visited on Garnish Island (Ilnacullin), a microclimate hosting an exotic garden of ornamental plants in County Cork.

An assemblage of fauna abounds in Ireland. In the Aran Islands, for instance, gray seals call the Atlantic waters home. Otters can be observed in the rivers, lakes, and most often in the rocky surface waters along the coasts. For animals of the larger variety, red deer have been reintroduced into the Connemara National Park, are abundant in the Killarney National Park, and the Glenveagh National Park. Hill walking throughout the countryside, you are sure to spot rabbits, including the swift Irish hare, along with the occasional hedgehog.

The most popular form of animal spotting in Ireland is dedicated to bird watching. Most species migrate from Iceland, Greenland, Africa, and the Arctic. Both shearwaters and the scarce corn cake are feathered visitors, as well as puffins, whooper swans, and white-fronted geese (best seen in the Wexford Wildfowl Reserve).

Ireland's Seasons, Weather, and Tourism

The lush and verdant valleys of Ireland come at a price—rain, and lots of it. When planning a trip to Ireland, consider the best times of the year that will decrease your chances of getting showered upon day in and day out. While this is much easier said than done, prepare yourself for variant weather patterns by bringing garments you can layer, a daypack, and perhaps a sturdy travel umbrella.

 Essential

When traveling in Ireland, try to not let the weather put a damper on your day. A short drive to your next destination might mean clear blue skies. Weather can vary from one hour to the next. If the sky is falling, head to a nearby café or pub and wait out the worst of it. Before you know it, you will be energized to head back out.

The season you choose to travel can affect the type of experience you may have. In the summer, namely July and August, throngs of people visit the Republic for its oceanic temperatures, festivals, and long daylight hours. The warmest and longest days of the year are April through October; at the summer's peak, daylight extends from 6 A.M. to 10 P.M. Travelers who plan months ahead for this season will benefit greatly from the best-priced airfare, top room choices, and tickets to main attractions.

Traveling in the wintertime is feasible, but has some disadvantages. Days are shorter and can feel more rushed, as driving distances often takes longer than expected. Winter brings with it more rain, wind, and even snow to the higher elevations. The coldest months of the year are November through March; the true wintry months are December through February. More precipitation and colder temperatures occur in the west and throughout the northwest during this unpropitious time.

 Alert

Traveling during the week before Christmas and through the New Year is most difficult. A large number of restaurants, B&Bs, monuments, parks, and sites are closed for the holidays. It is the only time that Ireland truly shuts down. Planning your trip with this in mind will ensure you are able to see, visit, and enjoy the sites much more.

Ireland in the spring or fall might be the best option. The last few years have brought amazing fall weather, even better than summer. With less chances of rain, longer days, cheaper prices, sites in full operation, and activities still occurring, traveling on either side of the peak summer months will benefit you greatly. With regard to the weather, one maxim holds true: The only certainty is uncertainty.

Temperature and Precipitation

The eastern coastline of Ireland receives less rainfall than its western half. Dublin receives about half as much precipitation as some of its western counterparts, such as County Kerry. The southeast of Ireland is enviable by all other regions for its sunshiny days, even in the colder months.

In and around Dublin, expect summertime peak temperatures to range between 18°C (65°F) and 24°C (75°F) with lows between 6 and 10°C (mid-40s–50°F). In the winter, expect highs around 6°C (mid-40s°F) and lows hovering above freezing to 5°C (42°F). Although rain falls throughout the year, it does more so in December and January. The relative temperature scale also applies to Belfast in Northern Ireland, although it does get 10–20 percent more rain.

Cork and Galway have similar summertime temperatures as Ireland's capital city, but slightly warmer winter months. However, in December, January, and March, expect 30 percent more rain. In the fall, especially in October and November, twice as much rain falls in the western half of Ireland than in Dublin.

 Fact

The Irish understand both Fahrenheit and Celsius, as they do kilometers and miles. Ireland inherited the imperial system from England, and many of the older generation continue to relay temperatures and distance in it. Officially, the European Union conducts its measurements in the metric system.

Holidays and Festivals in Ireland

Ireland abounds in craic, that is, pure light-spirited fun in music and drink. With music venues around every corner and inviting pubs on each street, it is easy to recognize that locals know how to have a good time. In addition to the fond memories of lush green pastures, your other mental mementoes will be those special times reveling in local festivities.

Ireland acknowledges several national and public holidays throughout the year. On these days, banks are closed, as are most businesses. Christmas and Easter are the biggest holidays. While the dates of the Easter holiday vary, Good Friday is observed by most businesses. Take note that many Europeans travel during the week before Easter, so book accommodations and certain restaurants well in advance. For Christmas, closings from December 23 to after New Year's Day are common. Saint Patrick's Day is on March 17. Businesses shut down on Mondays if a holiday occurs on a weekend.

Bank holidays in Ireland are nationally observed days off work. Most tourist hot spots and weekend-only venues in the off-season are open with extended hours during these times. Bank holidays include the first Monday in May, June, August (last Monday in Northern Ireland during May and August), and the last Monday in October.

 Essential

For the most up-to-date information regarding festivals and events throughout Ireland, check out *www.discoverireland.ie* and in Northern Ireland, *www.discovernorthernireland.com*. For Dublin, visit *www.visitdublin.com*. Your best resource will be regional tourist offices carrying publications with the latest information on concerts, theater, music, film, art exhibitions, and more.

Winter Festivals

In the winter months: Dublin hosts the Temple Bar Irish Music and Culture Festival (*www.templebartrad.com*) in January. During the same month, the ever-popular Yeats Winter School (*www.yeats-sligo.com*) takes place in Sligo Town. The Six Nations Rugby Tournament takes place in Dublin from February to April every other Saturday. Saint Patrick's Day (*www.stpatricksday.ie*) is celebrated throughout the country in March, so come prepared for days of carnivals, sports, and parades.

Spring and Summer Festivals

The Pan Celtic Festival (*www.panceltic.ie*), generally held in Donegal in each April, includes dance, song, sports, and parades. Commencing in May, Temple Bar (*www.templebar.ie*) is the scene of free open-air performances in theater, music, dance, film, and art throughout the summer. In June, Dublin also hosts the Bloomsday Festival (AKA James Joyce's Festival; *www.jamesjoyce.ie*), honoring Leopold Bloom, the protagonist in *Ulysses*. In Kilkenny, the Cat Laughs Comedy Festival (*www.thecatlaughs.com*) runs in the same month. In July, the Galway Arts Festival (*www.galwayartsfestival.com*) and the Galway Races (*www.galwayraces.com*), also in September and October, bring Ireland's west into the limelight.

In August, the Kilkenny Arts Festival (*www.kilkennyarts.ie*) is an ever-popular gathering, while the acclaimed Puck Fair (*www.puckfair.ie*) sees a goat crowned monarch for three days of exuberant festivities in Killorglin, County Kerry. In the same region, the Rose of Tralee International Festival (*www.roseoftralee.ie*) is a weeklong event bringing a pageant, street performances, horse races, and more to this central town.

Fall Festivals

The Galway International Oyster Festival (*www.galwayoysterfest.com*) is a world-renowned event with lots of activity in the latter part of September. The Dublin Theatre Festival (*www.dublintheatrefestival.com*) in October is a two-week drama-lover's dream. Also in October, gourmets should head to the world-famous Kinsale International Gourmet Festival (*www.kinsalerestaurants.com/autumn.php*) and County Cork, which plays host to the Guinness Cork Jazz Festival (*www.corkjazzfestival.com*).

The Emerald Isle Goes Green

While the green movement is moving ahead full force in Europe, Ireland is still working hard to meet all of the protocols. While

Ireland's population does not warrant extreme environmental measures, every little bit helps. Because Ireland receives millions more tourists than it has inhabitants, visitors do have an impact on Ireland's overall environmental well-being.

Alert

Visitors to Ireland should be conscientious of their impact on the local environment. By choosing eco-friendly establishments and restaurants listed in this guide, you will see that going green does not mean sacrificing amenities. Visit Carbon Neutral Ireland (www .carbonneutralireland.com) for the latest information on your carbon footprint.

By making a choice to stay in small, locally run establishments, you are avoiding the bigger chain hotels that have not put the environment at the forefront of their planning. Additionally, choosing to bike or walk certain areas of the country (or while in smaller towns and cities) is one way to not only save money, but also reduce traffic and gas consumption. Sustainable Tourism Ireland (www.sustourism.ie) is a noteworthy website indexing various green businesses, adventure centers, hostels, hotels, cottages, and parks.

One area of environmental interest is the Green Box (www .greenbox.ie), a zone occupying parts of Ireland's upper west and Northern Ireland's southern regions. Surrounded by water on each side, the goal of the place is to establish a world-renowned eco-friendly tourist locality. The area boasts the Kingfisher Cycle Trail (www.cycletoursireland.com), outlines ecotourism breaks, outdoor activities, and eco-centers of learning. Another cool eco-project is the Village (www.thevillage.ie) in County Tipperary and is Ireland's premier project to join Europe's Eco-Village Network (www.gen-europe.org).

Ireland's Premier Highlights

Even if you have never visited the Emerald Isle, Ireland is a familiar place to travelers from the United States. With a heartfelt connection to its land, people, politics, literature, and history, a trip here brings these facets to life. Moreover, Ireland is a relatively easy country to travel within: Its people are hospitable, its food and accommodations top-notch, and its landscapes mesmerizing. Only driving on the opposite side of the road with Gaelic-only signs might make you feel like an outsider!

Following are certain places around the country that stand out from the rest due to their location, archaeological attractions, eco-friendliness, and allure, and for the accommodations and the proprietor's hospitality. Additional information about each attraction is highlighted in county-specific sections.

TOP ANCIENT SITES

1. **Newgrange, County Meath**

   Known as Brú na Bóinne, Newgrange is a stellar example of how much we do not know about the ancient world. It was constructed well before the pyramids of Egypt and is thought to be a passage grave of astral importance. Don't forget to sign up for the lottery for your chance to stand inside the grave during the winter solstice.

2. **Hill of Tara, County Meath**

   One of the most holy spots of ancient Ireland, the Hill of Tara became the changing of the guard, so to speak, for the high kings of Ireland. The visitor center does a great job of outlining how this transition took place.

3. **Glendalough, County Wicklow**

   This ancient site known as the "Glen of Two Lakes" was the stomping ground of Saint Kevin. Now a national park of prominent size, visitors from Dublin can arrive here in less than two hours to walk trails, examine the Round Tower, graveyard, and beehive hut called St. Kevin's Cell.

4. Rock of Cashel, County Tipperary

Whosoever held the seat of the Rock of Cashel, also known as St. Patrick's Rock, was considered the high king of Munster. A visit here takes onlookers through this prominent European medieval structure, a graveyard of high crosses, a stunning Gothic cathedral, and hidden tombs held within its depths.

5. Aran Islands, County Galway

This set of three islands is most often accessed from County Galway, but some travelers have luck on the Ferry from Doolin, County Clare. All of the islands have awe-inspiring ancient sites and offer wonderfully peaceful days of meandering the ancient stone walls. The Dún Aengus and Dún Dúchathair forts on Inishmor and O'Brien's Castle on Inisheer Island are the most historically significant attractions.

TOP NATURAL ANOMALIES

1. Skellig Islands, County Kerry

Best visited during the summer months, the Skellig Islands are a pair of UNESCO-protected islands that are only accessible after crossing the rough, maniacal ocean. The price paid is well worth it; Skellig Michael features early monastic settlements from the sixth century complete with beehive huts and ancient gardens.

2. Giant's Causeway, County Antrim

Undoubtedly the most talked about spot in Northern Ireland, the Giant's Causeway is one of Ireland's geographical marvels. Stone columns of basalt formed by volcanic eruptions and cut by the wind and sea jut out over Ireland's northern shore; local lore claims it was the seat of a great giant named Finn MacCool.

3. **Twelve Bens, County Galway**

   Located in the Lough Inagh Valley of the Connemara National Park, the Twelve Bens are a set of mountains on the edge of Kylemore Lake. Reachable from Letterfrack Village, the mountains offer wonderful walking opportunities; those with plenty of energy can walk all twelve in one day. The highest peak is 730 meters (2,395 feet).

4. **The Burren, County Clare**

   A landscape like no other, the Burren conceals within its crags some of Ireland's most diverse plant and animal species. It is a great destination for those seeking rare, exotic flora unseen anywhere else in the world. While the terrain is rough to walk, it is not overly mountainous and exploring the place on a walking daytrip is the best way to witness this marvelous rarity.

5. **Marble Arch Caves, County Fermanagh**

   A system of Europe's most renowned caves, the Marble Arch Caves have put County Fermanagh on the map for its great variety of stalagmites and stalactites. Entrance to the cave occurs with a boat ride on the River Cladagh. An arch formation along the trail outside the caves gives the caves their name.

TOP TOURISTY SPOTS

1. **Guinness Storehouse, Dublin**

   One of Dublin's highlights, the Guinness Storehouse is a seven-story fermentation plant turned visitor center extravaganza. With high-tech and snazzy audio-visual exhibits throughout, the pinnacle point is a visit to the Gravity Bar.

From this top vantage point, you will have wondrous views of Dublin as you down your pint.

2. **Bunratty Castle, Folk Park, and Medieval Banquet, County Clare**
Great for the kids or the big kid in us all, the Bunratty Castle and Folk Park top the list for family fun. The medieval banquet is the best in all of Ireland. With two scrumptious dinners served nightly, the jesters and fair maidens await. The Traditional Irish Night is another option gaining in popularity.

3. **Cliffs of Moher, County Clare**
With such an investment by the local and national government, the Cliffs of Moher and its Visitor Experience are akin to the Giant's Causeway in their absolute grandeur. The Atlantic Edge Exhibition is a hands-on discovery center that is best done before venturing outside to walk along the mind-boggling cliff's edge.

4. **Ulster American Folk Park, County Tyrone**
A wonderful place to explore the American and Irish connection, the Ulster American Folk Park brings Ireland's bygone days to life. Some of the structures, including a small cottage, were brought over from the United States. The summer is the best time to visit. Actors teach visitors about the past and festivals occur almost daily.

5. **Blarney Castle, County Cork**
Not an easy feat, climbing the stairs of the Blarney Castle to kiss the distinguished Blarney Stone is a worthwhile task. The parks and surrounding gardens are fun to explore for a couple of hours; it is also a great spot for a picnic lunch. With a true tourist feel, you might see more crowds here than anywhere else.

TOP HIDDEN SPOTS

1. **Mourne Mountains, County Down**

   Located on the outskirts of Newcastle, the Mourne Mountains are truly a gem in Northern Ireland. The jaw-dropping ocean views and outdoor pursuits, all less than two hours from Dublin, are going to make this place boom. Locals are pushing for the place to be recognized as Northern Ireland's only national park in order to protect its future.

2. **Burren Walk, County Clare**

   For independent travelers, the outlined "Caher Valley and Gleninagh Mountain" route described in the *Best Irish Walks*, edited by Joss Lynam, takes you into the Burren's heart and hinterlands. The trail starts out slightly confusing, but then connects to the Burren Way (national trail) before extending cliff side on an ancient walking path dubbed the Green Road.

3. **Inishbofin Island, County Galway**

   A short distance from the tip of Connemara, the lightly inhabited isle of Inishbofin ("Island of the White Cow") has some superb summertime pursuits, including scuba diving, snorkeling, and fishing. Much like the Aran Islands, biking certain parts of the island is a great way to intimately explore its historical significance.

4. **Dingle Peninsula, County Kerry**

   Smaller and more remote than the Ring of Kerry, the Dingle Peninsula is a rewarding step back in time. The town itself is small, but it has a scattering of top-notch dining choices. Driving, biking, or walking are all excellent ways to see the various sites. The Dingle Way walking trail combines outdoor adventure with a historical melting pot of ruins, ring forts, and ancient churches.

5. Yeats Country, County Sligo

Exploring these environs opens a door to bucolic discovery like no other. Find out what inspired the Yeats brothers in their arts. A circuitous route around the area also brings travelers to Rosses Point, followed by an occasion to venture to Innisfree, an island that inspired a poetry collection known as *The Rose*.

TOP FIVE TOWNS AND CITIES

1. Dublin

An ever-popular getaway full of life, great music, art, pubs, accommodations, and restaurants, Dublin is one of Europe's most admired cities. With loads of things to see and do, you might have to make a trip solely to explore this accessible and fun city.

2. Galway City

Exploring this city's divergent past on a walking tour is the best way to see all the sites in one day. The small town is jam-packed with things to see and do: museums, cathedrals, and ancient walls are at every turn. Enjoy rustic ocean views along Galway Bay and Salthill's promenade. Expect exceptional food, music, dance, drink, and a young crowd to keep the night lively.

3. Kinsale, County Cork

Located at the estuary of the Bantry River, this small town is one of Ireland's most appealing and the perfect base for sailing pursuits. With seaside views at every corner, colorful townhouses, and a harbor that inspires artists, Kinsale is home to fine dining, a wonderful ghost tour, and the quaintest B&Bs.

4. **Adare, County Limerick**

   Although the English heavily influenced Adare's design, it still holds to its appellation as "Ireland's Prettiest Village." While other villages and fishing hamlets are more off the beaten path, Adare's manicured state makes it a wonderful place to visit or to lay your hat for the night.

5. **Kenmare, County Kerry**

   A town overshadowed by Killarney, Kenmare is an attractive base from which to explore the Killarney National Park and Muckross House. The town itself exudes character and its center comes to life each evening with local song, dance, and great pints.

CHAPTER 2

Ireland Travel Essentials

Planning your trip to Ireland can be a fun and adventurous endeavor. Ireland's established tourist resources, the friendliness of the people, its online accessibility, and the fact that everyone speaks English all contribute to make the undertaking easier than ever. From simply getting to Ireland to navigating its attenuated roads, this chapter will give you the confidence to plan ahead. So, prepare yourself for the trip of a lifetime!

Getting to Ireland

Getting to Ireland has never been easier. Flights from the United States are available from major hubs, while the budget-flight market in the United Kingdom and Europe is saturated with good deals. For those who like to travel traditionally, ferries depart Britain for both Northern Ireland and the Republic.

Flying into Ireland

Most flights coming into Ireland arrive at the Dublin International Airport (01 814 1111, *www.dublin-airport.com*). The two other major airports are Cork Airport (021 431 3131, *www.corkairport.com*) and Shannon Airport (061 712 000, *www.shannon airport.com*).

From the United States, Aer Lingus (via American Airlines) (1 800 474 7424 U.S., 0818 365 000 in Ireland, *www.aerlingus.ie*) has numerous flights, including departures from Los Angeles, New York, Chicago, and Boston. Delta Airlines (1 800 241 4141 U.S., *www.delta.com*) and Continental Airlines (1 800 231 0856 U.S., *www.continental.com*) both fly into Ireland. Flying into Shannon Airport is a less stressful option if you do not want to explore Dublin.

You can also fly into Dublin from London on British Airways (*www.ba.com*), Aer Lingus (*see above*), Air France (*www.airfrance.com*), and the budget carrier Ryanair (*www.ryanair.com*).

Other budget carriers include Easy Jet (*www.easyjet.com*) during peak months and bmi baby (*www.bmibaby.com*), which have routes that include Cork, Dublin, along with Belfast International and Belfast City airports.

 Alert

During the summer, expect the highest rates for roundtrip flights to Ireland. The high travel season is July to September. Also, expect to pay higher prices during the Christmas season. This coupled with the fact that numerous monuments, sights, and accommodations are closed on both sides of Christmas and the New Year's holiday means it may not be an ideal time to take your dream trip. So, be sure to check ahead.

In Northern Ireland, flights arrive at and depart from the Belfast International Airport (+44 (0) 28 9448 4848, *www.belfastairport.com*) and the much closer Belfast City Airport (+44 (0) 28 9093 9093, *www.belfastcityairport.com*). British Airways (1 800 403 0882 U.S.) flies from London Heathrow to Belfast as does British Midlands (+44 (0) 870 607 0555, *www.flybmi.com*). Flights also arrive from Liverpool, Stansted, Bristol, and Glasgow. You can even fly into Derry from Stansted, Manchester, and Glasgow.

Ferries

Ferries arrive from Britain at the Dublin Ferry Port (01 855 2222) and at the Dún Laoghaire Ferry Port (01 842 8864). Irish Ferries (0818 300 400, *www.irishferries.ie*) travel from both Holyhead (Wales) and Pembroke (Wales) to Dublin and Rosslare (County Wexford) respectively. They also travel between Rosslare and Cherbourg (France).

Stena Line (01 204 7777, *www.stenaline.ie*) travels from Holyhead in Wales to Dún Laoghaire in Dublin. They also travel from Stranraer (Scotland) to Belfast (Northern Ireland). Additionally, they sail the popular Fishguard (Wales) to Rosslare route.

Brittany Ferries (021 427 7801, *www.brittany-ferries.com*) has a variety of departures. They sail from Roscoff (France) to the Ringaskiddy Ferryport in Cork. They also operate from Dublin to Holyhead along with scheduled times to Rosslare from Fishguard and Pembroke. They, along with Norse Merchant Ferries (0870 600 4321, *www.norsemerchant.com*), sail to Belfast as well. Norse Merchant Ferries has services to Liverpool (England), as does P&O Irish Sea Ferries (01 638 333, *www.poirishsea.com*), who also sail to Cairnryan (Scotland), Larne (County Antrim), Cherbourg, and Rosslare.

All the ports in Ireland have buses, taxis, or trains to various destinations, including city centers. In Dublin, Bus Éireann is available at the main port, while the Dublin Area Rapid Transit (DART) is next to the Dún Laoghaire port.

Train and Bus

Combined train/bus and sea tickets from Britain to Ireland are available at most train stations in Britain or at any National Express (+44 (0) 870 580 8080, *www.gobycoach.com*) office. Eurolines (+44 (0) 870 514 3219, *www.eurolines.ie*) and Ulsterbus (+44 (0) 28 9066 6630, *www.translink.co.uk*) are the most well known companies offering hundreds of destination choices.

Transport Options in Ireland

Getting around Ireland by train or bus is a great way to see the country's sights if you are traveling alone or if you want to base yourself in various cities. Otherwise, renting a car is the preferred way to see Ireland's finest, most-hidden sights, especially if you are traveling with your family.

For those wanting to see as much of Ireland as possible without having to drive, the following options are your best bet. While flying can be expensive and is quick, taking a train is the easiest and most efficient way to get from point A to B. Taking the bus is the slowest and cheapest option.

Flying

Flying intra-Ireland can be expensive but it is possible. Aer Arann (081 821 0210, *www.aerarann.com*) flies into Dublin, Donegal, Sligo, Waterford, Knock, Galway, Kerry, Cork, and Derry.

 Alert

Many buses and coaches are a "request-stop only" service. Therefore, be sure to wave down the bus as it approaches or else it may not stop. This is best done with your arm extended, palm out, and waving downward.

Train

Irish Rail (Ianród Éireann) (01 836 6222, or recorded timetable at 01 850 366 222, *www.irishrail.ie*) has service from all over the Republic and into Northern Ireland. Most trains spread out from Dublin to major cities and towns. In Dublin, Heuston Station serves trains going to the west and south (Waterford, Cork, Limerick, Galway, Westport). Pearse Station has trains to the southeast (Wicklow and Wexford). And, Connolly Station serves trains to the north (Sligo and into Northern Ireland: Belfast, Portrush, and Londonderry). Donegal has no train service. Eurorail (800 722 7151, *www.eurail.com*) offer deals should you be traveling throughout Europe and want to include Ireland (but not the United Kingdom or Northern Ireland) on your itinerary.

Bus

Bus Éireann (01 830 2222, *www.buseireann.ie*) runs routes all over Ireland, including some smaller towns. Fares are half the price of its rail counterpart. In Ireland, a "coach" serves long-distance routes, while a "bus" serves inner-city routes. Translink (+44 (0) 28 9066 6630, *www.nirailways.co.uk*; called "Citybus" in Belfast) connects all of Northern Ireland. Buses are by far the best way to explore the west coast and the northwest of the Republic if you do not have a car.

Traveling by bus and train around the Irish mainland is more relaxing than driving. Trains are nicely equipped; some have outlets you can plug your laptop or music device into. Trains and buses are rarely off schedule and take you through some of Ireland's most pastoral settings.

Reduced Rates

The Emerald Card (*www.translink.co.uk*) allows unlimited travel on buses, rail, and metro in Ireland and Northern Ireland for eight days (during a fifteen-day period) or for fifteen days (during a thirty-day period). An Irish Rover Ticket, which lasts three, eight, or fifteen days is a better deal and must also be used within a certain travel period. The Freedom of Northern Ireland Card is good for one, three (during an eight-day period), or seven consecutive days and is only valid in Northern Ireland. The BritRail plus Ireland (866 BritRail, *www.britrail.com*) rail pass is more expensive and is only worthwhile if you plan to visit Wales, Scotland, and/or England during your trip. Backpackers and budget travelers who don't mind being on the move should check out Paddy Wagon Tours

(01 823 0822, *www.paddywagontours.com*) for great deals on multiday journeys.

Driving in Ireland

Having a car will mean a great amount of freedom during your trip. Since driving is done on the left-hand side of the street (with the driver driving on the right side), it can be tricky to get used to for people from other countries. Following the guidelines and advice here will help you feel prepared and therefore more confident on the road.

Renting

During the higher travel seasons, it is best to book your rental car before you arrive in Ireland. Try to not rent a car during your time in Dublin until you are ready to set out from the city.

 Fact

Your U.S. driver's license is valid in Ireland and Northern Ireland. If you plan on driving in other European countries, it is recommended you obtain an international driver's permit from an AAA (*www.aaa.com*) office in your area. You will need to have two passport-size photos and a current U.S. driver's license to apply.

When searching online for a rental car, read the fine print. You will want unlimited mileage, and renting for seven or more consecutive days will save you a significant amount of money. To rent in Ireland, the person signing for the car will have to be at least twenty-one years old and under the age of seventy-five. Some rental agencies will not rent to drivers under twenty-five or over seventy, or will augment the price with high "under age" or "over age" fees. The cheapest rentals are smaller, manual cars. The lowest weekly rental will cost between €250 and €500. Add a minimum €150 to this amount for an automatic car. Add €75+ if you want to return the car to a different location (more if in another country, such as Northern Ireland or mainland Britain). Gas in Ireland is two to three times more expensive than in the United States.

Most rentals require some sort of deposit blocked (but not charged) on your credit card. Often, you can purchase a collision damage waiver (CDW) at the time of rental. Don't assume that insurance provided through your credit card carrier will cover you in Ireland. Call before your trip to check on the details.

Tips for Driving

Ireland competes with only a couple of other countries in having the highest accident rates in western Europe. If you are cautious and follow the rules, your trip will go without incident.

Here are some important steps to fully prepare for driving in Ireland:

- Learn some of the road signs. One good resource for this is Irish Car Rental (*www.irish-car-rental.com*), which also provides other information to aid your journey.
- Practice driving a manual car if possible. In Ireland, the pedals and steering wheel are on the right-hand side of the car, and you will need to shift with your left hand.
- Remember to stay on the left-hand side of the road at all times. Most rental cars have signs on the dashboard indicating that you should remain on the left-hand side.
- Buy a good driving map of Ireland. The Michelin Ireland map is superb.

- Try not to overcompensate by staying too close to the right or to the middle of the road. Most Irish roads are narrow.
- Give yourself an average travel speed of 60 km/hour (40 miles/hour).
- Don't be afraid to ask for directions.
- Each person in the car must wear a safety belt, and children under age twelve are not allowed to sit in the front seat. The use of mobile phones while driving is against the law.

The Republic of Ireland now has all of its signs in kilometers per hour. Northern Ireland, on the other hand, has its signs posted in miles per hour. Most cars label both speeds, so heed the limits accordingly. When you enter into Northern Ireland, you probably will not be aware of it as there are no border markers. The same rules and regulations apply for driving in Northern Ireland as in the Republic.

Roundabouts and Intersections

You will find roundabouts at most intersections. Traffic inside the roundabout has the right-of-way. As you merge into the roundabout, look right to ensure no one is coming, then continue in a clockwise pattern. If there are two lanes merging side-by-side into the roundabout, the outer lane tends to be for those taking the first left exit, while the inner lane is reserved for those taking the second, third, or even fourth exit. If you are taking the first left exit at a two-lane entrance, use your left turn signal to show your intention. If you are on the inner lane of this two-lane entrance, signal right to show your intention to enter the roundabout completely. Before you turn out of the roundabout, signal left.

Speed Limits

When driving, you might wonder where all the speed-limit signs have gone. Speed limits are "understood" in Ireland.

SPEED LIMITS IN IRELAND

Road Type	Example	Max KPH	Max MPH
In towns	Kinsale	40–50 kph	30 mph
Rural roads	R-255	80 kph	50 mph
National roads and divided highways	N-3	100 kph	60 mph
Motorways	M-50	120 kph	75 mph

Parking

Parking in Ireland can be a little confusing. One yellow line on the road means no parking during weekly business hours (Monday–Saturday). Double yellow lines signify no parking. And, broken yellow lines means that you can park for a short amount of time. For ease, it is best to find "Pay and Display" parking lots. Parking ticket machines do not give change. Getting clamped or towed will run €85–175 or more for the car to be released. You can purchase "parking disks" in local stores that you can use in specified parking areas all over the country.

 Essential

Parking in Dublin can be expensive, especially if you want to leave your vehicle overnight or for a twenty-four-hour period. Bigger hotels provide parking, but smaller ones or hostels will not. Ask if your hotel has any deals with local lots. In major cities, search for Q-Park (*www .q-park.ie*) deals, which can save you 50 percent or more off regular parking fares.

Types of Accommodations

Whether you will be spending your nights in the lap of luxury or counting pennies, the hospitality of the Irish is unmatched. No matter where you dine or slumber, you really cannot go wrong.

If you plan to explore Ireland during off-peak seasons you can easily find rooms each night without booking ahead. For those with a limited amount of time and/or budget, planning ahead by e-mailing or calling the establishments will ensure your rooms are booked each night.

Hotels

From regular hotels to luxury spas, the choice is really dependent upon your budget and taste. Bigger chain hotels will have more amenities; some are near golf courses, offer babysitting, live music or nightclubs, and indoor and outdoor sporting pursuits.

 Essential

With the bed-and-breakfast boom, seemingly anyone can become recognized by the Tourism Quality Services and published by the Irish Tourist Board called Fáilte Ireland. Associated and approved B&Bs display a green shamrock beside their outdoor sign verifying their membership.

Bigger chain hotels, such as Jury's Doyle (*www.jurysdoyle .com*) will offer luxury, but less in the way of cultural immersion, while more lavish establishments afford the opportunity to sojourn in palatial castles, classy manors, and swank lodges. Hotels in the Republic of Ireland are inspected and rated according to a five-star system, a rating of five being the most luxurious. Hotels in Northern Ireland are rated on a four-star system in the same manner.

County Houses

Country houses are establishments that do not offer the same amenities as bigger or more luxurious hotels. These houses offer their clients a more intimate experience and an opportunity to feel a part of Irish culture and history. Prices for these types of accommodations can at times compare with their five-star counterparts. The value and *real* feel of it all is worthwhile.

 Fact

Both Ireland and Northern Ireland refer to rooms with an adjoining bathroom as "en suite." While you do not need to say it with a French accent, be sure to ask for it if you desire your own bathroom inside your room. An "en suite" room does not necessarily mean a bathtub, but usually a shower.

Bed-and-Breakfasts

Lining streets of tourist areas throughout Ireland are bed-and-breakfasts. With no shortage, these places (and their hosts) each offer a unique experience. The idea behind a bed-and-breakfast is to experience Irish hospitality with the friendly locals at a price that cannot be beat. Rooms tend to be charming, but not overly luxurious. Scrumptious breakfasts are generally the highlight. Costs vary but average between €35 and 70 per person, depending on the season. Since most B&Bs are small, be sure to ask whether they accept major credit cards (usually MasterCard or Visa).

Guesthouses

If you're searching for something between a B&B and a country house, you may consider staying in guesthouses as well. Guesthouses are homes or manors that have been refashioned for travelers passing through for one or more nights. They and their hosts are often known for excellent evening meals and breakfasts. In the Republic of Ireland, guesthouses can be rated as high as four stars, while in Northern Ireland they are graded accordingly with an A or B appraisal.

Castles

The highlight of any stay in Ireland would be spending at least one night in a fabled castle. Both historical and luxurious, castles such as Ashford Castle (*www.ashford.ie*) in Cong, County Mayo, offer amenities, fine dining, and incredible personal service. Spending a night in a castle is not only reserved for the well-heeled. Online deals and off-peak tourist prices can mean a stay at a portion of the regularly listed price.

 Alert

When searching for hotels, take the time to evaluate each place. Doing an online search with the keywords "Review of" plus the name of the hotel, guesthouse, B&B, or lodge will let you see what other travelers have said and think about the establishment. And, when arranging your trip to Ireland, reserve at least your first night's accommodations before you arrive. You will need this information for customs when entering the country.

Farmhouses

A truly genuine way to experience Ireland is a stay at an Irish family farm. These establishments tend to cater well to families with small children. One of the best resources is Irish Farmhouse Holidays (061 400 700, *www.irishfarmholidays.com*). Additionally, farmhouses make excellent bases from which to explore the surrounding countryside, especially for walkers or cyclists.

Self-Catering and Eco-Lodging

If you are an eco-minded traveler or simply want to have a spot to base yourself for exploration, then a self-catering apartment, house, lodge, or cottage might do the trick. Self-catering is an establishment that is rented for multiday stays, usually with a one-week minimum. Self-catering signifies access to a kitchen and appliances, which could save you money even if the rental fee is high. It also gives you privacy with a certain amount of comfort and luxury. Most self-catering cottages and eco-lodges, such as the newfound Tory Bush Cottages (+44 (0) 28 4372 4348, *www .torybush.com*) in the Mourne Mountains, offer a variety of activities (such as cycling and trail walking) to keep you occupied.

Hostels, Camping, and Caravanning

Ireland offers amazing hostelling and camping opportunities. Every big city or town has a camping area where you can pitch a tent or dock your motor home (called a caravan). Some of these spots are more popular than others, so try to book ahead during the summer months. This is also true for hostels, which are listed online and in the Independent Holiday Hostels of Ireland (*www .hostels-ireland.com*) and Independent Hostels Ireland Guide (*www.independenthostelsireland.com*). You can also check out those associated with the Irish Youth Hostel Organization (*www .irelandyha.org*).

Researching and Booking

One of the best websites to search for and book hotels is with Ireland Hotels (*www.irelandhotels.com*). They publish an excellent guide entitled *Be Our Guest* that can be obtained in bigger tourist offices. More luxurious accommodations can be found in *Ireland's Blue Book* (*www.irelandsbluebook.ie*) and in their published booklet of the same name: *Ireland's Blue Book: Irish County Houses and Historic Hotels and Restaurants*.

Another handy resource is the Hidden Ireland (*www
.hiddenireland.com*) website, which also releases a pamphlet
listing guesthouses, manors, and lodges. Budget accommodations can be arranged with organizations such as Hostel Bookers
(*www.hostelbookers.com*) and Hostel World (*www.hostelworld
.com*). Campers and those with caravans can visit the Caravan
and Camping Guide (*www.campingireland.ie*).

Gulliver to the Rescue

One of the best ways to ensure you are not scrambling at dusk
to find accommodations is to stop by a tourist office. Using a service
called Gulliver (066 979 2030, *www.gulliver.ie*), they will help you
find a room in your location and price range. The service searches
a wide variety of accommodations. Travelers are free to use Gulliver
online to research and book accommodations throughout Ireland.

Here are some tips to consider before you reserve your
accommodations:

- If you are a light sleeper or want something quiet, ask for
  rooms that are set apart from active areas. In regular hotels,
  this might mean a room that is not on the first floor near the
  check-in area, close to elevators or vending machines, near
  construction, facing a road or busy street, above a pub
  (especially with live music), or those who cater to families
  with infants.
- While nonsmoking is standard in most guesthouses and
  B&Bs, it might not always be the case in regular hotels.
- Find out if there are any additional fees (common in large or
  expensive hotels, but not B&Bs), such as service charges,
  which can increase the total bill by 15 percent or more.
- Find out if taxes are included. Europe uses a VAT (value-
  added tax) system that is around 14 percent in the Republic
  and nearly 20 percent in Northern Ireland.

- Understand if the cost you are quoted is per person or per room. Most accommodations, especially B&Bs are labeled on a per-person basis.
- If you need Internet access while in Ireland, find out if this is available where you will be staying. While even small establishments usually have the Internet available, some also claim WIFI (or wireless Internet) accessibility.
- Most establishments do not have queen- or king-sized beds. Rooms are referenced as "double room" (one to two people, double-sized bed) or a "twin room" (two twin-sized beds). Individuals traveling alone will most often pay a small supplement.

Getting the Best Deal

One of the best ways to save money is to travel in the off-peak tourist season. September and even October can be wonderful months to travel, as is April and especially May and June. Additionally, if you are reserving a room midweek (even in the higher season), look for or ask if they have discounted rates. Advertised rates are always the highest. Calling the hotel directly or e-mailing them will mean a reduction in price as opposed to booking through a hotel or hostel-booking website. You might also save by paying in cash.

Here are some handy reference terms to remember:

- **Half board:** One night's stay with evening meal and breakfast.
- **Full board:** One night's stay with lunch (usually packed), evening meal, and breakfast. On a weekend, this might include a special lunch with the host family.
- **Table d'hôte:** This French practice is becoming popular and refers to a special evening meal where guests and hosts dine together in a more formal setting. Generally, there is an extra cost and various courses served.

For self-catering accommodations, guesthouses, B&Bs, and even hotels, do not be reluctant to request a one-night complimentary stay after a five- to seven-night sojourn. Most hotels, B&Bs, and guesthouses include breakfast and might offer dinner at cost. This can be expensive, yet enjoyable.

Restaurant Guide

Ireland offers an array of dining experiences, some more expensive than others. From pub food to fish and chips to gourmet fusion fare, you will be delightfully surprised at the selections available.

Breakfast is still one of the main staples of the day for many of the Irish, especially farmers. A "full Irish breakfast" is generally composed of rashers (bacon), sausage, eggs, potatoes or tomatoes, eggs, black and white pudding, and brown soda bread with local butter. In most establishments, this is served alongside a continental breakfast of cereal, orange juice, and toast.

 Fact

Black pudding is oftentimes referred to as "blood pudding," which is a type of congealed blood sausage. White pudding is also a common Irish provision, which is composed of pork meat rather than coagulated blood. Try not to hate it before trying it—you might be pleasantly surprised!

In cities, lunch in Ireland is similar to elsewhere in Europe and North America: fast food. For travelers rationing funds, lunch is a good time to eat well, as prices are cheaper, even in fancier establishments. Often you will find menus with set prices, sometimes including beverages. Bistros, cafés, and pubs are preferred lunch-time pursuits.

Evening dining in Ireland varies greatly based on the region and your budget. Black-tie affairs can be had, while less-posh gourmet restaurants only require men to don jackets. Others, such as pubs and family restaurants are informal. Dining choices are as diverse as the Irish scenery; from castles to mansions to dinner theater, Ireland is chock-full of memorable dining experiences.

Essential

Tipping in Ireland is a common practice. If a waiter comes to your table, expect to pay a 10 percent to 15 percent tip. If you eat at the counter in a pub, a tip is not required. Check your receipt to verify the tip was not automatically included before leaving one on the table.

Making Reservations

During high season, make reservations for the finer establishments at which you plan to dine. Calling a couple days ahead of time tends to be sufficient but on weekends, plan well in advance.

Most guesthouses and manors (and some B&Bs) serve an evening meal. This can be a rewarding way to experience local cuisine. Additionally, most B&B and guesthouse hosts can recommend the best places to eat.

While credit cards might be accepted in larger restaurants, bring sufficient cash for smaller dining venues, such as local pubs, family restaurants, and B&Bs. Most dinners are served after 6:30 P.M. and until 9 P.M. in pubs. Most pubs stop serving drinks at midnight, while others stop at 2 A.M.

CHAPTER 3

Ireland
Defined

Ireland, like its varied landscapes, is a county of contrasts.
Its culture and heritage is an amalgam of the various groups
that settled here. From Celtic mythology to Saint Patrick, the
spiritual world carved its place in Ireland's history. Religion
gave way to political motive and oral tradition evolved into a
literature that was forever transformed. A country the size of
a small U.S. state, its rich history, its artistic contributions, and
its inspiring struggle that brought it liberty is nothing less than
mesmerizing.

Essential History
of Ireland

Ireland's history is one of the most interesting of all European
nations. The last 100 years is a lens that allows you to view a
culmination of the vital events that have shaped its people and
initiated its rebirth as a nation. The formation of modern Ireland is a direct result of the melting pot of language and culture that came together with the various peoples who made it
their home.

Imagine the Emerald Isle as the Glacier Isle! That is what covered the current Republic of Ireland about 16,000 B.C. It was not until 8,000 years later that Middle Stone Age nomads began perching here. Archaeologists who have unearthed huts and stone tools in the region believe they resided on Mount Sandel near Londonderry, Northern Ireland.

Three thousand years later, Neolithic farmers began settling the land, which had a greater impact on the once tree-filled landscape. What they left behind were megalithic structures, including impressive dolmens, and the method of their construction leaves modern man puzzled. Thousands of these types of structures dot the horizon, some such as the impressive Poulnabrone in the Burren, County Clare.

The Celts

By the time the Celts arrived in 500 B.C., they had brought with them a feudal system filled with hundreds of clans and no central government. The tribes eventually came to recognize a high king (*Ard-Rí*) and provincial leaders, but their organization was chaotic at best. Numerous paltry skirmishes took place; ring strongholds warded certain kinship groups better than others.

The Celts, descendants of those who fled Roman rule, offered tremendous advancement in regard to language, religion, art, poetry, and sports, along with developed technologies. When they weren't fighting for their lives, their cultural impact spread and is of historical repute. They were skilled in the use of iron and built structures and weapons that have withstood the test of time. With an established religion of Celtic polytheism, they forever changed the land and culture of *Éire* (Ireland).

The Rise of Christianity

While the Romans never vied for Ireland (most likely due to its climate), ancient Christians were all about spreading the Word to the farthest kingdoms. All heathens deserved their chance. The Celts did not know exactly what to think of the slow influx of these monotheistic believers. But, without much fuss the Celts accepted them and adopted their religion.

One persistent fellow named Maewyn Succat (later called Saint Patrick) was a Roman previously living in Wales who had been enslaved in County Antrim. He is credited with the conversion of the masses. Saint Patrick returned to the isle in the 430s A.D. with inspired fervor that not only cast away all snakes (old religion), but also converted and spread the Good News. His popularity and status grew. To the great pleasure of the pope, Ireland would become a primarily Catholic nation.

The Vikings

Because the local Celts were less affected during the rest of Europe's darker times (the Dark Ages), scholars, monks, priests, and intelligentsia came to Ireland in order to continue their progress as intellectuals. With them, settlers brought riches that made Ireland quite a little treasure trove unbeknownst to the world.

When the Vikings landed around A.D. 795, jaws dropped that no one had beat them to the punch. What they found was unprotected riches held in scant towers, which knew no defense. The highly educated were not equipped to withstand the Vikings, who pillaged with no regard. However, the Vikings, who were not the most literary bunch, left behind the scrolls, manuscripts, and books that would delineate the history of Ireland and the movement of Christianity therein.

The Vikings, who had pillaged all they could throughout the 800s, decided that Ireland was not that bad of a place in which to live. They began settling the land by the boatload. What they fortified were the major harbors on the eastern side of the Island, including Dublin, and west toward Limerick.

Fact

The turning point for the perturbed Irish natives was the Battle of Clontarft in 1014 led by the high king of Ireland named Brian Ború. With sole Viking rule out of the picture, Ireland moved ahead, eventually succumbing to the Roman Catholic Church's whims.

The Anglo-Normans

Wanting to unite Ireland when he had the chance, the king of Leinster, Diarmait Mac Murchada in 1169 called upon the help of Henry II, the Norman king of England, for military aid. Henry II knew the offer was too juicy to refuse, so he sent Richard de Clare, who would come to be called Strongbow. Following battles in Dublin and elsewhere, Strongbow's victories brought about his appointment as governor and also his marriage to Diarmait's daughter. This gave Britain a bloodline and stake to the Emerald Island's land, people, and inherent wealth. Strongbow took Diarmait's place as king of Leinster.

With Strongbow's rise, King Henry II became begrudgingly concerned about where he stood, so he claimed all of Ireland as his own. What ensued was an influx of unwelcome Anglo-Normans who congregated behind stone walls and scoffed at the primitive Irish clans surrounding them. But, by the later 1200s, the English were not maintaining their rule with ironclad force. Much too busy in France and on their own soil, the English ruled from afar—the Pale (or "ditch") surrounding Dublin marking their true dominion.

Fight or Flight: Gaelic Rule Ends

By the 1500s, Spain had attempted to oust England via Ireland, but had no luck. England would use Ireland as their base to send settlers and bring back fortunes from the New World, the Americas. When England metamorphosed into a Protestant nation under Henry VIII, the transpiring revolts from Catholic Ireland were all crushed and the land was given to English converts by Elizabeth I.

In late 1595, Hugh O'Neill and Hugh O'Donnell fought gloriously for their homeland, but eventually had to succumb to the raw might of Britain following their loss in the 1601 Battle of Kinsale. O'Neill's land was confiscated but then returned under royal decree. By 1607, he and other once-strong Gaelic liege lords departed their country for another home in Europe, chronicled as the Flight of the Earls.

Cromwell's Siege

Following Elizabeth I, King James I moved quickly to populate the northeast of Ireland with Protestant settlers. When England fell into civil war, however, the Irish again attempted to reclaim their land from the haut monde.

Oliver Cromwell, who became Lord Protector of England, Scotland, and Ireland with the beheading of his nemesis King Charles I in 1648, wanted to ensure his rule over the kingdom. The Irish were up in arms about another Protestant ruler and as a result, Cromwell invaded Ireland with thousands of men and went on a bloodthirsty rampage that still lives on in infamy. With millions of acres of land under his iron fist, Cromwell handed it all over to his Protestant brethren. As the 1700s arrived, English rule only grew in the country and penal statues ostracized everyone and everything Catholic.

Only Time Will Tell: The Next 200 Years

The 1700s brought with them relative peace. Dublin was the new London and Georgian delights reigned. In the backdrop, Ireland was gaining in strength and inspiration from the revolutions against Britain in both America (1776) and France (1789). The Irish lawyer, Wolfe Tone, arranged the gathering of thousands of French troops to aid Ireland, but was defeated in 1796 not by sword, but by storms. Upon their return, Britain squashed the attempt and Tone was sentenced to death. By the turn of the nineteenth century, the Irish Parliament was politically terminated.

In 1845, the Great Potato Famine (or *an Gorta Mór*, the Great Hunger) hit Ireland more violently than any war. The blight infested and destroyed the country's most important crop. Peasants, who were given the worst land, depended on the potato for survival, and the death of nearly 1 million people from starvation and related diseases ensued. The English (who did send nutritionally devoid cornmeal from India, but exported all other crops) did little to aid their vassals. Nearly 2 million impoverished Irish left their country in search of a better life. They headed west to America and Canada, while others ventured as far away as Australia. Currently, over 50 million people of Irish descent reside in the United States.

By the 1880s, Ireland was gaining backing for their desire for "Home Rule" (independence). Charles Stewart Parnell, an Irish national, was elected to Parliament and fought for tenant rights and worked for the unification of the Irish at home and abroad. When Home Rule was nearly passed, he was ridiculed for a love affair. This, along with the onslaught of World War I, meant the issue would be dropped but not forgotten.

Easter Rising and Beyond

Easter Monday on April 24, 1916, brought with it a light crew of 1,500 Irish Volunteers who, along with the Irish Citizens Army, marched on Dublin, took over the post office, raised a new flag, and officially declared the independence of Ireland. Britain swiftly reacted and Dublin became a war zone. With the harsh execution of those involved, which included their leader Patrick Pearse, the Irish became outraged.

What ensued was the election of an Irish Parliament headed by Sinn Fein who would not take their seats in London. With fervor and timing on their side the rebels, led by Éamon de Valera, alongside the cunning deputy Michael Collins (who infiltrated the British spy network and initiated urban guerrilla warfare tactics with the newly renamed Irish Republican Army) won Independence with the signing of the Anglo-Irish Treaty. The slightly disheartened Collins, who foresaw the treaty's compromise that left six mainly Protestant counties in the north (Northern Ireland) under the United Kingdom, knew more internal strife was to come. De Valera opposed, not accepting "partial" freedom for his nation.

Those who accepted the treaty battled those who defied it on the streets of Dublin. In April 1922, for eight days de Valera's anti-treaty forces fought against Collins's army. The anti-treaty's might was short-lived, but they were not yet stamped out. The fighting would continue in random skirmishes for the next year. De Valera distanced himself from the movement and went on to become president of Ireland. Collins was assassinated near his home a few months later. The Irish Free State officially became Éire, and thereafter known as the Republic of Ireland.

Those who remained in the de facto Irish Republican Army (IRA) decided to head into the United Kingdom's Northern Ireland. It was not until the 1970s that the nationalist, predominantly Roman Catholic organization regrouped and began a terrorist campaign to oust the Unionists, who were the Protestant majority controlling the region. After twenty years of violence on both sides, the Belfast Agreement (Good Friday Agreement) was signed in 1998. In 2005, the IRA dismantled their weaponry nucleus, bringing the power of the vote to decide its fate. The Republic of Ireland boomed throughout the 1990s and into the twenty-first century, and the Celtic Tiger (representing Ireland's economic boom) purred to the rhythm.

Mythology and Religion

Ireland's fervent religious past has played an important role in how the country perceives itself today. For much of Ireland's history, religion not only controlled politics, but actually was politics. Kings, queens, lords, landowners, priests, and commanders have all rationalized their skirmishes and battles in the name of God. Visitors to Ireland today will find a humble people holding to their values, but choosing balance and harmony over bloodshed.

 Fact

Cúchulainn is probably the most notable of all the warriors in Irish mythology. He was a demigod who, as a young lad, killed a feral guard dog in self-defense with his hurling stick and ball. He made an oath to protect the castle grounds until a new dog could be raised. His sobriquet, "Hound of Culann" (AKA The Hound of Ulster) stuck well. Later, he defeated Queen Maeve of Connaught in battle and became a hero.

The land of leprechauns, fairies, troublesome spirits, and mighty warrior gods has a deep-rooted oral history in Ireland. Storytelling was a way of life for the Celts, who passed on their knowledge to subsequent generations. For the ancient Gaels, giants constructed the mounds of earth and dolmens. Fairies protected such structures, and to touch or destroy one would bring about a lifetime of misfortune (one reason why such structures are still around today). If something could not be explained mystically, the druids (the priests and soothsayers) were the nonpareil storyweavers who would pass on legend and lore. In addition to the giants and diminutive mischief-makers, heroes (such as Cúchulainn) and villains of godlike stature controlled the spiritual world and often the fate of mankind. Other heroes such as Finn Mac-

Cool, the thumb-sucking prophet, the swan children known as the Children of Lir, and the miracles of saints all have their place in Ireland's oral past.

Religion Today

The modern Republic of Ireland is composed of nearly four million people; over 95 percent Roman Catholic. Conversely, the majority of Northern Ireland claims Protestantism, either Presbyterian or Methodist. The Catholic Church of modern Ireland still has its place, but with a country full of young, educated, well-traveled, and prosperous go-getters, Rome feels a world away.

While Sunday Mass is still a centerpiece of the week, especially in rural areas, Dubliners and other city-dwellers are focusing more on the present moment and their future rather than the afterlife.

Irish Literature

Ireland's art is oftentimes synonymous with its literature. The country's past brims with storytelling, manuscript recording and illumination (such as the venerated *Book of Kells*), along with the Celtic influence in language, festivals, and song has had a direct result on the profound contributions the small isle has made to the literary world.

The literature of the Gaels, or Gaelic literature, is said to be the oldest in Europe. Both oral and written, stories from the eighth to the twelfth centuries still survive. The mythos of character and plot, such as in the stories of Cúchulainn, appear in and have affected facets of even modern literary compositions (such as *Angela's Ashes* by Frank McCourt).

Gaelic literature slumped with the advent of Anglo-Irish literature, which was reared for and geared to the educated masses of London and Dublin. Writings in theater and drama blossomed.

Playwrights and those cultured felt much more English than they did Irish. This included Oscar Wilde, who attended Oxford, along with the likes of George Bernard Shaw and W. B. Yeats, who made London their home.

Travelers might consider reading a few of the greats before visiting Ireland:

Jonathan Swift

Swift's *Gulliver's Travels* is a satirical piece on government, religion, corruption, and modernity. Interestingly, the book is suitable for kids and adults alike due to its fantasy-world adventures and societal reflections. Most often, it is read as a children's book.

W. B. Yeats

Cofounder of Dublin's famed Abbey Theatre, W. B. Yeats was a poet and a playwright of such esteemed works as *Love Poems* and *The Tower*. A prolific writer in his own right, Yeats went on to win the Nobel Prize for Literature in 1923.

James Joyce

Famous for his new stream-of-consciousness writing style, James Joyce is best known for *Dubliners* (1914) and the epic *Ulysses* (1922). Joyce's works focus on regions of Ireland, notably Dublin, although he lived in other parts of Europe for most of his life.

Samuel Beckett

A writer, poet, and dramaturge, Samuel Beckett lived in France until his death in 1989. Intrigued with minimalism and extreme realism, his works such as *Waiting for Godot* were either loved or hated, but performed worldwide. What followed was a quasi-realist movement dubbed the "theater of the absurd." He won the Nobel Prize for Literature in 1969.

George Bernard Shaw

A staunch socialist who often mocked the system of government in the developed world, George Bernard Shaw was a copious playwright with such notable works as *Arms and the Man* (1894) and *Pygmalion* (1914), which became *My Fair Lady* on Broadway. He won the Nobel Prize for Literature in 1925 and an Oscar in 1938 for his screenplay of *Pygmalion*; he is the only person who has won both awards.

Bram Stoker

Best known for his 1897 writing *Dracula*, Bram Stoker wrote numerous other novels and short-story collections. He started out as a government clerk, but thereafter became a businessman, a well-received critic, and a manager of the Lyceum Theatre in London. *Dracula* inspired the German expressionist film *Nosferatu*.

C. S. Lewis

Born in Northern Ireland, C. S. Lewis is an esteemed twentieth-century author of such works as the volume *The Chronicles of Narnia*, which is his most famous. Religiously, Lewis dabbled in Celtic mysticism, but later became an advocate for Christianity—a theme seen in most of his works.

Brendan Behan

Known for his vociferous presence and drinking, Brendan Behan was a poet, novelist, playwright, and short-story writer. He was also a steadfast Irish Republican and a member of their army until his mid-twenties, an experience that lent itself to his work *Confessions of an Irish Rebel* (1965).

Roddy Doyle

Inspired by working-class Dublin, Roddy Doyle is one of Ireland's most celebrated modern authors. Working as a teacher, he released *The Commitments* (1989), which set the stage for his remarkable career. Following, in 1993, he won the Booker Prize for *Paddy Clark Ha Ha Ha*. His works have been made into successful films.

Brian Friel

Another modern Irish icon, Brian Friel is a short-story writer and playwright from Northern Ireland. His works focus largely on the "troubles" and post-colonial Ireland. *Dancing at Lughnasa*, for which he won the Olivier Award in 1991, and his most-famous work, *Translations*, are notable classics.

Frank McCourt

The author of the acclaimed *Angela's Ashes*, Frank McCourt was born in Brooklyn to Irish parents. During the Great Depression, the family returned to Ireland, and Frank details his life and times in destitute Limerick in his memoir. His succeeding book entitled *'Tis* relates his return to the United States.

Dialectal Dissection of Irish Gaelic

Irish Gaelic (often simply referred to as "Irish") is only one form of the Gaelic languages that exist in the world today. The Scotts have Scottish Gaelic, Wales has Welsh, Cornwall has Cornish, and Brittany regions of France speak Breton. With the onslaught of the English language (and its dominance in the twentieth century in Ireland), the Irish who currently speak fluent Gaelic (about 5 percent) are dramatically fewer than even a century ago.

At the turn of the twenty-first century, the Irish government passed new regulations to bring about a kind of rebirth of the nation's mother tongue. All signs would have to be in Irish or both English and Irish. As a tourist, you will surely experience slight frustration at the government-pushed movement to have directional, place name, and warning signs posted only in Irish in the Gaeltacht regions, which happen to be the most rural locations. It's a good idea to purchase a map that shows both languages.

With three main forms, the Irish language still thrives in parts of the country. In Counties Cork, Kerry, and Waterford, you'll hear Munster Irish; in Galway and parts of Mayo, you'll perhaps catch locals speaking Connaught Irish; finally in Donegal, you'll hear the chiming of Ulster Irish in nearly every part.

 Fact

Schools in Ireland have a mandatory component of Irish-language classes. At first, the strict Catholic manner in which it was enforced did not appeal to Irish youth. However, this approach has evolved to incorporate a more practical and pleasurable approach to teaching the language. Irish-speaking schools are sprouting up all over the country and culturally conscious parents are sending their kids to learn a language they may not even know.

'Tis Time to Talk

Parts of Ireland still speak Irish as their common, everyday tongue, namely in the Gaeltacht regions of Cork, Kerry, Galway, Mayo, and Donegal. You will also find the locals conversing in Gaelic in islands off of the west coast, namely the Aran Islands. Following you will find some handy charts to help you when attempting to speak a few words of Irish Gaelic with a local. Don't be shy; the Irish are an accepting bunch that will love to hear your attempts, especially over a pint, and if they teach you more of the local lingo, buy them one!

EXPRESSIVE EXPLORATION

Irish	Pronunciation	Meaning
An Lár	ahn lar	city center
Baile	bal-yeh	town/village
Bóthar	bohe-er	road
Caiseal	cashel	stone, ring fort
Cill	kill	church
Droichead	drockh-ad	bridge
Dun	dewn	fort
Gall	gahl	foreigner
Garda	gar-dah	police
Mór	more	large
Poll	pole	grotto/cavern
Slí	slee	footpath/trail
Sliabh	sleeve	mount/mountain range
Teach	tak	house/residence
Tur	tewr	tower/turret

 Essential

Interestingly, Irish does not include the consonants q, z, k, x, or j, nor does it have the sound th. An Irishman speaking English will pronounce the word *three* as "tree," regardless of whether he is fluent in Irish Gaelic or not. So, "tank you" for your time.

Here are some other phrases and words that will come in handy for everyday conversation:

FUN PHRASES AND WORDS

Irish	Pronunciation	Meaning
Fáilte	fault-shuh	welcome
Dia duit	dee-ah gwit	hello (God be with you)
Dia is Muire duit	dee-ah moyra gwit	hello (God and Mary with you)
Conas ta tu?	kun-as aw-taw too	how are you?
Go maith	goh-mah	okay/fine
Cad is ainm duit?	kod es ahnim dwit	what's your name?
____ is ainm dom.	____ es ahnim dohm.	____ is my name.
Cad é seo/sin?	kod ay shohw/shyn	what is this/that?
Maidin mhaith	maw-jin wah	good morning
Oíche mhaith	eek-heh wah	good night
Slainte!	slawn-cha	to your health (at a pub)
Craic	krak	fun/good times and conversation
Ceilidh	kaye-lee	Irish dancing and get-together
Trad	trad	traditional Irish music
Fleadh	flah	festival of song or music

Chatting with the Locals: Pub Culture

Pub culture in Ireland might be something of a misnomer; it might rather be titled Pub Life. Pubs in Ireland are not only a place to grab a pint of your favorite local stout, but also a place to unwind, to meet up with kinfolk and townsfolk alike, and to engage in lively conversation after a few rounds. When walking into a pub in Ireland, you'll be sure to find a friend. If a group is gathered talking around the bar, feel free to listen, buy a round, and join in.

For those of you drinking and eating out, pub grub is a fine accompaniment to any pint. Consisting of soups, brown soda bread, Irish beef burgers, and chips (fries), it is the place to get fresh, good food fast. Other types of food include seafood chowder, lamb stew, and meat-filled shepherd's pie, all of which will keep you energized for any adventure. Remember to eat by eight o'clock in the evening if possible. Pubs stop serving dishes once the thirsty regulars sojourn. Families with children are welcome for the early hours of the evening. Once 9 P.M. rolls around, families are often shooed out the door.

 Essential

> When someone invites you to a pub in Ireland, it is common practice for her or him to purchase the first drinks. But, you should bestow the next. Order the following round before others finish their drinks in order to keep the spirit, conversation, and your ability to be culturally one-step ahead from lulling. (It takes nearly two minutes for a Guinness to settle before the swilling can begin.)

Guinness is the most well known Irish beer, but the island has been brewing several other splendid concoctions for centuries. Try what is on tap at the various pubs you frequent for a true *taste* of the region.

Ireland's other beers (besides Guinness) include:

- Smithwicks (Kilkenny)
- Caffrey's Irish Ale (County Antrim)
- Beamish Red Ale (Cork City)
- Harp Lager (Dundalk)
- Murphy's Irish Stout (County Cork)
- Galway Hooker (Galway City)

Whether you stop by Abbey Tavern in Dublin, McGann's in County Clare, or Smuggler's Creek in Donegal, the pub is the place not only to meet locals, but to learn about each region's culture and heritage. Once the pub doors swing open, you'll forget about that tiring hill walk or the hours of driving tight roads and be truly absorbed in the friendliness exuding all around.

CHAPTER 4

Ireland
Itineraries

I reland is a small island; much can be seen in a short amount of time. Numerous factors will determine what type of trip you want to take and what area you want to explore. With seven days to two weeks, you will have a wonderful introduction to the Emerald Island's highlights. With more time (or with recurring visits), you can enjoy a slower type of travel that matches the laid-back lifestyle and culture of the Irish.

Which Itinerary
Is Right?

Whether you are traveling solo or taking a luxury honeymoon, Ireland's offerings will far surpass the time you have available. For those with time constraints, the best plan of action might be to break down your choices to a certain region or type of travel, or a mix thereof.

The first step when choosing an itinerary is to figure where you would like to start your vacation. Most flights from other European destinations arrive into Dublin. Flights from the United States can enter into the airports in Shannon or Dublin. Most likely, this will be the determining factor of where your trip will begin.

If you really want to travel the west side of Ireland, consider paying a little more to land in Shannon or Cork. Or, take a train

(3.5 hours), bus (4–5 hours), or rental car (4 hours) across the isle to begin your journey. If you are leaving Dublin right away, rental cars are available at the airport. If you are staying in Dublin for a period, it is highly recommended to use public transport options.

Alert

If your flight arrives in Dublin in the late afternoon during summertime, you might be able to hop into your rental and drive west without issue. Sunset in summer is at 10 P.M. If arriving later, however, resist the urge to drive at night. Simply book a room and wait for the next day.

Travel Goals

The best way to plan your trip is to focus on your personal vacation goals and travel style (along with those accompanying you). If your idea of a perfect vacation is to ramble in the great outdoors, consider one of Ireland's many "waymarked way" trails such as the Burren Way or Wicklow Way. On the other hand, a sightseeing tour that incorporates castles and forts is also plausible. If your ultimate goal is to get off the tourist path, focus your attention on Ireland's northwest.

The Way to Roll

Oftentimes your style of travel will be determined by age, mobility, energy level, past travel experiences, expectations, and for most, budget. Those traveling on a relatively average budget will find that B&Bs, guesthouses, and regular hotels will fit the bill perfectly (hostels and campgrounds are also realistic options). Others will discover that the numerous accommodations, such as castles and manors, are geared perfectly to their travel style and needs.

In Ireland, the most rewarding style of travel might be the simplest. Those who allocate a middle-range budget will be those who are culturally immersing themselves in the quaintest B&B, learning about the sport of hurling in a pub, and finding pleasure in the rolling green meadows lined with grazers. This is not to say that luxurious travel should not be had or promoted, but setting parameters on what you spend will directly influence what you explore. Splurging on certain amenities in the name of luxury is worthwhile, more so if it is amalgamated within an itinerary that helps to open yourself to Ireland's plentitudes.

Experts on Ireland: Tour Operators

Where there is travel there are tour operators. These companies work as on-the-ground liaisons to help you decide which itinerary might be best. Based on numerous factors, these tailored trips are perfect for a myriad of people.

Most vacationers who use a tour operator do so because they do not have enough time for planning or they simply want help in making all the arrangements. The various types of tours that might involve an operator include:

Coach or Package Tours

Tours involving a group on a large bus are coach tours. These package tours might include flight arrangements, entrance fees to monuments, an accompanying guide, some meals, and accommodations. These trips can be composed of groups who know each other or who do not. Irish Tourism (069 77 686 or 1 877 298 7205 U.S., *www.irishtourism.com*) has a listing of coach tours running throughout the year. EireBus (01 824 2626, *www.eirebus.ie*) arranges fully inclusive, guided, and customized tours as well.

Small Group Tours and Adventures

Itineraries composed with a limited number of seats (usually a max of twelve to sixteen) in which the group obtains a more intimate view of a country's people, traditions, and customs are considered small group tours. Some of these groups come together for a certain activity or event like hiking, rafting, cycling, photography, bird watching, or language training. Discover Ireland Tours (021 437 3624, *www .discoverirelandtours.com*) arranges a wonderful array of affordable small group and customized itineraries. For adventure, contact Vagabond Ireland (01 660 7399 Ireland; 1 870 619 4059 U.S., *www .vagabondtoursofireland.ie*). For fun day trips from Dublin, Over the Top Tours (01 860 0404 Ireland; *www.overthetoptours.com*) are well known in their field.

Alert

When traveling in Ireland, be sure to have travel insurance. Especially with adventure-tour operators, you will be required to show proof that you are covered before setting out on any excursions. This insurance can also cover airplane ticket cancellations, lost gear or luggage, and rescue services. Some of these matters are covered more thoroughly in Chapter 5.

Regional- or Activity-Specific Tour Operators

Regional tour operators are those who may not cover the entire country, but perhaps a specific tourist destination. In Killarney, for example, you will find both small and large companies bringing groups around the Ring of Kerry. This hotspot lends itself to these types of outfitters. In other areas, small activity-specific operators might run horseback riding or hill-walking excursions. In each chapter of this book, you will find recommended operators arranging various trips.

Private, Custom, Self-Guided or Independent, and Specialty Tours

All of these types of tours are related and might be mixed, yet distinct enough to mention. A private trip is set up for one or more people who want to travel together. It might be fully guided (or not) and with or without a driver. Along the same lines, a custom trip is usually private and designed and coordinated with an agency.

Self-guided or independent trips are ones in which an itinerary has been established with an operator (and accommodations reserved), but might include a rental car so that you can still explore on your own. Companies like Authentic Ireland (*www.authenticireland.com*) arrange these and other types of tours.

Finally, specialty tours tend to be activity based and can be geared for a certain audience. Some examples include gardening, golf, fishing, historical, folklore, ecological, and archaeological tours. A Celtic music, craft, and history operator such as Celtica Tours (*www.celticatours.com*) is just one fine example. For those traveling alone and searching for someone to join, contact the PATT Club (*www.thepattclub.ie*).

 Essential

> While Ireland is on the forefront of making itself totally accessible, it still has much work to do. You can find specialty tours geared for travelers with various mobility issues. These types of tours utilize disability friendly establishments, restaurants, and frequent monuments easily accessible by everyone. One operator offering such tours is Undiscovered Britain and Ireland (*www.undiscoveredbritain.com*).

Eco-Friendly Tours

Eco-tours tend to be ecologically friendly, nature-based, sustainable excursions encompassing a greener type of travel. Appealing on a variety of levels, eco-friendly travel does not mean amenities are spared. In fact, eco-friendly accommodations in Ireland often constitute luxurious comfort. Described in various listings of this travel guide, great effort has been made to search out, detail, and give preference to eco-friendly activities and accommodations.

 Fact

Known as a low-impact, culturally sensitive, and oftentimes educative initiative, green travel is gaining prominence worldwide. And Ireland is on the forefront of this movement. Guesthouses, castles, manors, and even small B&Bs are coming up with innovative ways to save energy without sacrificing service or comfort. Operators offering eco-tour packages focus on slow travel rather than overstuffing a trip with sights.

Green Box (071 985 6898, *www.greenbox.ie*) is one eco-tour operator leading the way in Ireland's northwest. In Northern Ireland, contact Ireland Eco Tours (+44 (0) 28 6865 9171, *www.irelandecotours.com*) for small group excursions in their veggie mobile. Sometimes eco-friendly travel and active travel correspond. One such operator is Go Visit Ireland (1 800 721 4672 U.S., *www.govisitireland.com*).

Online Trip Preparation

Online trip planning and preparation means that you are your own travel agent. From reserving plane tickets to accommodations and daily excursions, the Internet is your tool to virtually plan each leg of your journey. And, because Ireland keeps pace with the rest of Europe, using online resources to plan and book your trip has never been easier.

If you are looking for the best prices in airfare, try Expedia (*www.expedia.com*), which allows you to begin your journey within or outside U.S. borders. If starting your trip in the United States or Canada, Travelocity (*www.travelocity.com*) is comparable. On average, Aer Lingus (*www.aerlingus.com*) offers the overall best rates from the United States direct to Ireland.

Arranging your own accommodations is also easy. You will find top-notch, both luxury and affordable, listings individually reviewed in each chapter throughout this guide. Helpful hints on booking rooms can be found in Chapter 2.

Various types of rooms are available on Gulliver (*www.gulliver.ie*), which the Ireland Tourist Offices utilize, or a site such as Ireland Hotels (*www.irelandhotels.com*). The Fáilte Ireland (*www.ireland.com*) also has a massive database of accommodation listings. For Northern Ireland, consider Northern Ireland Tourism (*www.discovernorthernireland.com*) for your accommodation needs.

Ireland's Best Itineraries

A well-designed itinerary in Ireland will ensure your vacation timeline and room reservations work out in sync. However, do not forget that Ireland is a country of discovery. Resist the urge to plan out each day with maximum detail, but instead leave time to discover the hidden corners, historical nuances, and the picturesque villages that will be forever etched in your memory.

The following itineraries offer travelers well-paced routes that incorporate history, culture, the best cities, and the outdoors with a smattering of light activity. More active itineraries can be created in collaboration with the chapters dedicated to outdoor pursuits.

For explanations of places, monuments, natural sights and wonders, along with any accommodations and dining establishments mentioned, take a quick scan of the referring county chapters. The following itineraries are general outlines giving you the freedom to select how many days you might like to spend in each location.

Classic Ireland
(Seven to Ten Days)

Leaving Dublin, head to Glendalough in County Wicklow. Often skipped by those rushing southwest, this tranquil stopover will give you a moment to relax and refuel. The Wicklow Mountains are best seen in the daytime and en route you can visit the Powerscourt estate. If kids are along for the ride, stop by the town of Bray just across the Dublin border to the National Sea Life Centre.

Following Glendalough, head to Kilkenny City. This truly Gothic town is best viewed while on a walking tour of the city. A dinner following your day at the eerie Kyteler's Inn sets the mood.

Now it is off to County Cork, where you can visit the esteemed Blarney Castle, the historical town of Cobh, and medieval Kinsale. In Blarney, kiss the famous Blarney Stone to acquire the "gift of gab" that will help you for the remainder of your journey. In Cobh, the Titanic Walking Trail is a scenic highlight. Arrive in Kinsale before sunset; this sailing town is probably Ireland's most photogenic. The Fishy Fishy restaurant makes a mean dinner and while the night is young, attend the ghost tour from Tap Tavern to learn about the town's bone-chilling past.

From Kinsale, the N71 is an amazing coastal drive going past Galley Head and Skibbereen. Continue upward to Glengarriff and Kenmare. If you have time, the Beara Peninsula makes a timeless day of exploration. Killarney National Park is not far off; the Muckross House and Jaunting Cars are on hand. The Water's Edge B&B is a perfect point from which to access all the region's sights. Early in the morning, prepare for Ireland's most stunning driving route along the Ring of Kerry. The UNESCO-protected Skellig Islands are accessible from Valentia. The next day will bring you into another often-skipped treasure, Dingle. Drive over Conor's Pass if the weather is clear and enjoy one of the numerous walks available on this peninsula. The Pax Guest House is a top-notch establishment in Dingle offering splendid amenities with stellar views.

If time allows, continue onward to Limerick to enjoy a dinner theater presentation at the Bunratty Castle and Folk Park. Ennis makes a nice stopover point for the night. Following, it is off to the stunning Cliffs of Moher. A musical night can be had in Doolin, where the town extends its kindness and warm welcome to all passersby. The Rainbow Hostel and B&B are great for those on a budget, while continuing to Ballyvaughn Village might mean a stay at the posh Gregans Castle Hotel. Aim to spend at least one full day in the area to fully appreciate the Burren. Finally, for those with sufficient time, head to Galway City. Those departing from the west can do so from the Shannon Airport, which is one hour south of Galway. Additionally, driving or taking a train through the midland back to Dublin is an option.

Classic Ireland Extended (Two Weeks Plus)

The aforementioned route can easily be extended to two or more weeks. This will allow you time to explore the ancient attraction of the Aran Islands along with breathtaking Connemara and Ireland's northwestern gems.

Following Galway City, head to the Aran Islands from Rossaveal (one hour west of Galway City) or from Doolin (County Clare). A sunny day on the islands is considered a godsend, so hop on a bike to see Dún Aengus (*dún* means "fort"), ancient stone huts, and basking seal colonies. Other options include hiring a local driver with a van from the boat pier, or better yet, hop on a buggy, often pulled by a tractor with tours given by local fishermen turned seasonal tour guides. The Kilmurvey House B&B on Inishmor and the Radharc an Chlair B&B on Inisheer make great points from which to explore further.

Moving into the Connemara National Park, lands of heath, bog, and rolling mountains sprouting wildflowers make the trip exceptionally worthwhile. The towns of Roundstone and Clifden both make good base points. While in Connemara, visit Kylemore Abbey, along with its cathedral and mausoleum to learn about the Henry family's luxurious lives and wrenching losses. If staying in a castle tops your list, head over to Cong for a night in the elegant Ashford Castle and view the town where *The Quiet Man* was filmed.

 Fact

The 12km (8-mile) walk around small Inisheer is called the Inis Oírr Way. This is a splendid way to get around this isle; the loop takes you past the lighthouse and the Church of the Seven Daughters (Cill na Seacht nInín) with views of the O'Brien Castle and various burial mounds.

En route into County Mayo, a boat ride to Clare Island (or far-removed Inishturk Island) puts you in prime walking country, as does a venture up Croagh Patrick Mountain. Following, scenic Westport and Westport Quay offer their splendid views of the bay. Astounding Achill Island is accessible by car; its appealing remoteness is highlighted by some of Ireland's most hidden cliffside scenery.

An epitome of Ireland's true rustic nature, County Donegal is a must and will require some time to explore. The remarkable vistas along the Slieve League Range and stunning walking therein beckon hikers far and wide. Following, take a side trip to the folk village of Glencolmcille before sleeping at the extravagant, yet well-priced, Donegal Manor or the Inishduff House B&B in Kilcar.

Ensuing is the glorious drive through the Glengesh Pass and up to the Rosses before heading to the Glenveagh National Park, which can easily take up an entire afternoon. A drive (or climb) along the Errigal Mountain is an awe-inspiring adventure, as are the picturesque vistas afforded at the tip of the Bloody Foreland Head. The next day, steer around historical Inishowen Peninsula.

Northern Ireland Extension (Three Weeks Plus)

For those with the time, entering Northern Ireland via Derry is an uneventful transition. Continuing east, however, brings you to the Antrim Coast and along the famed Giant's Causeway. The three-hour cliff-side walk is stupendous. Photographing Ireland's smallest worship center, St. Gobban's Church in Portbradden, makes a cool souvenir. An appealing stop at the Dunluce Castle and the Carrick-a-Rede Rope Bridge makes it a full day. For dinner, the well-priced fare at the Nook near the visitor center is recommended. A night in the restful Valley View B&B makes the day a ruminative gem.

 Essential

This latter itinerary of Northern Ireland can also be done from Belfast or Dublin. Taking a black-taxi tour of Belfast's impressively sad and moving political and religious murals is a must. Following, the inner sanctums of Northern Ireland's Antrim coast is a gem, especially for those in pursuit of scenic outdoor delights.

Continue to Belfast if you desire, but a trip along the southeastern coast of Northern Ireland, topped by a visit to the Exploris Aquarium in Portaferry should be on the list if kids are on board. Then, it is down to Newcastle and the undiscovered Mourne Mountains. A few nights at the eco-friendly Tory Bush Cottages, walks in the Tollymore Forest Park, a visit to Newcastle, and biking around the uninhabited environs make a truly splendid vacation.

Pick up the color-coded walking routes (at the Newcastle Tourist Office) through the Mourne Mountains for true off-the-beaten path adventures.

Honeymoon Tour: Castles Galore (Seven to Ten Days)

A honeymoon tour tends to be designed with a theme of romance sprinkled with luxury in both accommodation and dining. A romantic journey of this nature might incorporate stays at castles, manors, and small, removed cottages. The possibilities are virtually limitless.

Couples might consider starting their trip in Dublin, followed by a trip slightly west into the horse country of Kildare for a night in the Kilkea Castle (*www.kilkeacastle.ie*). Head far southwest to Limerick to enjoy a stay at Glin Castle or in Ireland's prettiest town, Adare. Following, continue north into the Burren for a day or two of exploration. A stay at the Gregan Castle Hotel should top your list.

Following, enjoy historical Galway City and Connemara with a night at the incredible Delphi Lodge (*www.delphilodge.ie*). Finally, drive through Joyce Country and a stay in Ireland's premier luxury fortress in Cong, Ashford Castle. Honeymooners can continue onward to Dublin or north into Counties Mayo, Sligo, and Donegal.

A Family Route (Seven to Ten Days)

Ireland makes a pleasurable and exciting vacation for families of all ages. Whether it's history, culture, or wildlife that you seek, finding all of that and more will not be difficult. But, deciding what you can fit into your travel time might be!

When considering accommodations, pick some places the kids will not forget. Ireland has a plethora of farm hotels and guesthouses that make idyllic spots to run and play. Arguably, the best-suited place in Ireland for families is the southwest.

Cork makes a good entry point and from there you can get your bearings. Exploring the City Gaol (jail) and the Blarney Castle can easily take up a full day. Next, head east to the Fota Island Wildlife Park. Following that it is off to Kinsale for water sports and a thrilling ghost tour at night.

For another day, a hike around or a ride in a jaunting car at the Muckross Estate in the Killarney National Park takes up an afternoon. Stay at the Sea Shore Farm (*www.kenmare.eu/seashore*) or the fun-filled adventure land that is the Peacock Farm Hostel (064 33 557) off of Muckross Road. From Kenmare, you can also enjoy a seal-watching cruise.

Then, it is off to Dingle for the Dingle Oceanworld and a trip on the open seas to see Fungi the Dolphin. For those with extra days, extend your itinerary for an adventure into the Burren of County Clare, topped with a boat ride to the Aran Islands (from Doolin, Galway, or Rossaveal). A cycle around the islands is something the whole family can enjoy. Finally, Galway City makes a nice stop. Departures are possible from the Shannon Airport; a drive back to Dublin takes four hours.

Active with Mother Nature (Five or More Days)

Since walking is Ireland's national pastime, those looking for an active vacation will feel right at home. Ireland's rolling hills (and some surprising mountains) beckon travelers to come explore. Ireland also lends itself to cycling, golfing excursions, great fishing, and some serious trekking.

A full-on active itinerary for those without months to explore is best designed by choosing a region of the country that caters to the activity you want to do. Connemara (County Galway) is known for its mountain biking (such as the impressive Sky Road outside of Clifden), while the Burren Way (County Clare) trail is not as removed, but a thorough delight. A lesser-explored and easier trail is the Beara Way (Counties Cork and Kerry), while the truly off-the-beaten path county for cycling, surfing, and hiking is Donegal. Walkers on the Donegal Way will truly enjoy a surplus of solitudes. For those not wandering far from Dublin, the Wicklow Way (which includes a stint through Glendalough) is mesmerizing, but more crowded in the warmer months. The hidden outdoor delights in Northern Ireland's Mourne Mountains are also a short drive from Dublin.

History Buff's Delight (Seven to Twelve Days)

History buffs have a vast array of explorative pursuits in Ireland. The epicenter of English and Irish history is rooted in Dublin, while Saint Kevin's impressive impact on Glendalough can still be seen today. Visiting Wexford will mean exploring its Viking past, while continuing over to Kilkenny will afford a visit to stunning Kilkenny Castle, Roth House, Black Abbey, and St. Canice's Cathedral.

Continuing over to Tipperary, there is the mighty Rock of Cashel, which depicts the succession of those who once ruled over all of Munster. Finally, an excursion into County Cork will mean a visit to Cobh, Blarney Castle, and the Viking-settled town of Kinsale with Desmond Castle and St. Multose Church in its sanctum, along with Charles Fort on its outskirts.

For those with time in the southeast, take a few days to go through Kenmare, Dingle, and up into the west to experience the extraordinary Burren and end up in fortified Galway to see the Lynch Castle, Eyre Square, and Galway Cathedral.

Culture and Cuisine
(Five or More Days)

For travelers that believe good food is synonymous with a good trip, Ireland will not disappoint. Fine-dining and award-winning establishments are listed throughout this guide. What you will find is an abundance of guesthouses and manors that also have adjoining restaurants. Booking your accommodation and evening meals in the same location is one sure way to have the best of both worlds. A strong locally produced and organic movement thrives in Ireland. This is most likely due to the fact that in its recent past, importing food was cost-prohibitive, which resulted in a need to eat locally. Today, numerous top-notch dining establishments procure the finest and freshest ingredients from what is available nearby. This means that each county or region therein can offer its own unique flavors to tempt your palate.

Besides the fine dining and international fare available in Dublin, Ireland's southeastern corners proffer an abundance of restaurants that, in the high season, are brimming with locals and travelers alike. Small Kinsale hosts its annual Festival of Fine Foods alongside its Jazz Festival each year. Cork City offers the highest-grade cheese in the country, while the smoked fish (especially salmon) of this region is out of this world. Cork City also invites visitors to its famed English Market, while restaurants like the Ballymaloe House continue to set the highest standard with its restaurant and cookery school.

Genealogy Trips

A genealogical tour in Ireland is a personal journey through the sands of time to discover whom your ancestors were and perhaps from where they originated. Access to records in Ireland is open to researchers and family members; and the friendly staff at various genealogical centers listed in each chapter of this guide are not only helpful, but truly passionate and knowledgeable in their fields. One of the best websites to utilize as you begin your journey is the Irish Family History Foundation (*www.brsgenealogy.com*), which is working on a mammoth project to put all records of the country into their electronic database. Beyond that, the last names of your ancestors will aid greatly in searching for what county they might have lived in or from which one they emigrated.

CHAPTER 5

From the Experts: Travel Tips for Ireland

While Ireland is not an overly difficult country in which to travel, grasping a few of the finer subtleties will make your trip run much more smoothly. Ireland differs from other European destinations and being mindful of the helpful tips presented here will allow you to have more fun throughout your journey. From obtaining passport information to packing essentials, along with helpful advice on in-country practicalities, here is your chance to become a travel expert on the Emerald Isle!

Pre-Trip Planning

Nationals of numerous countries do need a passport, but not always a visa to enter Ireland or Northern Ireland. European and UK nationals do not need a visa to enter or work in Ireland, which is a part of the European Economic Area (EEA) and the European Union (EU). Americans, Canadians, Australians, and New Zealanders do not need a visa to enter any part of Ireland, as long as they have a passport that is valid for at least six months upon entry.

Citizens of the above-mentioned countries can stay in Ireland for up to three months, and six months in Northern Ireland.

To verify all visa and immigration information, visit the Garda National Immigration Bureau (*www.garda.ie*; click on "National Support Services," followed by "Specialist Units," and finally "Immigration (GNIB)") or the Home Office (*www.homeoffice .gov.uk*) websites.

 Fact

A passport is a photo ID verifying which country you come from that can be used for international travel. A visa is a stamp/certificate placed in the passport that allows the bearer to enter a country within certain parameters. Numerous types of visas exist. Most are for tourist purposes, while others are for work, medical, or familial reasons.

American nationals can obtain a passport by visiting their local post office or city hall for an application. You will need a minimum of two official passport photos, a birth certificate, a check for the application fee, and possibly other documents. Interested applicants can complete the Passport Application Wizard and check on current passport information by visiting the U.S. Department of State's Bureau of Consular Affairs (*www .travel.state.gov*).

 Essential

In recent years, upon entering Ireland, immigration officers automatically stamp a one-month validity for tourists. If you plan on traveling for more than one month in Ireland, let this person know. If you happen to overstay this written limitation, but have not been in the country more than the legally allotted ninety days, you will not have any difficulties.

Working in Ireland

Students of certain countries can work legally in Ireland through the Council on International Educational Exchange (*www.ciee.org*). For others who want to work or live in Ireland long term, you will have to apply with the Immigration Bureau and/or the Department of Enterprise, Trade, and Employment if you are being transferred with your job. Individuals with parents or grandparents of Irish nationality can obtain Irish citizenship rather easily (Americans can hold dual nationalities), which means you can live and work in any EU country.

Tourist Offices

Using a tourist office to help you locate a room should be considered only if you have had no luck on your own. Travelers' centers use the Gulliver System (*www.gulliver.ie*) to handle bookings, but will not be able to offer you any real critiques about establishments. Tourist offices do charge a fee for this service, keep proceeds from proprietors, and require an initial deposit.

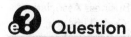 **Question**

Is there an Irish tourist office in the United States?
The national tourist office of Ireland abroad is referred to as Tourism Ireland (1 212 418 0800 U.S., *www.tourismireland.com*; 345 Park Avenue, New York, NY 10154). Funded by both the Fáilte Ireland and the Northern Ireland Tourist Board, they can be contacted for information regarding both countries.

The Dublin Tourist Centre (01 605 7700, *www.visitdublin.com*) is a one-stop all-Ireland shop with reference material covering the entire country. It is at St. Andrew's Church, on Suffolk Street in Temple Bar. On sale are Michelin (*www.viamichelin.com*) maps, which do a nice job depicting national and main highways, along with delineating counties and regions. Highly recommended is their smaller foldup, one-page map, which is great for driving and sightseeing. For highly detailed topographical maps, you can purchase Ordnance Survey (OS) maps of Ireland's regions (see Chapter 19).

Time Zones

Throughout the summer time, Ireland is on the same time as London, plus one hour in the spring and summer (called Greenwich Mean Time, GMT+1 or Universal Time Coordinated, UTC+1). This allows an extended amount of daylight for plenty of pubbing following a busy workday. In the winter months, Ireland reverts back to regular GMT/UTC time and is on par with London. Therefore, 10 A.M. in New York (EST) would be 3 P.M. in Ireland during the winter months and 4 P.M. in the summer.

 Fact

Detailed color maps of each major city are free at tourist offices. The Dublin Visitor Map published by the Dublin City Business Association (www.dcba.ie) is artfully illustrated. In Kilkenny, Cork, Limerick, and Galway City, the tourist offices have mass-produced, free color maps that are a handy reference tool. Staff members are willing to highlight places of interest.

The Perfect Packing List

Overpacking for any trip is something to be avoided. If you are renting a car, remember that European cars are smaller than American vehicles. Additionally, if you want to hand carry any gifts back home, you will want to have enough room. Everything that is available at home is most likely available in Ireland (perhaps under a different brand). For walkers, hikers, and bikers, read the thorough packing list in Chapter 19.

From the experts who travel to Ireland often, the following items are a few essentials you should bring along. Any item without a number beside it indicates that only one of those articles is recommended.

- ✓ T-shirts (6)
- ✓ Nice shirts (2)
- ✓ Regular pants (2)
- ✓ Hiking pants
- ✓ Pajamas
- ✓ Shorts
- ✓ Underwear (5)
- ✓ Socks (5 pair, not cotton, see "Fabric Types," below)
- ✓ Walking shoes/light boots (1 pair)
- ✓ Dress shoes (only if needed)
- ✓ Sandals (for bathroom use)
- ✓ Rain jacket
- ✓ Fleece/sweater
- ✓ Light gloves
- ✓ Light scarf
- ✓ Warm hat
- ✓ Bathing suit

And here is a list of essential materials and gear:

- ✓ Travel umbrella
- ✓ Watch
- ✓ Travel alarm clock
- ✓ Backup glasses/contact lenses
- ✓ Sunglasses

- ✓ Money belt
- ✓ Water bottle
- ✓ Daypack
- ✓ Earplugs
- ✓ First-aid kit
- ✓ Any medications (labeled with prescriptions)
- ✓ Sunscreen
- ✓ Notepad
- ✓ Toiletries and a towel
- ✓ Travel clothesline
- ✓ Emergency contact details
- ✓ Insurance details
- ✓ Extra credit/debit cards
- ✓ Passport
- ✓ Airplane ticket(s)
- ✓ Driver's license

Fabric Types

For some of the gear, such as T-shirts, socks, and underwear, avoid bringing cotton garments since they are heavier and take longer to dry. Light merino wool for socks and moisture-wicking products for T-shirts and underwear work nicely. For pants, bringing jeans along is fine, but you should also consider one or two pair of comfortable, quick-drying pants. Additionally, rain, bog, and wet grass are inevitable; bring breathable and waterproof (not simply water-resistant) shoes or light boots so your feet will stay dry.

Medications

Medications are allowed in the country as long as they are properly labeled in the correct container. Consider bringing along your doctor's prescription (detailing generic drug names) and a contact phone number. Pharmacies in Ireland are excellent sources of information. Should you need to purchase prescription drugs, your doctor will need to fax the proper forms. Or, you will have to visit a local physician to obtain one. Additionally, women travelers should bring ample supplies of birth control if they are taking it. Men should consider bringing their own supply of condoms. Obtaining these items in Ireland is not as hard as in the past, but it is much easier to bring your own.

Health and Safety

Besides some perilous roads and young (risk-taking) drivers keeping you alert, most likely your trip will carry on without disruption. However, it is always better to be prepared and understand what to do should an issue arise.

The police in the Republic and Northern Ireland are helpful and diligent in most cases. If your situation is not an extreme emergency, the police might take their time responding and may appear quite relaxed when dealing with your issue. Officers in Ireland are referred to as Garda and in Northern Ireland they are the Police Service of Northern Ireland (PSNI). If you have a problem, dial 999 in the Republic and 112 in Northern Ireland, which will connect you to all emergency response services.

If your children are old enough and have traveled with you before, they are probably used to a certain amount of rules and routine. If not, then consider bringing along their favorite books or games to help occupy them during driving and down times. Most accommodations cater to children, but a handful cannot provide for those under a certain age. Self-catering cottages, apartments, and lodges are great for families who want to prepare their own meals.

Be Aware

In the bigger cities, such as Belfast, Dublin, Galway, Cork, and Limerick, petty crime is a problem. Keep only your daily spending money and one credit card accessible. Store all other valuables in a money belt and in your room hidden in your baggage or in a safe. You will have no reason to carry your passport or plane tickets while walking around—a copy of any identity papers will suffice. If you have any medical conditions or allergies, be sure to keep this written down with your documents or wear the proper bracelet or necklace indicating the condition.

Alert

Traveling in Northern Ireland is as safe as anywhere in the United Kingdom. However, due to past strife, demonstrations do occur in the cities. Most often, rallies include marching and sit-ins. In mid-July, the Orange marches take place in Belfast, which can cause some public upheaval. Tourists are not targeted during any demonstrations, political unrest, or threats.

For other areas, use your common sense. Do not leave your car unlocked or in an insecure area. Do not walk down dark streets or walk alone in the late-evening and early-morning hours. Although drugs are not a huge issue in the cities, the problem persists where those under the influence rob the ill prepared.

Medical Insurance Issues

Quality travel insurance is a central component to safe travel. Well-rounded coverage will include lost or stolen baggage, plane delays or cancellations, medical expenses, and emergency transport (including airlift and repatriation). Obtaining the best insurance at an affordable rate will take some research and planning.

If you have medical coverage, be sure that your carrier will cover you while abroad. You might need to supplement your coverage for travel cancellation, emergency repatriation, and/or if you plan to be taking part in any adventure activities or backcountry hiking. One decent provider that receives good reviews for its performance and customer care is Travel Guard (*www.travelguard.com*).

When researching medical and travel insurance, find out who pays whom if an emergency arises. Most often, you will have to cover the cost and will be reimbursed once back home. Keep detailed, itemized receipts and original signed documents verifying all the charges for medication, transport, and any treatments.

Embassy and Consulate Information

To a minimal extent, an embassy and consulate will help one of its citizens while traveling abroad. For certain cases, the embassy or consulate will respond to (but not necessarily help much in) matters concerning indictment of one of their citizens. If you break the law in Ireland or in Northern Ireland, you are bound by their regulations.

For medical emergencies, the consulate or embassy might help you out slightly more. They can help notify your family and aid you in returning home (at your cost) if needed. For those in dire straits, the consulate will help get you a new or temporary passport. But, this can take several days. The U.S. Embassy in the Republic of Ireland is located in Dublin at 42 Elgin Rd., Ballsbridge, Dublin 4. Phone them at 01 66 88 777 and send fax correspondences to 01 66 89 946.

Money Issues

Traveling in Europe, especially the Emerald Isle, can be expensive, but it does not have to break the bank. Ireland uses the euro (€) as its main currency, while Northern Ireland uses the pound sterling (£). Since currencies can fluctuate a great deal, prices in this guide are listed in local tender.

Bring ample cash in dollars (or better yet, euro), debit and credit cards of various types (Visa or MasterCard are best), and phone numbers to your banking institutions. Know the pin numbers for each. And, call your bank ahead of time so they are aware of your travels. If you find your card is not accepted, you might have to call your bank or credit card company to release it. Finally, have an emergency account or credit card with accessible funds available from the United States: $2,000 to $5,000 for couples and more for families.

Traveler's Checks

Once the ultimate form of travel currency, traveler's checks are no longer accepted or appreciated the world over. Irish banks and some hotels will accept them, but do not bring all of your funds in the form of traveler's checks, as smaller B&Bs and guesthouses, restaurants, and shops will not accept them. American Express has shut down their main office in Dublin, so that is no longer an option.

Lost Cards

If you lose your credit or debit card while traveling in Ireland or it is stolen, report it immediately. Write down the phone numbers from the back of the credit card with the last four digits and expiration date on a separate piece of paper. If you do not have this information available at the time an incident occurs, check the Internet for any phone numbers for your bank and/or credit card agency.

 Fact

The currency converter found on XE (*www.xe.com*) will give you an idea of the current rate of exchange. In Ireland, banks offer the best rate, while post offices come close. Exchange bureaus offer the worst rates, but they are often open for longer hours.

Twenty-four-hour phone numbers to major credit-card issuers are listed below. The first number listed is the corresponding office in the United States. The second number listed is the respective office within Ireland.

- **American Express:** (623) 492-8427 (US) 1850 88 2028 (Republic of Ireland)
- **Visa:** (410) 581-9994 (US) or 1800 55 8002 (Republic of Ireland)
- **MasterCard:** (636) 722-7111 (US) or 1800 55 7378 (Republic of Ireland)

When calling any of these credit card companies, state your problem and wait for them to connect you to the proper representative. Following, you will most likely have to answer various security questions (your social security number, home phone and address, birth date, etc.). You should not be responsible for any fraudulent actions on your account and should receive a replacement card within a couple of days.

Running on Empty

If you find yourself in need of fast cash, friends or family back home can send you quick funding via any international transfer service. These include Western Union, American Express (Amex), or Thomas Cook. Such services charge a fee, keep a commission, and often offer the worst rate of exchange. However, for emergency situations, they often work flawlessly.

Taxes, Refunds, and Customs

In Europe, each purchase has a value-added tax (VAT) that is usually above 20 percent. This percentage adds up over time, especially if shopping is high on your list. If you do not work or live in Ireland (or Europe), you are entitled to receive a refund on a portion of this tax. Some larger sellers can automatically deduct the tax when you are purchasing an item, so simply ask.

 Essential

Contact your insurance company about the coverage you might have on your valuables while traveling. Most agencies will charge a supplemental fee to cover your items while you are on the road. If you travel often, buy a yearly plan that is well worth the small investment. What warranties do not cover, there is a good chance that insurance will.

Knowing about the VAT refund is important before you go because you will need to ask each seller if they are able to provide you with the necessary form(s), signature, or stamp.

The steps for obtaining this tax credit are:

1. The seller of an item should help you complete the tax-free shopping document.
2. At the airport upon leaving Ireland (or any other European country), find the agent in the airport who deals with VAT refunds. This is most often done before going past security into the duty-free lobby. If you have purchased large or restricted items, make sure you do not check your baggage before the customs officer verifies your purchases.
3. The next step can vary, but most often sellers of items work with an agency called Global Refund (*www .globalrefund.com*), which you can either locate at larger airports or mail your documents to. If your refund is claimed in person, you can obtain cash or have credit applied to your credit card. If mailed, you will have to supply the credit card number used for most of the purchases. The credit might take a few months to appear on

your statement. For any other information about bringing items back to the United States, read over the U.S. Customs and Border Protection (*www.cbp.gov*) website.

If you have taken valuable merchandise with you abroad, such as cameras, computers, or jewelry, then you might be required to pay duty fees on these items if you cannot prove that you bought them within the United States before your trip. For this reason and as a precaution, consider registering your items with customs before departing on your journey.

At the airport, visit customs and obtain a Certificate of Registration, which will allow you to enter without issue on items you have brought along. If you do not register them with customs, bring original receipts or a copy of your insurance policy that verifies all that you own.

 Fact

Electric shavers can be used in various B&Bs, hotels, and guesthouses that have an American style outlet in the bathroom. These are labeled with a small shaver icon and display that their output is 110–115 volts. Many rooms offer hairdryers, but ask your host at the time of booking if this is a concern.

Electricity and Electronics

Electricity in Ireland is 240 volts at 50 cycles, which is common throughout Europe. In most cases, electronics from the United States will work fine on 240 volts. Check the fine print in the user's manual for details. Laptops and portable DVD players are fine with a prong adapter (not a voltage converter). Irish plugs are the same as those in the United Kingdom (which are not typical European plugs): two large, square front prongs and one equally sized at the top.

Communication

Keeping in contact with your friends and family back home while you are on the road will not be that difficult in Ireland. If you have your own laptop, many hotels, B&Bs, and guesthouses have WIFI available. Some provide a computer for guests to use. Otherwise, the options of snail mail, mobile Internet, and telephoning home are options.

Calling Ireland and Back Home

In order to access an international line (or to dial out of country) on most landline phones in the United States, you will have to first dial 011. Following, you will have to enter the code of the nation you wish to call. Ireland's country code is 353. Next, you will have to enter the region code and phone number, dropping the first "0" of the establishment you wish to reach. As an example, follow this scenario:

1. You wish to call the Aran Islands to reserve a room at a B&B.
2. The phone number listed on the website is +353 (0)99 555 5555.
3. Dial 011 followed by the country code, 353.
4. Next, drop the first "0" and enter the region code of the Aran Islands, which is 99.
5. Enter the phone number: 555 5555.
6. The entire number would be dialed as: 011 353 99 555 5555.

Once you are in Ireland, you will not have to enter 011 or the country code. If you are dialing within country, the phone number would be entered as simply 099 555 5555, which is how numbers are written in this guide.

In order to call Northern Ireland from the United States, you will have to follow the same steps above, except you would use the United Kingdom's country code +44 (44).

To call Northern Ireland from the Republic, replace the 028 (everywhere in the UK region of Ireland has this prefix) with 048.

Once you are in Northern Ireland, simply dial the phone number without a regional prefix (i.e., drop the 028 and dial the number).

To call the United States from Ireland, you will have to dial the country code to the United States (+1, or 001), plus the area code and phone number (i.e., 001 212 555 5555).

VoIP Services

The way of the future is to make calls over the Internet (using a VoIP service). The most popular programs are Skype (*www.skype.com*) and Google Talk (*www.google.com/talk*). Yahoo! Voice (*www.voice.yahoo.com*) is a similar service in conjunction with Jajah (*www.jajah.com*). These services allow you to make inexpensive calls anywhere in the world, have voice mail, and a local U.S. (or other) phone number that rings over your computer or phone no matter where you are in the world. Certain companies are releasing mobile phones with this software preinstalled.

Mobile Phones

Besides VoIP services, the best alternative if you are going to be in Ireland for ten days or more would be to purchase a mobile phone upon your arrival, which will come with some pre-paid credit. Phones in Europe use a GSM 900/1800 system that is not compatible with all U.S. phones. Call your provider to see if your phone will function on the European wavelength or if it will work with a SIM card. If your company indicates your phone cannot be "unlocked," various shops in Dublin can *manipulate* it for a reasonable fee.

Alternatively, your provider might be able to open your phone to "roaming," although this is an expensive option. Renting a phone in the United States and bringing it along with you is possible on a number of websites.

Having a local phone number will allow you to more easily call hotels to verify reservations, secure seats at restaurants and shows, or in the unlikely event you have an emergency. The phone will work across Europe, Australia, and parts of Asia. In Ireland, Vodaphone has the best coverage, followed by O2, and 3 (pronounced *tree*).

Another option to consider while in the country is to buy phone cards that can be used with public phones. These can be purchased in tourist offices or newspaper shops around the country. Acquire an international phone card if possible, which is good for in-country calls and those to other countries. Not all cards are the same, so ask which has the best rate to the country of choice.

Mobile Internet

Ireland has entered the age of the mobile Internet where connecting on the go has never been easier. With a small USB toggle, Vodaphone offers the best coverage, but they require a two-year minimum contract. The company called 3 offers mobile, prepaid Internet at a great price with good customer service. Plus, your coverage extends into Northern Ireland. Only in removed locations in the west and northwest of the country will you have no connectivity, although that might change as coverage is expanded. Most companies' software is compatible with Mac OSX, Windows, and Linux.

Traveler's Corner

Traveling independently in Ireland is an enjoyable way to intimately experience the country; however, traveling alone is not the cheapest option in Ireland (unless you plan on staying in hostels and using the excellent bus or train network), and hotels will actually charge you more if their regular rates are per person, adding a single supplement charge of 15–50 percent on the tariff.

 Alert

Hitchhiking is not openly recommended in Ireland. While it is reasonably safe in rural areas, travelers who hitchhike are taking a risk in any part of the world. That said, most Irish locals will pick up hitchhikers in certain situations, such as in bad weather or if far removed from a town or village.

Senior Citizen Travel

Senior citizens traveling to Ireland might be able to find discounted rates on airfare through various organizations, such as the AARP (*www.aarp.org*). Once in Ireland, you can save money on nearly all sites and attractions, paying equal to that of a student. Seniors over the age of sixty qualify, so carry a copy of your passport or simply present your driver's license and ask for a senior discount. Seniors also receive excellent deals on exhibitions and theater presentations.

Student and Youth Travel

With a majority of its population under the age of twenty-five, student travel is a prevalent business in Ireland. And, with vast numbers come quality discounts. The one key possession that students traveling in Ireland will need is an International Student/ Youth Identity Card through ISIC (available at *www.statravel.com* or *www.isiccard.com*). This youth card, which is available to individuals under the age of twenty-six, will allow students and youths to benefit from reduced rates on public transportation, theater, museums, and more.

Gay Travel

With the end of its political strife and a coming-of-age with the expansion of Europe, homosexuality has become more accepted in Ireland, and it was officially legalized in the early 1990s. Nevertheless, gay travelers in Ireland will still face glances from more conservative folks, especially in rural areas. And, even in more liberal cities (such as Galway, Belfast, or Dublin), gay couples should try to prevent overt public displays of affection. A bunch of groups, clubs, B&Bs, guesthouses, and other businesses cater to gay travelers, so finding them is easily done online. One resource is Outhouse (01 873 4932, *www.outhouse .ie*), with an office at 105 Chapel Street in Dublin. Other resources include the Gay Switchboard in Dublin (01 872 1055), and the International Gay and Lesbian Travel Association (IGLTA, *www .iglta.org*).

Special-Needs Travelers

Travelers with disabilities or other special needs can still enjoy certain sites and activities in Ireland. While regulations at smaller B&Bs and guesthouses are changing to accommodate for diverse clients, all have not yet met the requirements. For Europe, Ireland is still far behind in this part of its travel sector. If you are in a wheelchair, visit local tourist offices to find out which accommodations are accessible to those of reduced mobility. Many of the cottages and one-story eco-lodges described in this book are compatible to diversified clientele.

As old buses are being retired, new ones are equipped to handle a variety of travelers with special needs. Specially equipped rental cars are available; contact the larger companies referenced in this guide about the options. Train cars have been updated throughout the country with the help of the European Union; they now meet the needs of the mobile, hearing, and seeing impaired. One quality web resource is Disability Ireland (*www.disability .ie*). Additionally, various operators catering to this travel sphere are Accessible Journeys (*www.disabilitytravel.com*), Access-Able Travel (*www.access-able.com*), and accessatlast (*www.accessatlast.com*). The latter lists hotels able to assist those with various needs. Assist Ireland (*www.assistireland.ie*) outlines some handy travel resources and references Accessible Ireland (*www.accesibleireland.ie*) as an especially handy resource.

Dublin Metro Area

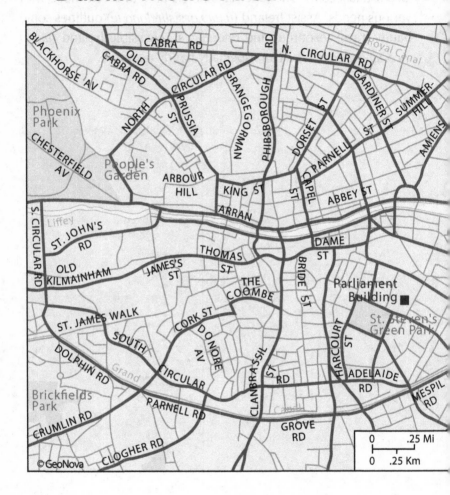

CHAPTER 6

More than Pubbin': Everything Dublin

Dublin is the pulse of Ireland. A city of old born again, it has a richness not originating in its recent financial uprising. Dublin is a vibrant city where the people are busy by day but relaxed in a cozy pub by night. Dublin revitalizes the traveler's spirit and offers a view into the soul of Ireland.

Getting to Dublin

It is no surprise that over half the travelers coming from North America fly directly to Dublin. Because of its central location, it is an unrivaled starting point.

Exploring eastern Ireland from Dublin is a good way to orientate oneself to the country. Belfast, in Northern Ireland, is 160km (100 miles) away; the interstate (with partial toll road) or train makes the trip rather quick. The pastoral hills of Wicklow and the timeless medieval city of Kilkenny are respectively one and two hours away. Dublin is 300km (185 miles) from Killarney and 215km (133 miles) from County Galway, roughly four hours by car.

Flying

The Dublin International Airport (01 814 1111, *www.dublin airport.com*) is the largest travel hub in Ireland. Other major airports are Cork Airport (021 431 3131, *www.corkairport.com*) for internal flights and Shannon Airport (061 712 000, *www.shannonairport.com*). From the United States you can often find deals with Aer Lingus (via American Airlines) (1 800 474 7424 U.S. or 0818 365 000 in Ireland, *www. aerlingus.ie*) from New York, Chicago, and Boston. Delta Airlines (1 800 241 4141 U.S., *www.delta.com*) and Continental Airlines (1 800 231 0856 U.S., *www.continental.com*) also fly into the Republic.

You can also fly into Dublin from London on British Airways (*www.ba.com*), Aer Lingus (*see above*), Air France (*www .airfrance.com*), and the budget carrier Ryanair (*www.ryanair.com*).

Ferry

Ferries arriving from Britain come into the Dublin Ferry Port (01 855 2222) and at the Dún Laoghaire Ferry Port (01 842 8864). You can find out more through Irish Ferries (0818 300 400, *www .irishferries.ie*) or the international group of Stena Line (01 204 7777, *www.stenaline.ie*).

 Alert

If you will be starting your trip in Dublin, it is recommended that you do not rent a car while in the city. With congested traffic, one-way streets, and expansive highways that change names every few miles, your trip will be much more relaxing if you take advantage of the public transport options available.

Train

The Irish Rail (Ianród Éireann) (01 850 366 222, *www.irishrail.ie*) has service from all over the Republic and Northern Ireland into Dublin. Heuston Station serves trains coming from or going to the south

(Cork and Killarney) and west (Mayo and Galway). Pearse Station serves trains coming from or going to the southeast (Wicklow and Wexford). And, Connolly Station serves trains coming from or going to the north (Belfast) and northwest (Sligo and Northern Ireland, but not Donegal). You can save money by booking trips online.

Bus and Car

Bus Éireann (01 836 6111, *www.buseireann.ie*) runs express routes to and from all major cities in Ireland from the Bus Aras (Busáras) station on Store Street (on the other side of the Trading House premises off of O'Connell Street). Bus Éireann offers discount rates to students holding a Student Travel Card (*www .studenttravelcard.ie*). If you are driving into the city, the M50 circumnavigates the greater Dublin area, while the East Link and West Link (toll roads, €2–3) allow you to skip the busier city center.

Getting into the City Center

AirCoach (01 844 7118, *www.aircoach.ie*) departs every fifteen minutes (every hour after midnight) from the airport to the city center (Grafton Street and Trinity College). It costs €7 one way, €12 roundtrip for adults, and €1 for children under twelve.

Airlink Express (01 844 4265) runs every twenty minutes but does not currently offer service after midnight. It runs to the Dublin city center, to the Heuston and Connolly Railway stations, and to the Bus Aras (Busáras) central bus station. It costs €4 for children and €7 for adults one way.

The Dublin Bus (01 873 4222, *www.dublinbus.ie*) has connecting routes from the airport to the city center and costs €6 one way. Bus 747 goes from the airport to the city center at O'Connell Street, while bus 748 goes from the airport to the Tara Street Station, Aston Quay, Wood Quay, and the Heuston Rail Station. The Travel Information Desk is helpful with any questions. Taxis are also available and will cost €30-plus. Tip taxi drivers a minimum 10 percent.

Getting Around the City

Dublin Bus has routes throughout the city and is the cheapest way to get around. Nearly all the buses start on or near Abbey Street and O'Connell Street on the north side, while College Street and Aston Quay are central points on the south side.

It operates Monday–Saturday, 6:00 A.M.–11:30 P.M.; Sunday, 10:00 A.M. –11:00 P.M. Fares €1.50-plus. Multiday passes are available. Nitelink bus runs Thursday–Saturday, midnight–3:00 A.M. Fares €5 flat.

 Alert

> If you spot the bus you want, stick out your arm and wave your hand to flag down the bus. Have exact change or you will receive a receipt in lieu of change, which can be cashed in at the central bus station (59 O'Connell Street) during normal business hours.

A hop-on, hop-off Dublin sightseeing bus (01 605 7705, *www .irishcitytours.com*) has multilingual tours of the city for those who want to see all the sights with ease.

Dublin Area Rapid Transit (DART)

The rapid transit train, known as DART, will take you from the city center at Pearse, Tara Street, and the main Connolly Station. The DART goes all the way to Howth and Malahide to the north and extends south all the way to Greystones. It operates Monday–Saturday, 7 A.M.–midnight; Sunday, 9:30 A.M.–11 P.M. Fares €1.80-plus. Multiday passes available.

LUAS Tram

The LUAS Tram (*www.luas.ie*) runs where the DART does not. It goes through the city center at Connolly Station and down south at St. Stephen's Green. The main use of the LUAS for travelers would be getting to and from Connolly Station to Heuston Station. It operates Monday–Saturday, 5:30 A.M.–12:30 A.M.; Saturday, 6:30 A.M.–12:30 A.M.; Sunday, 7:00 A.M.–11:30 P.M. Fares €1.50-plus. Multi-day passes available.

Things to See and Do

Orienting yourself with the River Liffey will help you keep your bearings in the city. The river is divided into quays. Temple Bar is just south of Crampton and Aston Quay. Dublin is divided into various postal codes. Odd number designations, such as Dublin 1 and Dublin 3, are north of the River Liffey. Even number designations, such as Dublin 2 and Dublin 8, are south of the river.

Temple Bar and Stephen's Green

Cobbled streets line Dublin's most animated zone known as Temple Bar (01 679 3477, *www.temple-bar.ie*). Located between the Christ Church Cathedral and the Bank of Ireland, this area showcases Dublin's heightened diversity in people, culture, art, and cuisine. An information center can be found at 12 East Essex (01 677 2255, *www.visit-templebar.ie*). Stephen's Green (open daily) is an expansive park of nearly 11 hectares (27 acres) that can be found at the top end of Grafton Street.

If you're interested in the alternative art scene of Temple Bar, see the Irish Film Institute (01 679 5744, *www.irishfilm .ie*), which presents outdoor screenings in the summer at Meetinghouse Square. The Temple Bar Gallery (01 671 0073, *www .templebargallery.com*) exhibits works by up-and-coming artists. If you are into avant-garde, check out the Project Arts Center (01 881 9613, *www.project.ie*). The Gallery of Photography (01 671 4654, *www.galleryofphotography.ie*) presents local and international photographers.

Temple Bar and Stephen's Green highlights include:

- One of the top sights in Temple Bar, the famed Chester Beatty Library (01 404 0750, *www.cbl.ie*), has earned such titles as Museum of the Year (2002) and is home to an awe-inspiring array of masterful works of art. Entrusted to the state upon his death, Sir Alfred Chester Beatty, a mining tycoon from America, collected objects of the highest esteem, including Babylonian tablets nearly 6,000 years old, along with invaluable artifacts from the east. Located in the Clock Tower Building, Cork Hill. Open Monday–Saturday, 10 A.M.–5 P.M.; Saturday, 11 A.M.–5 P.M.; Sunday, 1 P.M. Closed October–April. Admission free.
- Although the hub of British rule over Ireland for nearly 800 years, the Dublin Castle (01 645 8813, *www.dublincastle.ie*) does not stand in its former grandeur. The only remaining structures of old are the Record Tower. A tour, which runs twice per hour, can be worthwhile, but government meetings might cause some delays. Located on Cork Hill. Open Monday–Friday, 10 A.M.–5 P.M.; Saturday–Sunday, 2 P.M. Closed Good Friday, December 25–26, January 1. Admission €2–3.50/4.50.
- A vast collection of paintings makes up the well-established National Gallery (01 661 5133, *www.nationalgallery.ie*). With collections of both Irish and other European art, the highlight of the museum is the Yeats Collection by Jack B. Yeats, Ireland's most distinguished painter. Located on W. Merrion Square. Open Monday–Wednesday and Friday–Saturday, 9:30 A.M.–5:30 P.M.; Thursday, 9:30 A.M.–8:30 P.M.; Sunday, noon–5:30 P.M. Admission free.
- Home to a memorial dedicated to Jonathan Swift, author of *Gulliver's Travels*, and the supposed location where Saint Patrick baptized Irish infidels in a well, St. Patrick's Cathedral (01 475 4817, *www.stpatrickscathedral.ie*) has been

around since at least 1225. You can also listen to the choir sing on certain days (September–June, Monday–Friday, 9:40 A.M.; 5:30 P.M. daily, except Wednesday). Located on St. Patrick's Close. Open daily. Admission €4/6.

- The Christ Church Cathedral (01 677 8099, *www.cccdub.ie*) dates back to 1038 when a wooden church was erected here. Strongbow, a Norman warrior, rebuilt it in stone in 1171. The chamber holds artifacts that will surely spark contemplative theories. Located on Church of the Holy Trinity road. Open daily; hours of operation vary throughout the year. Admission €3/5.
- What is considered one of Dublin's splendid Georgian homes, the Leinster House (01 618 3000, *www.irlgov.ie*) is currently presided by the Irish Parliament, and Lower and Upper House. Designed and constructed by Richard Cassels in the mid-1700s, it was made with two façades, a country house and a town house. Tours are available. Open November–May: Tuesday, 2:30 P.M.–8:30 P.M.; Wednesday, 10:30 A.M.–8:30 P.M.; and Thursday, 10:30 A.M.–5:30 P.M. Admission free.

Museums

Dubbed the "dead zoo," the Natural History Museum (01 677 7444, *www.museum.ie*) is dedicated to Ireland's flora and fauna. The museum, basically unchanged since its debut in Victorian times, displays the skeletons of human bodies, along with peculiar stuffed animals. Located on Merrion St. Open Tuesday–Saturday, 10 A.M.–5 P.M.; Sunday, 2 P.M.–5 P.M. Admission is free.

Another worthwhile museum is the National Museum of Ireland—Archaeology and History (01 677 7444, *www.museum .ie*), which houses some of the grandest examples of Bronze and Iron Age artifacts in Europe. The Tara Brooch, Ardagh Chalice, and Crucifixion Plaque are especially of note. Located on Kildare St. Open Tuesday–Saturday, 10 A.M.–5 P.M.; Sunday, 2 P.M.–5 P.M. Admission free, donations appreciated.

One kid-friendly museum is Dvblinia (or Dublinia) (01 679 4611, *www.dublinia.ie*), which has interactive exhibits geared toward teaching children the history of Dublin. Located on St. Michael's Hill, Christ Church. Open daily 10 A.M.–5 P.M. Closed December 23–26 and March 17. Admission €5/6.

 Essential

While many sights are free, you might consider buying a Dublin Pass (*www.dublinpass.ie*) at any tourist office. A one-day pass costs about €40 per adult and €18 for a child. Multiday passes are available. The card does allow you to jump ahead of certain lines.

Trinity College

Founded in 1592 by Queen Elizabeth I, the University of Dublin, with its famed Trinity College (01 677 2941), was set up initially as a Protestant college. Only in the 1970s did Catholics begin to attend its 16-hectare (40-acre) grounds. Alumni of the college include Jonathan Swift, Oscar Wilde, and Bram Stoker. The university is a retreat from the hustle and bustle of the Dublin city center. South is Grafton Street, lined with its trendy shops and cafés, and outside the front gates are the city's handsome Georgian government buildings. The most significant monuments and sights of the college are:

- The Campanile is a dominating 30-meter (100-feet) bell built by the architect of Queen's University in Belfast, Sir Charles Lanyon. Once you have entered, pass the statues of Oliver Goldsmith and Edmund Burke; continue through the main entrance and into Parliament Square (which sits over the college's invaluable wine cellar).
- The Long Room, constructed in 1732, is a magnificent hall-like edifice housing over 200,000 antique objects, including

Ireland's oldest harp, which became the iconic crest of Guinness. Most of the collection is comprised of ancient texts. You will also find busts of scholarly or literary notables, such as Shakespeare.

- The Old Library contains the *Book of Durrow*, along with the most celebrated and one of the oldest books in the world, the *Book of Kells* (01 608 2308, *www.bookofkells .ie*). This lavishly decorated book contains the first four books of the New Testament in Latin. It was illuminated by cenobites who fled the small island of Iona, Scotland, before fleeing to Kells, in County Meath, Ireland, and about forty miles north of Dublin, around A.D. 806. Open daily May–September, Monday–Saturday, 9:30 A.M.–5 P.M.; Sunday, 9:30 A.M.–4:30 P.M. (Sunday, noon–4:30 P.M., October–April). Closed 23 December until 3 January. Admission €7/8.

Essential

A walking tour is one of the best ways to get a full viewing and understanding of the college's intricacies. The tours take place every forty minutes from Parliament Square from mid-May through September. It does not include access to the Book of Kells. Tours Monday–Saturday, 10:15 A.M.–3:30 P.M.; Sunday, 10:15 A.M.–3 P.M. Admission €10.

O'Connell Street and Greater Dublin

Passing over the Ha'penny Bridge brings you to Dublin's O'Connell Street and into a new medley of sights to explore. The LUAS can take you farther afield to the edge of Phoenix Park (with public gardens and walking/jogging areas), which is home to the Dublin Zoo (1 800 924 848, *www.dublinzoo.ie*). Additionally, exploration closer to Four Courts brings you to the Old Jameson

Distillery (01 807 2355, *www.jamesonwhisky.com*), which is a massive museum giving tours of the making of the "water of life." Enjoy a sampling of old-world whiskeys.

 Fact

For such a small country, in both size and population, it is a statistical miracle that the Nobel Prize for Literature has been awarded to three Irishmen: William Butler Yeats in 1923, George Bernard Shaw in 1925, and Samuel Beckett in 1969.

If you want to experience Dublin's past literary figures, then a visit to the Dublin Writer's Museum (01 872 2077, *www.writersmuseum.com*) and the nearby James Joyce Cultural Centre (01 878 8547, *www.jamesjoyce.ie*) is a must. Yeats ran the popular Abbey Theatre (01 878 7222, *www.abbeytheatre.ie*). A visit to the Shaw Birthplace (01 475 0854), a short walk from Stephen's Green on Synge Street, and to the Oscar Wilde House (01 662 0281, *http://tinyurl.com/oscarwilde*) are compelling additions to any literary crawl. Discount combined tickets for the Writer's Museum, Cultural Center, and Shaw Birthplace are available.

Pub Crawls, Walking Tours, and Folklore

For access into Dublin's great pubs combined with tales of its literary geniuses, tag along on the Dublin Literary Pub Crawl (01 670 5602, *www.dublinpubcrawl.com*). The tour begins at the Duke Pub (01 454 0228) at 9 Duke Street. April–November, begins daily, 7:30 P.M.; Sunday, noon and 7:30 P.M. (all year); November–March, Thursday–Saturday, 7:30 P.M. Admission €10/12.

If you are not into a literary pub-crawl, wet your whistle for a Musical Pub Crawl (01 475 3313, *www.discoverdublin.ie*). Additionally, Historical Walking Tours of Dublin (087 688 9412 or 087 830

3523, *www.historicalinsights.ie*) meet in front of the Trinity College front gate May–September at 11 A.M. and 3 P.M.; April and October at 11A.M. only; November–March, Friday–Sunday at 11 A.M. If a night of magical folklore tops your list, enjoy a candlelight dinner at the Brazen Head Pub (1800 251 052 or 01 492 2543, *www.irishfolktours .com*) while learning about Irish life of times past. Bookings available at the Dublin Tourist Office.

Kids' Activities
The Ark Cultural Center (01 670 7788, *www.ark.ie*) is brimming with learning activities, and the Lambert Puppet Theatre and Museum (01 280 0974, *www.lambertpuppettheatre.com*) was brought to Dublin by the ventriloquial genius Eugene Lambert. Check websites for hours and book ahead.

St. Michan's Church
St. Michan's Church (01 872 4154) offers a ghoulish glimpse into the chambers of the ancient dead. The guided tour of the church, its grounds, and its secret depths will surely delight. Learn more about the aristocrats, crusaders, nuns, and the horrendous deaths of those forever entombed in its eerie cavity. Located on Lower Church Street (near Four Courts). Open March–October: Monday–Friday, 10 A.M.–12:45 P.M. and 2 P.M.–4:45 P.M.; Saturday, 10 A.M.–12:45 P.M.; November–April: Monday–Friday, 12:30 P.M.–3:30 P.M. Admission €3/4.

Guinness Storehouse
The most-visited site in all of Dublin, the Guinness Storehouse (01 408 4800, *www.guinness-storehouse.com*) was a fermentation plant until 1988. Thereafter, the building, internally shaped like a giant pint glass, became the masterpiece it is today. Each of the seven stories is dedicated to a central theme. The seventh floor is the Gravity Bar, offering a free pint and a crowning 360-degree view of Dublin. Located at St. James's Gate

Brewery. Open daily, 9:30 A.M.–5 P.M., until 8 P.M. July–August. Closed Good Friday, December 24–26, January 1. Admission €6–10/15.

Fact

Guinness lovers the world over claim that no better "pull" of Guinness exists elsewhere than in Ireland. To ensure this, the Guinness company sends experts throughout the island to test various "pulls." So, a visit to a pub for a pint of the dark stuff is an essential component to any Irish experience.

Kilmainham Jail

The removed Kilmainham Gaol (jail) (01 453 5984, *www .heritageireland.com*) offers an astonishing walking tour of the premises, alongside a compelling oration on the jail's history. Many famous Irish leaders spent time here, including the renowned Charles Stewart Parnell and Joseph Plunkett. The tour starts each hour and takes a little over one hour. Located on Inichicore Road, which is past Heuston Station. Take the bus from Aston Quay in town. Open April–September: daily, 9:30 A.M.–5 P.M. October–March: Monday–Saturday, 9:30 A.M.–5:30 P.M.; Sunday, 10 A.M.–6 P.M. Admission €3/6.

Irish Museum of Modern Art

Once the Royal Hospital of Kilmainham and now the Irish Museum of Modern Art (01 612 9900, *www.imma.ie*), the impressive structure was envisioned by William Robinson and completed in 1687. Its original purpose was a home for wounded soldiers. In 1991 the residential quarters were transformed into a museum housing Irish and international art. Located on Military Road (take the bus from Aston Quay). Open Tuesday–Saturday, 10 A.M.–5:30 P.M.; Wednesday, 10:30 A.M.–5:30 P.M.; Sunday, noon–

5:30 P.M. Closed Good Friday and December 24–26. Admission free. Free guided tours available, Wednesday, Friday, and Sunday, 2:30 P.M.

Accommodations

If you prefer quaint B&Bs or want five-star luxury, the accommodation options in Dublin are endless. Hotels located near the city center are going to be more expensive. Plenty of quieter, less-expensive establishments are available within a ten-minute walk or five-minute bus or taxi ride from the city center.

Waterloo House

Waterloo Road, Dublin 4
01 660 1888
www.waterloohouse.ie
€120+; S/D/T/F. MC/V

This four-star establishment set in Georgian architecture holds true to its character. The furniture, beds, plush carpeting, and spotless interiors make this a great choice for those looking for a bit of luxury without breaking the bank. The rooms overlooking the back garden are all en suite and offer splendid tranquility. Off-street parking is provided. Located ten minutes walking distance from Stephen's Green.

Azalea Lodge

67 Upper Drumcondra Road, Dublin 9
01 837 0300 or 087 243 4589
www.azalealodge.com
€50–60+; S/D/T/F. MC/V

This lodge is rated highly both online and off for its historic charm and unequalled personal service at incredible prices. The Azalea Lodge is situated comfortably from the city center (ten minutes by bus) and provides parking. If rooms are not available here, try the affordable Ashling House, a neighboring B&B owned by the same proprietors.

Jacob's Inn

21-28 Talbot Place, Dublin 1
01 855 5660
www.isaacs.ie/jacobs-inn-dublin
€50+; S/D/T/F. MC/V

Jacob's Inn is setting a high-caliber standard for budget accommodation in Dublin. It has spic-and-span en suite accommodations with amenities you will find at no other hotel in its price category. Rooms have flat-screen TVs, well-equipped bathrooms, open-faced armoires, along with proper towels and sheets. The hostel keeps its spirits alive offering various activities all week long. Check out Jacob's downtown brother at the Isaac's Hostel (01 855 6215, *www.isaacs.ie/isaacs_hostel*) at 2-5 Frenchman's Lane, Dublin 1.

Other Accommodations

Here are some other accommodations you might consider while in Dublin.

(In the listings that follow, € = around 25 euros per person).

- **€ Aishling House. 19/20 St. Lawrence Rd.**
  01 833 9097
  www.aishlinghouse.com
  The establishment has an antique charm. The proprietors, a husband and wife team, serve excellent breakfasts, and will ensure you a warm and welcoming stay.

- **€€€ Cassidy's Hotel. Cavendish Row, on Upper O'Connell St.**
  01 878 0555
  www.cassidyhotel.com.
- **€€ Castle Hotel. 3-4 Great Denmark St.**
  01 874 6949
  www.castle-hotel.ie.
- **€€€€€ Clarence Hotel. 6-8 Wellington Quay.**
  01 407 0800
  www.theclarence.ie.
- **€ Four Courts Hostel. Merchants Quay.**
  01 672 5839
  www.fourcourtshostel.com
  For a true hostelling experience at a great price, this is the pick. This excellent hostel's staff is personable and quite hip. Geared for a younger crowd. Temple Bar is only a five-minute walk away.
- **€€ Jury's Christchurch Inn. Christ Church Place.**
  01 454 0000
  www.jurysdoyle.com.
- **€€€ Lynham's Hotel. 63-64 O'Connell St.**
  01 888 0886
  www.lynhams-hotel.com.
- **€€€ Number 31. 31 Leeson Close.**
  01 676 5011
  www.number31.ie.

Restaurants and Pubs

The apex of Irish cuisine is Dublin. From international fusion that looks more like art to good old shepherd's pie, Dublin is a gourmet's rush.

DUBLIN'S BEST RESTAURANTS, CAFÉS, AND PUBS

Name	Address	Phone Number	Cost	Type
Bad Ass Café	Crown Alley, Temple Bar	021 452 2000	€	Pizza, burgers
Epicurean Food Hall	Lower Liffey St.	N/A	€	International stalls
Gruel	68a Dame St.	01 670 7119	€	Organic, pasta, fish
Cornucopia	19 Wicklow St.	01 677 7583	€€	Vegetarian
Avoca Café 11-13	Avoca Café St.	01 672 6019	€€	Pizza, salad, deli
Chapter One	18-19 Parnell Sq.	01 873 2266	€€€	Gourmet
Unicorn 128	Merrion Ct.	01 676 182	€€	Italian/ Mediterranean
Eden Meeting House Sq.		01 670 5372	€€	Sirloin steaks
Roly's Bistro	7 Ballsbridge Terrace	01 668 2611	€€	Fish, scallops, lamb pie
O'Neills	2 Suffolk St.	01 679 3656	€	City Center pub
4 Dame Lane	4 Dame Ln.	01 679 0291	€	Pub
Globe	11 S. Great George's St.	01 671 1220	€	Bar and café
The Grave Diggers	1 Prospect Sq., Glasnevin	01 605 7700	€	Pub
Peter's Pub	1 Johnson's Pl.	01 677 8588	€	Pub

KEY

€ = under 25 Euro per person
€€ = 25-35 Euro per person
€€€ = 35-50+ Euro per person

For some of Dublin's ongoing entertainment listings, pick up the *Irish Times*, the *Tribune*, and *Hot Press*. The *Event Guide* can be found at most pubs and clubs as well. To book tickets for theater and concerts, contact Ticketmaster (0818 71 9300; warning:

high-commission charges per ticket for credit card payments), the Dublin Tourist Office (01 605 7700) on Suffolk Street, or the HMV (01 679 5334) at 65 Grafton Street for all the insider information. Here are some of Dublin's best entertainment venues:

DUBLIN'S NIGHTLIFE: FILM, THEATER, AND CLUBS

Name	Address	Phone Number	Type
Irish Film Institute	6 Eustace St.	01 679 5744	Independent film
Cineworld Cinemas	Parnell St.	01 872 8444	Alternative/ independent
Screen	D'Olier St.	01 672 5500	Independent
Abbey Theatre	Abbey St. Lower	01 878 7222	Theater
Focus Theatre	6 Pembroke Place	01 676 3071	Theater
Laughter Lounge	Eden Quay	1800 266 339	Comedy/ international
Project Art Center	39 East Essex St.	01 881 9613	Theater
Helix	Collins Ave.	01 700 7000	Opera/recitals
Gate Theatre	Cavendish Row	01 874 4045	Opera/theater
Gaiety Theatre	South King St.	01 677 1717	Jazz/blues
Village	26 Wexford St.	01 475 8555	Club: mix
Rogue	64 Dame St.	01 675 3971	Club: techno/ house
Rí Rá	Dame Ct.	01 671 1220	Club: gay-friendly/mix
Dragon	South Great George St.	01 478 1590	Disco/bar: gay-friendly
Spy	South William St.	01 677 0014	Nightclub

Shopping in Dublin

The best shopping in Dublin is concentrated in two areas, each on either side of the river. Grafton Street in the south is by far the touristier venue, but offers the trendiest shops. To the north, you will find stores lining the renowned thoroughfare of Henry Street, which is perpendicular to O'Connell Street.

For Dublin's best shopping that won't break the bank, visit:

DUBLIN'S BEST SHOPPING

Name	Address	Phone Number	Type
Brown Thomas	88-95 Grafton St.	01 605 6666	Department store
Carroll's Irish Gift Stores	57 Upper O'Connell St.	01 873 5709	Souvenirs
Kilkenny Shop	6 Nassau St.	01 677 7066	Irish crafts/silver/clothing
Smock	5 Scarlet Row (Temple Bar)	01 613 9000	Int'l women's wear
Powerscourt Center	59 S. William	01 679 4144	Shopping center
Stephen's Green Center	West St. Stephen's Green	01 478 0888	Shopping center
Antique Prints	16 S. Anne St.	01 671 9523	Antiques
Cultivate (Eco-Store)	15-19 Essex St. W.	01 674 5773	Living/learning center
Powerscourt Townhouse	S. William St.	01 671 7000	Galleries/stalls

Traveler's Tidbits

Here you will find the necessary information for Dublin. The best websites to check out information on Dublin are *www.visitdublin.ie* and *www.discoverdublin.ie*. Tourist offices are open during regular business hours.

DUBLIN TOURIST OFFICES

Name	Address	Phone Number	In Operation
Dublin Airport Tourist Office	Dublin Airport	1850 230 330	All year
Dublin Tourist Office	Dun Laoghaire	1850 230 330	All year
Dublin Tourist Office	O'Connell St.	1850 230 330	All year
Dublin Tourist Office	Suffolk St.	1850 230 330	All year

Following is further relevant travel information. In the case of an emergency, dial 999 anywhere in the Republic of Ireland.

TRAVEL INFORMATION

Name	Address	Phone Number
Garda (Police) Headquarters	Phoenix Park	01 666 0000
Dublin St. Vincent's Hospital (south side)	Elm Park, Dublin 4	01 269 4533
Beaumont Hospital (north side)	Beaumont Rd., Dublin 9	01 837 7755
American Embassy	42 Elgin Rd., Ballsbridge	01 668 8777
Dublin Post Office	O'Connell St.	01 705 7600
American Express Office	41 Nassau St.	1890 205 511
Outhouse (Gay Resources)	105 Capel St.	01 873 4932
Central Library (Internet)	Henry St.	01 873 4333
Central Cybercafe	6 Grafton St.	01 677 8298
Genealogy Research (Register Office)	Joyce House, 8-11 Lombard St. E.	01 671 1000

CHAPTER 7

Counties Meath
and Louth

County Meath (An Mhí) and County Louth (Lú) have several small towns and stunning monuments worth exploring. Meath boasts Newgrange, Trim Castle, and the Hill of Tara, while Louth holds one of Europe's most pristine religious sites at Monasterboice. If bedazzling monuments and heart-warming villages giving way to mountains melting into the Irish Sea sound appealing, a short drive from Dublin will allow you to experience a mélange of history, myth, religion, and a powerful political past that the Irish of this region hold dear.

Getting Around Counties
Meath and Louth

Counties Meath and Louth are not far from Dublin, so getting there to explore the sights in one day is feasible. While areas right across the Dublin border are considered nettlesome burbs of urban sprawl, keep traveling to discover the magical realms these counties still possess.

Train, Bus, and Car

The central towns of Drogheda, County Louth, or the smaller, business-oriented Dundalk are accessible from Dublin's Connolly or Pearse Stations. Irish Rail (01 836 6222, *www.irishrail.ie*) has services throughout the day.

Bus Éireann (01 836 6111, *www.buseireann.ie*) is more versatile with daily scheduled routes to Kells, Navan, and Slane, Tara, Trim, Drogheda, Dundalk, and Carlingford.

If you want to head directly to Newgrange, Bus Éireann connects from Drogheda in twenty minutes. Over the Top Tours (01 836 42 4252, *www.overthetoptours.com*) leaves from the Dublin Tourist Office to Newgrange twice daily.

If driving, Drogheda is accessible off the N1, which then leads to the worthwhile Boyne Valley along the N51 west. If you plan on skipping Drogheda, then take the N2 from Dublin to Slane and onward to the Boyne Valley. If heading to the notable Hill of Tara, head toward Navan on the N3, which then connects to the N51 toward Boyne.

County Meath's Tidy Trim

The charming market town of Trim (Baile Átha Troim) is one of Meath's top draws. The region was so highly esteemed by the crown that Elizabeth I contemplated establishing Trinity College here. It might be luck that Dublin won out; the township has maintained a hushed appeal that the few tourists get to savor.

Market Street holds the town's finest cafés, eateries, and shops. From here, there it is easy access to Lornan Street, where you will find St. Patrick's Church (046 943 6698), a nineteenth-century chapel with a fifteenth-century tower, door, baptismal stoup, and window. The Trim Heritage Centre (046 943 7227) at the Town Hall has an audiovisual presentation that brings the history of the town to life. The place is also home to the genealogy heritage department of Meath. Open Monday–Saturday, 9:30 A.M.–5:30 P.M.; Sunday, noon–5:30 P.M.

A famous spire known as the Yellow Steeple is so dubbed for the amber glow of its stones at sundown. This fourteenth-century structure once held a sacred wooden statue of the Virgin Mary, but was lost when Cromwell's men burned the place down. The nearby abbey is now referred to as the Talbot Castle, named after Sir John Talbot. He was famously defeated by Joan of Arc and notoriously regarded in France during the late 1420s. Interestingly, Jonathan Swift later inhabited the place. Open daily. Admission free.

Trim Castle

Trim's most prized possession is Trim Castle (046 943 8619), a grand Anglo-Norman edifice founded by Hugh de Lacy, which took well over thirty years to complete. Built within an already existing moat, the castle was started in 1172 but torn down at least two times, the second when King John visited in 1210. The walls in some places are well over 3-meters (9-feet) thick with a curtain wall and towers with gates encircling the entire complex.

 Fact

Trim is home to the hot-air ballooning multiworld record holder Pauline Baker. She founded the company Irish Balloon Flights (046 948 3436, *www.balloons.ie*), which have offices all over the Republic and Northern Ireland. The Irish Hot Air Ballooning Championship was hosted here in 2001 and 2002.

Interestingly, this stronghold was a backdrop for scenes in the movie *Braveheart*, starring Mel Gibson. Get here early to enjoy a guided tour, capped at twenty people per session. Open Easter–October, daily, 10 A.M.–6 P.M.; November–March, Saturday–Sunday only, 10 A.M.–5 P.M. Access for those with disabilities is limited due to steep stairs. Admission €1.30/2.60/3.70.

County Louth's
Darling Carlingford

With Carlingford's (Cairlinn; *www.carlingford.ie)* allure as one of Ireland's prettiest and most petite fishing hamlets, County Louth will never lose its appeal. The town sits at the base of the Cooley Peninsula's Slieve Foye Mountain, along the banks of Carlingford Lough, and looks across the border into Northern Ireland. A town of cobblestone streets, soft whitewashed country houses, and the remains of King John's Castle in view give it a medieval and removed feel.

 Essential

If you are in Carlingford during the summer, enjoy one of many adventures with the Carlingford Adventure Centre (042 937 3100, *www .carlingfordadventure.com*). Activities include sailing, windsurfing, kayaking, raft building, along with rock climbing, archery, and team challenges. During the last weekend in August, all are welcome to partake in Ireland's largest oyster festival.

The Holy Trinity Heritage Centre (042 937 3454) is stationed in a wonderfully refurbished medieval house of worship. From here, walking tours of the town are often available that chronicle its Viking roots. En route is a visit to King John's Castle, the sixteenth-century mint, friary, and medieval gate known as Tholsel.

Things to See and Do

Often overlooked, both County Meath and County Louth have some tantalizing monuments and wonderfully removed places to explore. The most popular sites are Newgrange, the Hill of Tara, and Monasterboice. While a visit to the main points of interest is recommended, so is a drive around the Cooley Peninsula as well as a peaceful jaunt into its mountains.

Brú na Bóinne: Newgrange, County Meath

The most stunning passage grave in Western Europe and one of Ireland's most mythical attractions, the UNESCO World Heritage Site of Newgrange (041 988 0300, *www.knowth.com/newgrange.htm*) deserves every bit of flattery it receives. Built in 3200 B.C., before the Egyptian pyramids, the massive kidney-shaped mound went unnoticed until the end of the seventeenth century when it was partially pillaged, then left alone for another few hundred years before excavation began in the 1960s.

Archaeologically, Newgrange remains a modern marvel. Made up of over 200,000 tons of stone, standing well over 12 meters (40 feet) and 75 meters (250 feet) in diameter, the structure is completely watertight. Massive quartzite stones were brought from County Wicklow, over 60km (37 miles) away, while other granite boulders were brought down from Northern Ireland. Transportation most likely took place on the water; the wheel had yet to be invented.

 Fact

If you hope to be one of the few and proud bestowed entrance and flooded with winter's first light, enter the lottery. The Brú na Bóinne Visitor Centre has applications on hand. Statistically viable, if your name is drawn, you are entitled to bring one friend along. Winners are drawn in September or October each year.

Newgrange's front façade holds one of the most decorated curbstones marking the passageway into what many historians consider to have been holy burial grounds. Other stones throughout are decorated with spirals and geometric configurations. Celtic legend proclaims this large drumlin as the childbed of Cuchúlainn. Continuing inward, the small slit below the roof box is quite wondrous; during the winter solstice, it is the only time that daybreak's rays enter the main chamber, lightning it up for a total of seventeen minutes.

The stones aligning the passageway before the side chambers are of regionally obtained slate, while the cavity's impressively high ceiling tapers to the capstone, which weights roughly six tons. A large basin was a sacrificial reservoir of sorts and would have once held human remains, most likely cremated bones. Entrance is permitted by guided tour only in groups of twenty-four persons, so get there early. Tickets issued at the Brú na Bóinne Visitor Centre. Open May, 9 A.M.–6:30 P.M.; June to mid-September, 9 A.M.–7 P.M.; October and Febuary–April, 9:30 A.M.–5:30 P.M.; November–January, 9:30 A.M.–5 P.M. Combined admission to Newgrange, Knowth, and Exhibition €4.50/7.40/10.30.

 Essential

For families with kids, the Newgrange Farm (041 982 4119, www .newgrangefarm.com), located in the picturesque Boyne Valley, is a 130-hectare (330-acre) educational family farm run by Willie "Farmer Bill" Redhouse. Children and adults can enjoy playing with baby pigs, throwing feed to ducks, and petting ponies, all before frequenting the aviary house of rare birds. In mid-July, they host an annual Teddy Bear Picnic.

Knowth and Dowth, County Meath

After visiting Newgrange, a visit to Knowth and Dowth are the icing on the historical cake. An equally impressive passage tomb, the Great Mound of Knowth has a corbeled roof chamber with rooms jutting off to each side. It also contains prehistoric artwork formed with geometric designs. Around the area, numerous smaller tombs have been discovered, a few of which are open for viewing. Visit by guided tour only from the visitor center.

The Dowth Megalithic Passage Tomb, called the "Fairy Mound of Darkness," is not nearly as mind-blowing as Newgrange and Knowth, but is definitely more off-the-beaten-path. With a diameter of nearly 85 meters (280 feet) and 15 meters (50 feet) high, the cairn offers some eerie exploration; climbing down the ladder to the lower chamber is not for the claustrophobic. A basin similar to Newgrange and other chambers are worth exploring. A visit here is free of charge; simply drive from Slane on the Drogheda road and park on the north bank of the river. Feel free to wander around the site.

 Alert

Government developers want to run the M3 motorway directly through the Hill of Tara. A group of concerned activists have organized themselves into TaraWatch (*www.tarawatch.org*), whose aim it is to preserve what truly is one of Europe's most historical monuments. Irish government officials attending the winter solstice event at Newgrange are often inconvenienced and reminded of this potential folly by TaraWatch's attending activists.

Hill of Tara, County Meath

Another spot to freely amble about is the Hill of Tara (*Teamhair*). Although its name has a ring to it, the site itself requires some creativity to imagine the importance it once held. At one point in time, Tara was the most hallowed spot in primitive Ireland. Celtic legend holds that the place was a doorway to the spiritual world. Regarded as holy ground before the fifth century, it later became the ceremonial seat of the sovereign high kings of Ireland; royals were officially appointed here. Located off of the Navan and Dublin Road, The Hill of Tara Visitor Centre (046 902 5903 or 041 988 0300) has an audiovisual presentation and guided tours available. Hill of Tara is open all year. Visitor Centre open mid-May–mid-September, 10 A.M.–6 P.M. Admission €1.10/1.30/2.10.

Hill of Slane, County Meath

The Hill of Slane is not as impressive as that of Tara, but its mythic history is phenomenal nonetheless. The Hill, which is really more of a mound, was the location where a pagan king ordered that no flame be lit near this holy place. In defiance, Saint Patrick lit an Easter flame to proclaim Christianity's unstoppable spread. Later, a convert from the king's men, Saint Erc, founded a monastery on the site; the scant remains of his friary rest on the ground.

Monastic Sites in Kells, County Meath

Besides being the storage place of the illuminated *Book of Kells* (see Chapter 6), the town holds some compelling attractions. Set up by Saint Columba in the sixth century, the Kells Monastery was officially founded in 804 by the monks (slash scribes) who fled Iona. A century later, Vikings pillaged the place. The famed manuscript was stolen in the early eleventh century but recovered a few months later in a field; its gold encasement was the only portion missing.

 **Essential**

Outside of Kells, a venue worth a visit is Loughcrew Cairns (www .loughcrew.com/cairns.htm). Designated the "Hill of the Witch" (Slieve na Calliagh), it is an otherworldly necropolis of burial chambers; Cairn G, K, and the most notable Cairn T are the largest. Built around the same time as Newgrange, roaming around is a noiseless lesson in civilizations long gone.

From the monastery, the church grounds are worth a visit for its lofty Round Tower and splendid high crosses. The tower was the scene of the murder of Murchadh Mac Floinn in 1076, before he claimed his right to Ireland's throne. The nearby and best-preserved high cross of Patrick and Columba depicts scenes of Adam and Eve, Cain and Abel, and Daniel in the Lion's Den. The opposing side depicts Judgment Day.

Three other crosses in the yard depict various religions and secular scenes. Further afield off of Church Street is St. Columba's House (AKA St. Colmcille's House), a monastic commune and oratory with vaulted chamber, which is thought to have been a residence for scribes.

Off of Cross Street in town, the Market Cross has been in its same position for centuries; some historians believe that its current location was not its first. As a crime for sins, British forces used the cross as a gibbet at the end of the eighteenth century. Depicted at its base are biblical scenes and an inscription by the artist who carved the holy monument. All of these places of interest are well described in the Kells Heritage Centre (046 924 9336), open daily.

Exploring County Louth

An easy place to arrive from the capital city, Drogheda is County Louth's most appealing yet overlooked town on the tourist trail. Perched along the River Boyne, it is an enchanting place to enjoy pure Irish craic before heading deeper into the Boyne Valley and the Cooley Peninsula.

One of the highlights of the town is the Millmount Museum and Martello Tower (041 983 3097, *www.millmount.net*), which is considered the city's oldest structure. The exhibits on hand include banners from the 1700s, looms, gramophones, a folk kitchen, and an archaeological section containing rocks from every European country. The impressively designed tower is easily seen from town and is thought to have once been a burial tomb before the Normans constructed a castle on the premise. Guided tours and escorted walks are available. Open Monday–Saturday, 9:30 A.M.–5:30 P.M.; Sunday, 2 P.M.–5 A.M. Closed during the Christmas holiday. Combined admission to museum and tower €3/4/5.50.

Another site worth attention is the Old Mellifont Cistercian Abbey (041 982 6459, *www.heritageireland.ie/en/midlandseastcoast /OldMellifontAbbey*). A branch of the Benedictines designed what became the first of its kind in Ireland. Built in 1142 and sanctified in 1157, the monastery housed well over 350 monks practicing their strict faith. While the imagination is left to reconstruct the edifice in its full glory, the remains are still a big draw. Research conducted on the facility discovered an unusual burial vault under the abbey's west end. The lavabo washing room is the best remaining feature. Located off of the R168 in Tullyallen. Visitor Centre open daily from June–end of September, 10 A.M.–6 P.M. Admission €1/2/3.

Monasterboice, County Louth

An esteemed religious site in Ireland and north of Drogheda, Monasterboice is composed of two extraordinary high crosses known as Muiredach's Cross and the West Cross. Finely sculpted and featuring holy writ, Muiredach's Cross stands nearly 6 meters (20 feet) tall and fits together like a puzzle piece with a sandstone base and tenon capstone. Truly a phenomenal construction feat in the tenth century, the base illustrates Adam and Eve, while the capstone renders the meeting of Saint Anthony and Saint Paul. Throughout the center are other scenes depicting Moses and the Judgment Day. The West Cross is considered the largest of its kind in Ireland. A vast burial ground composed of two chapels and a round tower encircles these sites, along with a sixth-century monastery founded by Saint Buite. Open all year.

The Cooley Mountains and Peninsula, County Louth

Overlooking the Irish Sea, the Cooley Peninsula is a remarkable area to explore by car, bike, or foot. The best place to begin is to start out at the quaint town of Carlingford; just northwest of town are wonderful views afforded from the Slieve Foye Forest Park.

 Alert

The highest mountain in Cooley is the 589-meter (1932-feet) Slieve Foye (Sliabh Feá). Parking your car at the tourist office is the best way to start your ascent of the "Mountain of the Giant." Additionally, the trailhead can begin on the Táin Trail. While the map available at the tourist office might suffice, it is always a better idea to invest in an Ordnance Survey (OS) map.

Leaving Carlingford, the environs of the Cooley Peninsula and Mountains give way to magnificent views of the Mourne Mountains, scattered dolmen remnants, and loughs. Drive the coast around the R173 through the Windy Gap forming a loop by continuing onward to Rathcor, Grange, and Ballagan point. Driving the whole area takes about four hours, so pack a lunch and enjoy the finest scenery north of Dublin.

A popular and well-marked circuitous walking route from Carlingford is the 40km (25-mile) Táin Way. Possible in one day, but more relaxing over two, the trail meanders up the south side of Slieve Foye and has panoramic wonders overlooking the River Cronn and Rockmarshall Forest. The trail is composed of notable forest paths, ancient green paths, plus a few back roads. Additionally, the Cooley Bird Watching Trail is also a popular diversion for birders; the tourist office in town has all the latest information.

Fact

The *coolest* activity in Cooley is to delve into regional lore on the Táin Cycling Trail. The route is a full-on 589km (365-mile) loop that retraces the famed mythical war story of *Táin Bó Cúalgne*, or the "Cattle-Raid of Cooley." In the tale, Queen Maeve battles Celtic icon Cúchulainn for the right to possess the Great Brown Bull of Cooley.

Accommodations

The variety of accommodations in County Meath and County Louth are as noteworthy as in any other county on the island. Selections topping the list are guesthouses and castle hotels set in picturesque surroundings unmatched in more-populated areas. Like anywhere in Ireland, the quality and spirit put into the design and running of each establishment make each unique. Likewise, various lodgings offer dining options that will mean less time driving and more time feasting.

Bellinter House and Restaurant
Navan, Co. Meath
046 903 0900
www.bellinterhouse.com
€80–110+ per person; suite €150 + per person; S/D/T/F. MC/V

An eighteenth-century Palladian jewel with sleek, modern touches, the Bellinter House is a luxury hotel joining the eco-friendly ranks—another example of how sumptuous green can be. A famed architect in Ireland, Richard Castle, added his imprint in a picture-perfect spot along the River Boyne. Through the day, enjoy walking or biking trails working up an appetite for aperitifs at the Wine Bar followed by dining elegance at the award-winning Eden Restaurant.

Trim Castle Hotel

Castle Street, Trim, Co. Meath
046 948 3000
www.trimcastlehotel.com
€100–250+ per room; S/D/T/F. MC/V

Offering great rates in the off-peak season, the Trim Castle Hotel is a luxury four-star establishment with a bed-and-breakfast feel. The hotel makes a wonderful base from which to explore the surrounding sites, including Trim Castle, the Yellow Steeple, and Newgrange. Golfers will be in heaven; the castle receives reduced rates at local courses, six of which are ranked in the top 100 in Ireland.

Beaufort House

Ghan Rd., Carlingford, Co. Louth
042 937 3879
www.beauforthouse.net
€50–70+ per person; S/D

A five-diamond and well-priced guesthouse, the Beaufort House distinguishes itself as one of County Louth's finest. Deserving all the awards it has received, the Caine family work endlessly to ensure each guest rests comfortably along their calming shores.

Mourne View B&B

Belmont, Carlingford, Co. Louth

042 937 3551

www.mourneviewcarlingford.com

€45–65+ per person. S/D/F

With views unsurpassed, the Mourne View B&B sits on the Irish side of the bay and overlooks the town's lough, Carlingford Mountain, and the resplendent Mourne Mountains of Northern Ireland. The hostess, Lyn Grills, is known to go beyond the call of duty to ensure her guests have had a cozy night and a sumptuous breakfast. A well-priced venue, it is the premier B&B in the region.

Castle Arch Hotel

Summerhill Rd., Trim, Co. Meath

046 943 1516

www.castlearchhotel.com

€70–130+ per room; S/D/T/F. MC/V

The Castle Arch Hotel, a part of the Cusack Hotel Group, was an undiscovered gem until now. Excellent prices and services render this one-of-a-kind eclectic guesthouse as good a deal as any in Europe. The bar and restaurant carry drinks and dishes from home and abroad.

Other Accommodations

Here are some other accommodations you might consider while in Counties Meath and Louth. (In the listings that follow, € = around 25 euros per person.)

- €€ **The Old Forge B&B. Rathfeigh, Co. Meath.**
  041 982 5855
  www.theoldforge.ie

- €€ **Athlumney Manor. Athlumney, Navan, Co. Meath.**
  46 907 1388
  www.athlumneymanor.com
- € **Millrace Lodge. Old Rd., Athlumney, Navan, Co. Meath.**
  046 902 8222
- €€€ **Best Western Boyne Valley Hotel and Country Club. Drogheda, Co. Louth.**
  041 983 9188
  www.boyne-valley-hotel.ie
- €€ **Scholar's Townhouse Hotel. King St., Drogheda, Co. Louth.**
  041 983 5410
  www.scholarshotel.com
- €€ **Grove House. Market Square, Carlingford, Co. Louth.**
  042 937 3494
  www.grovehousecarlingford.com
- €€€ **Rampark Farmhouse. Carlingford, Co. Louth.**
  012 957 602
  www.atramparkfarmhouse.com
- € **The Foy Centre Hostel. Dundalk, St., Carlingford, Co. Louth.**
  042 938 3624
  www.carlingfordbeds.com

Restaurants

Both inland and coastal regions of Counties Meath and Louth have an array of eateries to tantalize the taste buds. Dundalk, Carlingford, and Drogheda have excellent seafood restaurants. The restaurants listed here, while leaning toward pricey, offer the best food around. If you are in the area, splurging on any of these eateries is well worth it. For those on a budget, plentiful pubs abound and venturing into one of the more rural locales will mean good stories, music, and quite possibly new friends. (In the restaurant listings that follow, € = around 25 euros per person).

The Kingfisher Bistro

Dundalk Road, Carlingford, Co. Louth
042 937 3716
€€€

Claire and Mark Woods have refurbished an old mill into what has become a popular local and tourist venue. With Asian food and vegetarian delights, among more traditional fare, the assorted menus make it worth a stop. Various wines on hand enhance the flavors of its continental delights.

Ghan House

Carlingford, Co. Louth
042 937 3682
www.ghanhouse.com
€€

A culinary school, luxury guest lodge, and fine-dining restaurant make the Ghan House a favorite in Carlingford. Having received top honors and raving reviews, this could be your best meal in Ireland. Using local produce helps maintain the bursting flavors that are guaranteed with each bite. With its popularity, it is recommended to book well in advance. Packages for accommodations and cookery school are available. Check to see if your visit to Ireland might coincide with one of their limited eight-course private gourmet nights.

The Loft Restaurant
Trimgate Street, Navan, Co. Meath
046 907 1755
€€

International fare makes the Loft Restaurant a popular eatery among Navan's locals. Cajun chicken, fajitas, and buffalo wings are a few of the savory items served. Early-bird dinners are available as is a tapas bar to help take the edge off.

Franzini O'Brien's
French Lane, Trim, Co. Meath
046 943 1002
€€

The vista of Trim Castle alone makes Franzini O'Brien's worth the investment. This swank restaurant will tempt you with its international cuisine and lively ambience. Their homemade soups and multinational dishes will surely please. Make reservations ahead in the summer, especially for weekend dinners.

The Ground Floor
Bective Square, Kells, Co. Meath
046 924 9688
€€

With choices galore, the Ground Floor offers a charming setting with inspiring fare. The early-bird menu offers the best deals; each day's catch brings fresh fish, while the rest of the menu depends on a rotating and seasonal carte du jour.

Traveler's Tidbits

Here you will find the necessary information for Counties Meath and Louth. The best websites to check out information are *www .meath.ie* and *www.countylouth.com*.

Tourist offices are open during regular business hours.

COUNTIES MEATH AND LOUTH TOURIST OFFICES

Town	Address	Phone Number	In Operation
Newgrange Tourist Office	Brú na Bóinne Visitor Centre, Co. Meath	041 988 0305	All year
Drogheda Tourist Office	Mayoralty St., Co. Louth	041 983 7070	All year
Dundalk Tourist Office	Jocelyn St., Co. Louth	042 933 5484	All year

Following is other pertinent travel information. In the case of an emergency, dial 999 anywhere in the Republic of Ireland.

TRAVEL INFORMATION

Name	Address	Phone Number	Web Address
Louth County Hospital	Dublin Rd., Dundalk	042 933 4701	
Louth Post Office	Togher, Drogheda	041 685 2151	
Genealogy Heritage Centre of Meath	Town Hall, Castle St, Trim	046 943 6633	*www.meathroots .com*
Meath-Louth Family Heritage Centre	High St., Trim	046 36 633	*www.meathroots .com*

CHAPTER 8

The Three W's: Wicklow, Wexford, and Waterford

The southeast of Ireland has all the magic of the Emerald Isle within a day's drive from Dublin. The rolling hills of magical Wicklow with its superbly marked trails at Glendalough are an easy adventure for travelers with or without cars. The coastal beauty of Wexford and Waterford beckon sun-seekers during the long summer days. They are ideal destinations, especially if you are traveling during the off-season, when rain in the west might flood out your outdoor pursuits.

Getting Around Wicklow, Wexford, and Waterford

Getting to the southeast of the Republic is easy due to its accessibility from Dublin. Bray, at the northern tip of Wicklow, for example, is only 20km (12 miles) from the southern tip of Dublin. Wexford is farther down the coast at 140km (86 miles) from Dublin and only one and a half hours from Wicklow. Waterford is west 65km (40 miles) from Wexford and 160km (100 miles) southwest of Dublin.

Train and Planes

Getting to Wicklow from Dublin is easiest on Irish Rail (01 836 6222, *www.irishrail.ie*) from the Connolly or Pearse stations. You can also take the DART train from Dublin to Bray, County Wicklow. Rosslare Strand, Wexford (Europort Station), is easily accessible to and from Waterford or Dublin. The Plunkett Train Station in Waterford serves Kilkenny, Dublin, and Limerick.

The airport at Waterford (051 875 589, *www.flywaterford.com*) receives flights from several European destinations with Aer Arann (0818 210 210, *www.aerarann.com*). They also operate flights to and from Galway and London, among other locations.

 Alert

No current bus routes connect to the Waterford Airport. Outside the terminal, if no cabs are available, try the Waterford Taxi Co-op (051 877 778) or Rapid Cabs (051 858 585). If you are staying at a hotel or B&B, contact them beforehand about transport options into town, especially if arriving at night.

Bus

On Bus Éireann (01 836 6111, *www.buseireann.ie*), you can get to Wicklow, including the towns of Arklow and Bray. St. Kevin's Bus (01 281 8119, *www.glendaloughbus.com*) is another good way to get from Dublin into and around Wicklow. Bus Éireann (053 33 114) also continues onward to Wexford and Rosslare Strand. From Waterford, they go to Carlow, Wexford, Cork, Dungarvan, and up to Dublin, which takes about three hours.

Ferry

Arriving at Rosslare Harbour, County Wexford, is an option from Britain on Stena Line (053 916 1555, *www.stenaline.com*) and Irish Ferries (053 33 158, *www.irishferries.com*).

Car

Once on the south side of Dublin, you can take the scenic R755 to Glendalough, County Wicklow, or continue along the coast on the N11 through Wicklow town, Arklow, and down to Wexford and Rosslare harbors. If skipping Wexford, turn onto the N30 in Enniscorthy to head toward Waterford.

County Wicklow

With its proximity to Dublin, County Wicklow is a popular weekend and holiday getaway for locals and tourists alike. Its rolling hills, remarkable walking trails, and the magical glens make it the "Garden of Ireland." Day trips are available from Dublin with companies such as Wild Wicklow Tours (01 280 1899, *www .discoverdublin.ie*), but to truly explore and experience its harmony, spend at least one night in its tranquil environs. With sights such as the Avondale House and Forest Park (0404 46 111, *www.coillte.ie*) in Rathdrum, along with the wonderful Mount Usher Gardens (0404 40 205, *www.mount-usher-gardens.com*) in Ashford, there is plenty to keep travelers occupied.

Wicklow Town is a fine point from which to explore the county. The area does claim a charming pebble beach, an eerie jail at the Wicklow Historic Gaol (0404 61 599, *www .wicklowshistoricgaol.com*), along with the Black Castle ruins on the edge of town. Farther south, Arklow is Wicklow's most bustling town, but does not have a lot to offer save the Maritime Museum (0402 32 868).

Bray, on Wicklow's northern edge with Dublin, is anything but placid. However, Bray Head, with its calmer ambiance and cliff-side views, is a more attractive base to peruse Powerscourt and to venture into the Wicklow Mountains. At the lower edges of the Sugar Loaf Mountain, Bray is home to the impressive Killruddery House (01 286 3405, *www.killruddery.com*), a mansion with an amazing garden designed by Frenchman Bonet.

Take the kids to the National Sea Life Centre (01 286 6939, *www .sealife.ie*) where they can decode messages to learn more about the secrets of the deep. South of Bray is the pleasant region of Greystones, which makes a great base for those seeking solace.

County Wexford

Known for its pristine beaches, curving streams, and the Blackstairs Mountains to the west, County Wexford (*www.wexfordtourism.com*) beckons sun-seeking sightseers. Conquered first by the Vikings and Normans from the ninth through the twelfth centuries, it was Cromwell who battled for the land in the 1600s. In certain sections, especially around Wexford Town and near Rosslare Harbour to Kilmore Quay, you might hear remnants of the Yola dialect.

 Question

What is Yola?
Yola (meaning "Olde") was a dialect spoken in parts of south Wexford that combines the languages of English, Welsh, Irish, and even Flemish. It evolved mostly from Middle English and was thought to come about due to geographic isolation. Some broken phrases and words still remain in daily use. Visit the Yola Farmstead Folk Park (053 913 2610, *http://homepage.eircom.net/~yolawexford*) for more insight.

Wexford Town is abuzz in the summer, even at the expansive Curracloe Beach. For the tourist, this small city holds the historically significant relics of the county. This includes the St. Iberius Church (053 43 013) built in 1660 and the nearby Bull Ring (with Friday market) where in 1798 the initial declaration of the Republic of Ireland was announced. Farther along is the

Selskar Abbey, where Henry II made amends for having Thomas à Becket killed. The Franciscan Friary and Westgate Heritage Tower (053 46 506) have a well done, but drawn-out film of Wexford's history. Just outside of Wexford Town in Ferrycarrig is the notable Irish National Heritage Park (053 912 0733, *www.inhp.com*) that neatly jams 10 millennia of the Irish experience into one place.

 Essential

The Wexford Opera Festival (053 912 2400, www.wexfordopera.com) is held in mid-October each year. It provides a deeper look at the cultural highlights of the county. This popular venue has already become Ireland's foremost operatic extravaganza. The streets and pubs are filled with stage performers. Book well in advance.

If bird watching is on your list, then visit the Wexford Wildfowl Reserve (053 912 3129) in the North Slob district of Wexford. Open daily, the reclaimed 100-hectare (250-acre) reservation is home to geese and swan, present from April through October. A boat ride up the River Slaney to the seal colony at Raven Point is a real treat.

The town of Enniscorthy (Inis Córthaidh) has plenty of sites to behold. A visit to the National 1798 Centre (053 923 7596, *www.1798centre.ie*) outlines the United Irishmen's plight against the British and sets the scene for further exploration.

If you want to stay along the coast, the quaint village of Kilmore Quay with its thatched-roof cottages might be the loveliest seaside town in the southeast. It has a Maritime Museum (053 912 1572), and walking trails at Forlorn Point make a truly peaceful afternoon. Moreover, it is a popular scuba-diving venue with shipwrecks galore.

County Waterford

The Vikings first settled the strategically located County Waterford in the eighth century. The Anglo-Normans vied for it in the 1100s, ousting the already ruthless settlers. Centuries later, as Cromwell's wrath appeared on the horizon, the inhabitants and soldiers surrendered without much fuss.

The Waterford coastline is especially notable as it extends from town through Dungarvan and onward to Youghal Bay. To fully appreciate the beauty of the coastal landscape and picturesque villages, drive or bike following the southeasterly drive, signposted along the R675 from Tramore to Youghal. Tramore Bay is not particularly interesting but does offer some very good surfing points.

 Essential

To save time traveling between Counties Wexford and Waterford, take the water crossing provided by the Passage East Ferry Company (*www.passageferry.ie*). Routes are April–September, 7 A.M.–10 P.M.; October–March, 9:30 A.M.–8 P.M. (open 9:30 A.M. on Sundays all year). You can cross from Ballyhack in County Wexford (off the R733) to or from Passage East, County Waterford. Cost is €8/€12 one-way/roundtrip for car and passengers.

Just across the bay from Hook Head is Dunmore East. Composed of nearly 2,000 inhabitants, the harbor town is very much alive. The views are hypnotic on a clear day. The beaches here are popular with locals, especially Counsellor's Beach, with a backdrop of sandstone cliffs.

The town of Dungarvan (Dùn Garbhán) does have some claims to fame, such as the Waterford County Museum (058 45 960, *www.dungarvanmuseum.org*) and the well-preserved St. Augustine's Church. Outside of town, Helvick Head is on the R674. It provides stunning views of the sea with a backdrop of the sublime Comeragh Mountains.

Things to See and Do

From walking journeys to monuments, each of Ireland's southeastern counties affords visitors an opportunity to indulge in the land and culture. Visiting Glendalough will truly take you away from the hustle and bustle of the capital. A drive or bike around Hook Head and a visit to the Kennedy Homestead highlight the activities available.

Powerscourt House and Gardens, County Wicklow

Located in Enniskerry, the nearly 400-hectare (1,000-acre) Powerscourt House and Gardens (01 204 6000, *www.powerscourt.ie*) provide an afternoon of absolute splendor. Richard Cassels designed the house originally in 1731. However, a disastrous fire in the mid-1970s destroyed a bulk of the interior. Parts of it have been rebuilt and are no longer open to the public. The Georgian Ballroom is magnificent and the gardens, designed by Irishman Daniel Robertson in the mid-1700s, are the true gem of the grounds. It contains Japanese gardens that were once bog land, Triton Lake, which mimics a popular Roman design, and the Italianate stairway known as the Perron. The Dolphin Pond, Pet Cemetery, and Bamberg Gate from Vienna all add to the estate's overall richness.

The Powerscourt Waterfall is only 7km (4.5 miles) away and is said to be the highest at 120m (400 feet) in Ireland. The estate is open daily, 9:30 A.M.–5:30 P.M.; until dusk in winter. Closed December 25–26. The waterfall is open May–August, 9:30 A.M.– 7 P.M.; March–April and September–October, 10:30 A.M.–5:30 P.M.; November–December and January–Febuary 10:30 A.M.–4:30 P.M.

Closed two weeks before Christmas. Admission €5–7/8, waterfall €3.50–4.50/5.00.

Glendalough and Wicklow Mountains National Park

Including Glendalough proper, its valley, and Glendalough Reserve, the Wicklow Mountains National Park (*www.wicklownationalpark.ie*) fills 20,000 hectares (50,000 acres) and was founded in 1991. The park is located just south of the famous Military Road. The road was constructed by the English in 1798 and is now the R115. This famous route takes travelers through Sally's Gap overlooking bog lands and streams. From here, you can access the Glenmacnass Waterfall.

 Fact

Glendalough (Gleann da Locha) means "Glen of the Two Lakes." But, as early as 9,000 years ago, the area was made up of only one lake. Due to the buildup of silt caused by erosion from the surrounding slopes, the one lake was partitioned and thereafter named by the local agrarian population.

The sequestered religious center still has some impressive ruins, including the inaccessible Church on the Rock (Teampall na Skellig), which sits on an island and was Saint Kevin's original settlement. Closer to the visitor center is an impressive round tower standing 30m (100 feet) surrounded by a graveyard bearing Celtic crosses, along with the Cathedral of St. Peter and St. Paul. Farther along is the small cave that was St. Kevin's Bed and the beehive hut known as St. Kevin's Cell.

The visitor center has free parking where maps costing 50 *cents* are available. Pay parking is available at the Upper Lake, which puts you closer to the trailheads. Entertaining guided tours of the monastic sights and nature walks are available from the center throughout the year.

 Fact

> Known as a hermit and now a saint, Saint Kevin came to Glendalough in the sixth century and lived out his solitary life dedicated to his faith. His solemn lifestyle made him well known throughout Europe. A church was founded here in his name and honor and over the centuries those seeking Christian enlightenment used it as a hub for higher learning.

Walking in Wicklow and Glendalough

In the Glendalough Valley, nine trails dedicated to the Spinc (*An Spinc* means "pointed hill") circle in and around the park. Choices range from forty-five minutes to over four hours, each having their own draw of waterfalls, wetlands, valleys, and mountain ridges. One of the best walks is the four-hour Spinc and the Wicklow Way (red trail). This route combines the two trails into what starts as a graded hill walk but ends as a stroll through vast evergreen forests. Local wild animal and bird life, such as deer, goats, jays, merlin, and kestrels may be spotted on this trail as well. This route gives walkers a workout over the Lugduff Mountain (and the 600 steps) that take you to a most rewarding view over the entire valley and lakes.

Take caution and leave personal belongings in the hotel or B&B, even if you are checking out.

For those more adventurous, consider walking the entire Wicklow Way (*www.wicklowway.com*). This 120km (75-mile) trail is one of Ireland's favorites. The well-marked route takes walkers through swampy bogs, over rolling hillocks, and through quaint villages.

Alert

Due to the popularity of the Wicklow Mountains and their proximity to Dublin, you will find ample signs advising travelers not to leave valuables in the car.

Saltee Islands, County Wexford

Great Saltee and Little Saltee make up the privately owned bird haven known as the Saltee Islands. These are home to cormorant, gannet, puffin, and more species, mostly viewable during migratory periods through spring and the first two months of summer. The islands are historically significant in that they have been hideouts to smugglers, pirates, and even famed revolutionaries such as Bagenal Harvey and John Colclough, who led the 1798 insurrection. You can reach the islands from Kilmore Quay at the harbor. During peak travel seasons, expect several boats per day that charge around €25 per person and €12 per child, roundtrip.

Hook Peninsula, County Wexford

Jutting out between Waterford Harbor and Bannow Bay, the Hook Peninsula (*www.thehook-wexford.com*) is one of southeast Ireland's hidden promontories. Dotted with rocky terrain, the headland extends to expansive, sandy beaches. The Wexford Coastal Path walkway extends through many of the prominent sights. If you are driving the circuit (also a great cycling route) start at Wellington Bridge on the R733, then continue around the Ring of Hook as it begins on the R734.

Europe's Oldest Lighthouse

The drive from Fethard to Hook Head affords wonderful vistas across the bays. The lighthouse here is said to be Europe's oldest. The area was first used as a beacon in the fifth century by monks residing there and modernized with time. It was functional until the mid-1990s and thereafter replaced with an automated unit. The visitor center (051 397 054) gives an informative half-hour tour. On site is a refreshing café and craft shop. The visitor center is open daily all year. Guided tours of the lighthouse are available throughout the day starting at 10 A.M., except November–February. Admission €3.50–4.50/6.00.

 Fact

> The first significant sight along the route is Tintern Abbey (051 562 650). Funded by William Marshall, he vowed to God during a storm at sea that he would erect a Cistercian friary if he lived through the horrendous event. The edifice was completed in the thirteenth century and the trails around the 40-hectare (100-acre) estate are well maintained.

Duncannon Fort and Dunbrody Abbey

Going up north to the small resort town of Duncannon (*www.visitduncannon.com*), visitors can find some interesting monuments, including a star-shaped fort often referred to as the Duncannon Fort, a medieval Knights Templar church, and in July, home to the premier Duncannon International Sand Sculpting Festival. Back on the R733, the Dunbrody Abbey (051 388 603, *www.dunbrody abbey.com*) is an impressive twelfth-century Cistercian cloister often referred to as the Abbey of St. Mary de Port. Kids will surely enjoy the yew-hedge maze and mini-golf course. Abbey and Maze open May–September, 10 A.M.–6 P.M. Abbey admission €1/2. Maze admission €2/4.

Kennedy Homestead and Kennedy Arboretum, County Wexford

The Kennedy Homestead (051 388 264, *www.kennedy homestead.com*) can be accessed down a small lane out of Dunganstown. The place was the childhood home of Patrick Kennedy, the great-grandfather of John F. Kennedy. The scant grounds hold value for those wanting to explore the Kennedy-family past via a short film and an exploration of the grounds. The tour leader is a relative of the family. Open July and August, daily, 10 A.M.–5 P.M.; May, June, and September, Monday–Friday, 11:30 A.M.–4:30 P.M. Admission €2.5-3.50/5.

The Kennedy Arboretum (051 388 171) is located in New Ross off the R733, just a short distance from the homestead. It contains thousands of species of hedges, plants, and trees. The 252 hectares (623 acres) of woodland is dedicated to JFK and was funded by influential Irish-Americans. Open May–August, 10:00 A.M.–8:00 P.M.; September and April, 10:00 A.M.–6:30 P.M.; October–March, 10:00 A.M.–5:00 P.M. Prebook guided tours April–September. Admission €1.30–2.10/2.90.

Dunbrody Famine Ship, County Wexford

Also near the Kennedy Homestead, you will find the Dunbrody Famine Ship (051 425 239, *www.dunbrody.com*). The vessel is a reassemblage of the ship that sailed between 1846 and 1865 from Ireland to the United States. Originally, the ship was not designed for people, but for cargo. Around 50 percent of the human traffic that took the long, crowded trip across the Atlantic never made it due to sickness. The Visitor Experience displays the Emigration Wall of Honour and has an electronic database holding over 1 million names of those who crossed during the two-decade period. Open April–September, daily, 9 A.M.–6 P.M.; October–March, 9 A.M.–5 P.M. Closed December 24–26. Admission €4.50–6/7.50.

Waterford Town, County Waterford

Waterford Town has some memorable sights worth exploration. One highlight is the Waterford Treasures Museum (051 30 4500, *www.waterfordtreasures.com*), located on Merchant's Quay. The museum outlines Waterford's Viking past to Strongbow's marriage to Aoife, and its rise to becoming one of the world's foremost crystal manufacturing centers. The museum is open daily all year, June–August, 9:30 A.M.–9:00 P.M.; April, May, and September, 9:30 A.M.–6:00 P.M.; October and March, 9:30 A.M.–5:00 P.M.

Another highlight of the city is the churches, two of which were designed by John Roberts. The Protestant-built Christ Church Cathedral (051 858 958) at Cathedral Square is home to the James Rice tomb. The Holy Trinity Cathedral (051 875 166) is Roberts's second claim to fame. This Catholic church is famous for its oak pulpit and ten Waterford crystal chandeliers. Both open Monday–Saturday, 10 A.M.–6 P.M.

Some other sights in Waterford include:

- **Reginald's Tower:** The circular turret of Reginald's Tower (051 304 220) was possibly constructed by Reginald the Dane around 1003, but it is credited as a Norman tower. First used as a mint, then as a prison, the current structure houses a fine museum. Open daily 10 A.M.–5 P.M. Closed during the Christmas period. Admission €1.10–1.30/2.10.
- **Waterford Crystal:** The Waterford Crystal (051 332 500, *www.waterfordvisitorcentre.com*) is located in Kilbarry. A tour of the Waterford Crystal Factory is a fascinating encounter with the artisans and craftspeople behind the scenes. Watching molten glass being transformed into some of the finest crystal is an eye-opening experience. Factory tours run January–February, Monday–Friday, 9:00 A.M.–3:15 P.M.; March–October, Monday–Sunday, 8:30 A.M.–4:15 P.M.; November–December,

Monday–Friday, 9:00 A.M.–3:15 P.M. Closed December 23–27. Admission €7–7.50/10.

- **Garter Lane Arts Centre:** Off of O'Connell Street, the Garter Lane Arts Centre (051 855 038, *www.garterlane.ie*) is one of Ireland's voluminous arts exhibition halls. With various independent films and documentaries, the Garter Lane Theatre presents contemporary works in dance and music as well. Open daily; ticket prices for showings and classes vary.

Accommodations

Finding a picture-perfect hotel, B&B, or guesthouse in Wicklow, Wexford, or Waterford will not take that much effort—finding one that is not full on a holiday weekend or in the high travel season might. Because Dubliners head south whenever an opportunity arises, book your accommodations before you go, especially in places such as Glendalough, Arklow, Hook Head, Kilmore Quay, and Dungarvan.

Riversdale B&B and Cottage

Glendalough, Co. Wicklow

0404 45 858

www.glendalough.eu.com

€80+ per room, €300+ weekly cottage,

S/D/T/F.

If you long for heaven on Earth; the sounds of birds chirping, gentle gurgling brooks, and a picture-perfect forest out your window, then the Riversdale B&B will suit you perfectly. The well-designed B&B has six en suite rooms available, including two triples and one quadruple with satellite television. A private, self-catering cottage that sleeps three to four is also available for weekly rentals. Riversdale B&B

is at the doorstep of the Wicklow Mountains National Park. Locate Riversdale B&B by following the R756 from Laragh.

Bracken B&B

Anamoe Rd., Co. Wicklow
0404 45 300
http://homepage.eircom.net/~brackenbb
€35+ per person, S/D/T/F

You will have a hard time finding a nicer couple than those running the Bracken B&B, just outside Laragh, near Glendalough. Conveniently located near the center, it is only a five-minute drive or fifteen-minute ride to the Glendalough visitor center and trailhead. This quaint B&B has both en suite and shared bathroom rooms available and is family friendly. For a relaxing evening, sink into one of the leather couches beside the fireplace in the living room.

Woodbrook House (Eco-Lodging)

Killanne, Enniscorthy, Co. Wexford
053 925 5114
www.woodbrookhouse.ie
€75+ per person, S/D. MC/V

Just outside of Enniscorthy, the Woodbrook House is a finely decorated Georgian house set in the shadow of the Blackstairs Mountains. The historically significant house is brimming with Irish hospitality and a luxurious air that rests the soul. The house has recently made some eco-friendly conversions, including solar-heated water, pellet-burning stoves, and bio-fuel transport.

Dunbrody House

Arthurstown, Co. Wexford

051 389 600
www.dunbrodyhouse.com
€135+ per person, S/D. MC/V

This house hotel, award-winning restaurant, and day spa provide luxury-seeking globetrotters with life's most enjoyable treats. Not only does the house sit on a 120-hectare (300-acre) parkland, but the meritorious service surpasses all expectations as well. Special weekend and low-season packages are available.

Gaultiere Lodge
Woodstown, Co. Waterford
051 382 549
www.gaultier-lodge.com
€65+ per person, S/D. MC/V

Built originally for Lord Huntington, the Gaultiere Lodge has awe-inspiring sea views set among tranquil, sunny environs. This eighteenth-century B&B is near Dunmore East and is easily accessible from the Passage East ferry port. Golf and sea fishing are available. Additionally, this establishment is one of the rare dog-friendly lodges in Ireland.

Foxmount County House
Passage East Rd., Co. Waterford
051 874 308
www.foxmountcountryhouse.com
€65+ per person, S/D.

The proprietors, Margaret and David Kent, will make sure your stay is nothing less than fabulous at the renowned Foxmount Country House. Not only is the award-winning breakfast going to last you a full day, but the pleasing purlieus of the area inspire exploration. The fastidiously kept rooms make this a truly top-notch, first-class B&B.

Other Accommodations

Here are some other accommodations you might consider. (In the listings that follow, € = around 25 euros per person.)

- €€€ **The Old Milking Parlour (eco-friendly).**
  Kilbride, Co. Wicklow
  040 448 206
  www.ballymurrin.ie
- € **Derrymore House. Lake Rd., Co. Wicklow.**
  0404 45 493
  www.glendaloughaccommodation.com
- € **The Old Presbytery Hostel. Fairgreen,**
  Rathdrum, Co. Wicklow.
  0404 46 930
- €€€ **Ferrycarrig Hotel. Ferrycarrig, Co. Wexford.**
  053 912 099
  www.ferrycarrighotel.ie
- € **Maple Lodge B&B. Castlebridge, Co. Wexford.**
  053 915 9195
  www.maplelodgewexford.com
- € **MacMurrough Farm Hostel & Cottage.**
  New Ross, Co. Wexford.
  051 421 383
  www.macmurrough.com
- € **Cairbre House. Abbeyside, Dungarvan,**
  Co. Waterford.
  058 42 338
  www.cairbrehouse.com

- **€€ The Coach House. Butlerstown, Co. Waterford**
  051 384 656
  http://homepages.iol.ie/~coachhse
- **€ Beach Haven. Tivoli Terrace, Tramore, Co. Waterford**
  051 390 208
  www.beachhavenhouse.com

This family-run business offers three different accomodations on separate premises: Beach Haven Studios (self-catering), Beach Haven House (B&B), and Beach Haven Holiday Hostel.

Restaurants and Pubs

The southeast coast of Ireland has wonderful seaside venues serving the freshest, mouth-watering seafood fit for a king. Other fine eateries serve traditional and modern Irish cuisine, and a pub is always to be found even in the most remote corners. All the cities have their international influences such as Italian and Asian eateries. (In the restaurant listings that follow, € = around 25 euros per person.)

The Hungry Monk
Church Rd., Greystones, Co. Wicklow
01 287 5759
www.thehungrymonk.ie
€€

The Hungry Monk serves the best catch of the day in summer and winter. In summer, the menu boasts the finest fish and in the winter months they serve wild pheasant and mallard, along with venison.

The Strawberry Tree

Macreddin Village, Co. Wicklow

0402 36 444

€€

Even in its infancy, this first-rate organic restaurant received its fair share of awards. Located near Rathdrum, between Aughrim and Aghavannagh, this mid-priced eatery will have any gastronome guessing what fine flavors will tantalize the palate next.

Kitty's of Arklow

56 Main St., Arklow Center, Co. Wicklow

0402 31 669

http://homepage.eircom.net/~kittysofarklow

€–€€

Well priced and well prepared, the food, drink, and cheery atmosphere at the restaurant and pub at Kitty's of Arklow is top-notch. With diverse lunch and dinner menus, families might find this a particularly attractive dining option. The seafood chowder and pan-fried tiger prawns come highly recommended.

The Lobster Pot Seafood Bar

Carne, Co. Wexford

053 913 1110

€€€

Located outside of Rosslare, the Lobster Pot Seafood Bar was voted the Best Seafood Bar of the Year in 2009 by the famed culinary critic Georgina Campbell. Gourmet seafood set in an amicable ambience is not hard to find, but this place does it with comfortable style. For travelers looking for the best in seafood, reserve ahead, especially on weekends.

The Bohemian Girl

Selskar St., Wexford Town
053 24 419
€

With a name derived from the title of the popular opera by Michael William Balfe, the Bohemian Girl pub not only has a catchy name, but also excellently priced food. From oysters to burgers, this Tudor pub is a great place for lunch or a cheap pub dinner.

Limeleaf Restaurant

Henrietta Street, Waterford Town
051 852 624
www.limeleaf.ie
€–€€

Off the quaint quays of Waterford City, the Limeleaf Restaurant serves affordable Asian cuisine with the freshest, home-sourced ingredients. From spicy squid to Thai hot-and-sour broth called "Tom Yum," this family friendly establishment also serves meat-based dishes and poultry delights. The Early Evening Menu will save you time and money.

La Palma

20 The Mall, Waterford Town
051 879 823
www.lapalma.ie
€–€€

The Italian restaurant La Palma receives excellent reviews in every sphere. From the locals of Waterford to food-loving travelers, this gem is worth a visit. The early-bird menu is served from 5:30 P.M –7:00 P.M. The luscious Gamberi and finely prepared Filetto made with Irish beef are definite pleasers.

Traveler's Tidbits

Here you will find the necessary information for Wicklow, Wexford, and Waterford. Tourist offices are located in each major area. The best websites for these areas are *www.visitwicklow .ie*, *www.wexfordtourism.com*, *www.waterfordtourism.org*, *www .discoverireland.ie/eastcoast*, and *www.discoverireland.ie/southeast*.

In the Tourist Office chart below, "Seasonal" designates offices generally open May through September. Tourist offices are open during regular business hours.

AREA TOURIST OFFICES

Town	Address	Phone Number	In Operation
Wicklow	Fitzwilliam Sq.	0404 69 117	All year
Arklow	Parade Ground	0402 32 484	Seasonal
Gorey	Main St.	053 942 1248	All year
Enniscorthy	Castle Museum	053 923 4699	All year
Wexford	The Quay Front	053 912 3111	All year
New Ross Dunbrody	Heritage Centre	051 421 857	All year
Waterford	The Granary, The Quay	051 875 823	All year
Tramore	Railway Square	051 381 572	Seasonal
Dungarvan	The Courthouse	058 41 741	All year
Lismore	Heritage Centre	058 54 975	All year

Following is additional pertinent travel information. In the case of an emergency, dial 999 anywhere in the Republic of Ireland.

TRAVEL INFORMATION

Name	Address	Phone Number
Wexford Police	Roches Road	053 22 333
Waterford Police		051 30 5300
Wicklow Hospital	Glenside Rd., Wicklow Town	0404 67 108
Wexford General Hospital	Richmond Terrace	053 42233
Waterford Holy Ghost Hospital	Cork Rd.	051 374 397
Waterford Regional Hospital	Dunmore Rd.	051 848 000
Wexford Library (Internet)	Redmond Sq.	053 21 637
Wexford Post Office	Anne St.	053 22 587
Waterford Post Office	Parade Quay	051 317 312
Waterford Genealogy Heritage Survey	Jenkin's Lane, Waterford Town	051 876 123
Wexford Genealogy Centre	Yola Farmstead, Tagoat	053 923 2610

CHAPTER 9

Kildare, Kilkenny, and Tipperary

The luck of the leprechaun has truly settled on this part of Ireland. It can be seen in the abounding lushness of the landscapes and the good fortune of the people who call it home. From world-renowned stud farms to Ireland's most prized monument, known as the Rock of Cashel, Kildare, Kilkenny, and Tipperary are all inland gems tucked into some of Ireland's most pristine settings.

Getting Around Kildare, Kilkenny, and Tipperary

Getting around the central east and south is facilitated by the transportation available in and around Dublin. Kildare, with its wealth and steady urban growth, is already referenced as another burb of the capital. Trips to Kilkenny and Tipperary, however, have their own, old-world feel and while not right outside the capital, make excitingly rewarding destinations.

Train

Irish Rail (01 836 6222, *www.irishrail.ie*) has scheduled routes to Kildare and takes thirty-five to forty minutes. If you are heading on Irish Rail (056 772 2024) to Kilkenny, you can depart the Dublin Heuston Station and get off at the McDonagh Station. Depart the same station in Dublin to take the Irish Rail

(052 21 982) to the Tipperary Station, off of Bridge Street, which is on the Waterford and Limerick train route.

Bus
Getting to Kildare by bus is possible on Bus Éireann (01 836 6111, *www.buseireann.ie*) and Dublin Bus (01 873 4222, *www.dublinbus.ie*), which serves Maynooth. Bus Éireann (056 776 4933) runs services to Kilkenny from Dublin, dropping passengers at the McDonagh Station. The same bus continues onward to Clonmel, County Tipperary. Other buses are available to Thomastown and Bennettsbridge. The bus station in Tipperary, off of Abbey Street, is a pick-up and drop-off point for the Limerick/Waterford line, serving Cahir and Cashel.

Car
To get to Kildare by car, take the N7 or the N4 from Dublin. Depending on where you are coming from, numerous routes run from Dublin toward Kilkenny; the more-direct N78 makes the trip quick, as does the N9. Getting to Tipperary from Dublin is best done on the N76 to Clonmel or the N8 to Tipperary Town.

Kildare City

Just outside of Dublin, County Kildare is Ireland's horse country. Known for its wealth in both fertile land and its thriving stud-farming business, County Kildare is close in distance but still a world away from Dublin.

Kildare City was founded by one of history's earliest feminists, Saint Brigid, now home to the St. Brigid's Cathedral, which was during her time a coed monastery. The 40-meter (120-feet) round tower is akin to that in Glendalough (County Wicklow) in stature, but unlike in that this one is climbable (after paying the hefty €4 admission fee). It affords a chance to use the fabled "wishing stone." Both the city and cathedral grounds are worth a jaunt if you have extra time to spare. The cathedral is open daily from May through September. Donations appreciated. Outside the exurb is where Kildare's magic ignites. Following are the best sights just near the city.

Curragh Racecourse

One of Kildare's best sights is the expansive Curragh Racecourse (*www.curragh.ie*) in Newbridge, Ireland's premier racing headquarters. Races run from spring to October. Whether you want to gamble gaily on the Irish Derby or learn more about the industry, this phenomenal locale efficiently entertains and educates at the same time.

 Essential

Curragh in Gaelic Irish can refer to a traditional Irish fishing boat or the land of running horses. The courses of this area have been used since the 1700s for thoroughbred racing. Interestingly, the grounds of the Curragh are thought to have been home to chariot races as early as the third century.

National Stud Farm, Japanese Gardens, and St. Fiachra's Gardens

County Kildare is also home to the National Stud and Museum, Japanese Gardens, and St. Fiachra's Gardens (045 521 617, *www.irish-national-stud.ie*) in Tully, near Kildare Town. The government-subsidized bloodstock farm was founded by Colonel Hall Walker, who based the worth of his breeds on his horses' relationship to particular celestial bodies. Notwithstanding, the 1,000-acre farm has produced some of the world's most impressive equines. Lunch at the restaurant is a treat. The grounds are also home to the Stud Museum and serene Japanese Gardens and St. Fiachra's Gardens. Open daily February 12–December 23, 9:30 A.M.–5 P.M.; 9:30 A.M.–3:30 P.M. Admission €5–8/10.

Kilkenny City

Rightfully proud that it has maintained its Middle Ages allure, Kilkenny attracts travelers from across the spectrum. While considered a city, it truly feels more like a town with shopping, first-rate pubs, and superb sights all within walking distance.

The center of Kilkenny is a pedestrian-friendly freeway for the masses. While walking, you might notice the slender passageways known as "slips" and other iconic establishments such as Kyteler's Inn (056 772 1064, *www.kytelersinn.com*) off of Saint Kieran's Street.

Dame Alice Kyteler and her maid, who were pronounced guilty of being witches, made this inn and cellar bar famous.

 Fact

Dame Alice Kyteler was pardoned for the death of her four previous husbands. When eerie events brought on further accusations of her evil craft, she was able to escape, but her maid was burned at the stake. Look for the sign of a black cat with a quarter moon over its head. That's the place.

Departing from the Kilkenny Tourist Office, Tynan's Walking Tour (087 265 1745 or 056 776 3955) is a popular venue and a valuable historical stroll through Kilkenny's best sights. Tours depart from mid-March to October, Monday–Saturday, 10:30 A.M., 12:15 P.M., 3 P.M., and 4:30 P.M.; Sunday, 11:15 P.M. and 12:30 P.M. Admission €5.50/6. The must-see sights of Kilkenny City are highlighted in the following sections.

Rothe House and Garden

Built during the rule of the Tudor dynasty, the Roth House (056 772 2893, *www.rothehouse.com*) is representative of a merchant's townhouse during the fifteenth to seventeenth centuries. Containing special artifacts and costumes of the era, the house is now owned and operated by the Kilkenny Archaeological Society. The estate Gardens is a reconstruction of an Irish urban garden. Open April–October: Monday–Saturday, 10:30 A.M.–5:00 P.M.; Sunday, 3:00 P.M.–5:00 P.M.; Open November–March: Monday–Saturday, 10:30 A.M.–4:30 P.M. Admission €4/5. Combination tickets with admittance to St. Canice's Cathedral are available.

Kilkenny Castle

The painstakingly restored Kilkenny Castle (056 770 4100, *www.kilkennycastle.ie*) was first constructed circa 1200. The home's most prominent owners were the wealthy Butler family. Restored during the Victorian era, the castle has passed through various restoration stages over the years. Nearly decrepit, the castle fell into the hands of the local government, who have worked for decades to complete its full restoration. Nearly complete, the informative and guided tour will sweep you back in time. Open June–September, daily, 9:30 A.M.–7:00 P.M.; October–May, daily, 10:30 A.M.–5:00 P.M. Closed Good Friday and Christmas. Admission €2–4/6.

 Essential

One of the antiquities you will learn about on a tour of the Kilkenny Castle includes a decorated heat screen used by women sitting near the fireplace. Resting with one's face shielded from the heat meant a lady's wax makeup would not run. This act eventually led to the coining of the term "saving face."

Black Abbey

Depicting the hardships of its past, the aptly named Black Abbey (056 772 1279) was a Dominican abbey founded in 1225. Thereafter ransacked by Cromwellian forces in the 1650s, it was reopened as a holy place of worship in the early 1800s. Restoration was complete by 1979. The church now stands in its full glory, one of the highlights including a massive stained-glass window completed in the 1890s. Open April–September, daily; October–March, Monday–Saturday. Closed during worship services. Admission free. Donations appreciated.

St. Canice's Cathedral

Also known as Kilkenny Cathedral, St. Canice's Cathedral (056 776 4971) beckons visitors with its dominating view over the city. The current edifice was constructed circa 1200 but was originally established by the patron saint of Kilkenny in the sixth century as a sort of diocese. The round, topless tower sits on the spooky cemetery. Open April, May, September: Monday–Saturday, 10 A.M.–5 P.M.; Sunday, 2 P.M.–5 P.M.; June–August: Monday–Saturday, 9 A.M.–6 P.M.; Sunday, 2 P.M.–6 P.M.; October–March: Monday–Saturday, 10 A.M.–4 P.M.; Sunday, 2 P.M.–4 P.M. Admission €3–4/5. The climb up the round tower costs extra. Admission to Rothe House included with combination ticket.

 Alert

Climbable by the truly fit and brave, the tower of St. Canice's Cathedral is 30 meters (100 feet) high and 14 meters (50 feet) in girth. A relatively tight fit in some sections, prepare to spend much of your time climbing on all fours. Think twice before taking any children on this climb.

Tipperary

With the famed WWI melody "It's a Long Way to Tipperary" on your tongue, Tipperary's secret as a trove in the land-locked central south is surfacing. With stunning mountains, walking trails, and the acclaimed Rock of Cashel (see "Things to See and Do") on the list, it is no wonder that travelers are including a few days here as a part of their planned route.

The town of Tipperary or the somewhat congested central town of Clonmel is situated for easy access to the wondrous purlieus farther along. The Glen of Aherlow (*www.aherlow.com*) offers walking, scenic drives, or cycling along the R663 into the Comeragh Mountains or the Nire Valley. From Clonmel, you can find all the signage, including the aptly named Knockmealdown Drive.

From this point, walking also tops the list with low-level options through the Glen or more advanced walking through the Galtee Mountains, Ireland's highest midland range. The Tipperary Heritage Trail is a nearly 60km (100-mile) route that cuts through the Vee and extends north to Cashel. For detailed trail maps and information visit the Glen of Aherlow Fáilte Society (062 56 331) off of Coach Road in Newtown. Open June–October, daily, 9:30 A.M.–6:00 P.M. Some intriguing attractions in Tipperary include:

Cahir Town, Park, and Swiss Cottage

Known for its lively market, Cahir sits along the Suir River. The main avenue of Castle Street is lined with excellent pubs and if the rain is coming down, submit to any dry watering hole for a relaxing pint. Follow the 2km (1.3-mile) footpath along the River Suir, which will lead you to the impressive Swiss Cottage (052 41 144) and adjoining Cahir Park. Built as a pastoral two-story getaway for the prestigious Richard Butler, known as Lord Cahir, and his wife, the thatched roofs and picture-perfect verandahs set the Elysian scene. Days and hours of operation vary throughout the year. Admission €2/3.

Cahir Castle

The true claim to fame of this humble town is the awe-inspiring Cahir Castle (052 41 011), which was handed over to the Butler family near the latter part of the 1300s and taken by the Earl of Essex at the end of the sixteenth century. Handed over to Cromwell in the mid-seventeenth century, it is now one of Ireland's impressive sights for castle lovers the world over. Open mid-June to mid-September, 9:30 A.M.–7:00 P.M.; mid-March to mid-June and mid-September to mid-October, 9:30 A.M.–5:30 P.M.; mid-October to mid-March, 9:30 A.M.–4:30 P.M. Admission €2.50/3.

Cashel Town

Overshadowed by the impressive Rock of Cashel, the eponymous town (*www.cashel.ie*) has a kid-friendly Folk Village (062 62 525), and the Bolton Library (062 61 944) showcases a wide array of literary works and maps. Outside of town is the Hore Abbey (named after the gray hoarfrost mornings) with a fifteenth-century tower that makes a nice excursion from the famed Rock.

Things to See and Do

Ireland's purest countryside is right outside Dublin's door. Rolling fields of the greenest grass and bogs give way to castles and cathedrals. The villages and friendly people enhance the area's old-world charm.

Castletown House, County Kildare

One of the splendid highlights of County Kildare, the Castletown House (01 628 8252, *www.heritageireland.ie* and *www.castletown.ie*) was built in 1722–25 in true Palladian form. Drafted and overseen by Alessandro Galilei for William Connolly, the variegated highlights are the Print Room, the Rococo stuccowork of the Staircase Hall, the Long Gallery, and the Red Drawing Room. The grounds include an obelisk, which are viewable from the gallery, while the "Wonderful Barn" with encircling spiral staircase sits off the main property. Located off the M4 in Celbridge. Days and hours of operation vary throughout the year. Access is via guided tour only. Admission €3.50/4.50.

Moon High Cross, Co. Kildare

Another highlight in County Kildare often skipped by travelers is a visit to the Moon High Cross, the remains of a cross that is 5 meters (17 feet) high, displaying Celtic art alongside biblical carvings. Founded by Saint Columba and located just outside the town of Moone off the N9, the eighth-century monument was an early Christian monastery. The high cross depicts the stories of Daniel, Adam and Eve, and the Crucifixion, among others.

Off the same road, you will also find the Irish Pewtermill (059 862 4164), which is worth a stop. The place has a nice showroom display, reprints, and elucidations of the Moon High Cross depictions, and handsome pewter ware for sale. You can watch the artisans at work if you arrive early enough. Open Monday–Friday, 10 A.M.–4:30 P.M.; Saturday–Sunday, 11 A.M.–4 P.M. Admission free.

Larchill Arcadian Gardens, County Kildare

A real treat for families, the Larchill Arcadian Gardens (01 628 7354, *www.larchill.ie*) are a fully restored ornamental farm with available trail walks, scenic views, and an adventure playground to boot. In the summer, enjoy archery lessons, theater presentations, and falconry displays. The lake highlighted by the two mock-Gothic ruins is a real treat, as is the restaurant serving lunchtime treats, including ice cream. Located in Kilcock. Days and hours of operation vary throughout the year. Admission €5.50–6.50/7.50.

Dunmore Cave, County Kilkenny

Located outside Kilkenny City, the signage leading to Dunmore Cave (056 776 7726, *www.heritageireland.ie/en/South-East/DunmoreCave*) is a testament to the popularity of this sight over the last few years. The limestone caverns are accessible only via an informational guided tour. The cave was the site of a massacre by Godfrey and the Vikings in 928 in which over 1,000 people were killed. Naturally partitioned into three sections, some of which are impressively adorned with stalagmites. Located off the N78 in Bally-foyle. Days and hours of operation vary throughout the year. Admission €1.50–2.50/3.

 Alert

Dunmore Cave is a wonderful adventure, but bring warm clothes even in the summer. The cave can get chilly as it hovers around the same cool temperature of 15°C (60°F). Children should also be closely monitored both inside and outside of the grounds.

Monastic Sights, County Kilkenny

One can only imagine a historical area such as Kilkenny having some of the most impressive medieval, cloistral sights awaiting discovery. Both the Duiske and Jerpoint Abbeys, which housed Cistercian practitioners, have been carefully restored in an attempt to match their former glory.

Duiske Abbey, County Kilkenny

Located in the hard-to-pronounce town of Graiguenamanagh, the fine Duiske Abbey (059 972 4238) was established by William Marshall for the Cistercians as early as 1207. Fully restored in the 1970s, the priory has undergone various facelifts over the years and remains today Ireland's best-kept abbey of this more-strict Benedictine branch. The figure of the thirteenth-century Knight of Duiske is preserved in the entranceway of the parish. Within are two granite high crosses that have been brought in from the outdoors to protect them from the weather. The visitor center is worth investigation. Open daily at 8 A.M.

Jerpoint Abbey, County Kilkenny

Just outside of Thomastown, Jerpoint Abbey (056 772 4623) was founded as early as 1158 for the Benedictines but later used by the Cistercians in 1180. Jerpoint passed to the Earl of Ormand following the Dissolution of the Monasteries during King Henry VIII's rule. The cloister sits atop effigies of highly regarded saints and knights. Moreover, tombs of the most worthy have been enshrined throughout the church. Open March–October, daily, 10 A.M.–5 P.M.; November–February, daily, 10 A.M.–4 P.M. Closed during the Christmas period. Admission €1.50–2.50/3.

Kells Priory, County Kilkenny

Located on the outskirts of the charming town of Kells, the Kells Priory (056 772 4558) was founded in 1193 by Augustinian priests. Sitting off on its own, the grounds are open for exploration, although group tours are available by appointment. The church is composed of an altar area and nave; the structure itself is topped with a square tower. In addition, the 2 hectares (5 acres) were at one time heavily fortified. You can walk around the grounds and spot the remains of old living quarters and a kitchen. Located outside of Kilkenny on the R699 with signage to Kells. From town, follow the Stonyford Road. Open daily. Admission free.

The Rock of Cashel, County Tipperary

With the sobriquet of "St. Patrick's Rock," the Rock of Cashel (062 61 437, *www.cashel.ie*) tops many a visitor's vote for Ireland's most impressive site. More than just a "big rock," the craggy outcrop has a magnificent cathedral, tower, and chapel tucked into its middle. Once visited by Saint Patrick, who converted King Aenghus c. 450, the Rock represents a powerful succession of rule of kings who claimed it as their own. It was first settled by a clan from Wales who were victorious in ruling much of Munster. Later, it survived total destruction by Cromwellian forces, and what remains is a complex amalgam of history, lore, and stunning artifacts.

 Fact

With the baptism nearly over that would convert King Aenghus of Cashel to a Christian, Saint Patrick accidentally stabbed the king through the foot with his bishop's staff. Believing it to be a part of the ceremonious ritual, the king phlegmatically maintained his stature as the liturgy continued uninterrupted.

Before heading up to the Rock, gander around the engaging Brú Ború Heritage Centre (062 61 122) and Sounds of History Museum located near the car park. Authentic Irish music is presented here daily; the summer brings evening alfresco performances that cannot be beat. There is also a restaurant and gift shop on site. Open daily, 9 A.M.–5 P.M. Admission to center free, €4/6 museum.

A tour of the Rock of Cashel will include these highlights:

- **St. Patrick's Cross and Cormac's Chapel:** The once-formidable St. Patrick's Cross bears a carving of the saint. While this replica must withstand the winds, the real cross is now housed in the museum. Just nearby, Cormac's Chapel, constructed from 1127 to 1134, is adorned with Romanesque features (the first of its kind in Ireland) and displays a centaur donning a helmet and preparing his bow for battle. The church is highly decorated both inside and out, with several motifs interacting simultaneously displaying the church's influences from abroad.
- **Gothic Cathedral:** Missing a roof, yet still impressively intact, the cathedral is unique in that the choir section is larger than the nave. This was most likely due to the cathedral's positioning when built. The north wing of the cross-shaped,

transept interior is aligned with sixteenth-century tombs with anomalous animal engravings.

- **Round Tower:** Constructed about the same time as Cormac's Chapel, the Round Tower, used primarily as a lookout point and for the storage of religious treasures, was once ruined after being struck by lightning.

 Essential

The Gothic cathedral contains many secrets. These include secret passages and deep walls, not to mention a "leper's squint," where those socially denied conventional service rites could still partake in Mass. Additionally, the grave of Miler Magrath, known as the "Scoundrel of Cashel," is here, since he converted to Catholicism on his deathbed.

Accommodations

From eco-lodging to castles set in medieval cities, Kildare, Kilkenny, and Tipperary all have an assemblage of fine establishments that will surely please. You will find no seaside resorts in these land-locked gems, but country, guest, and farmhouses that bring visitors ever closer to Ireland's natural soul abound.

Coursetown House

Stradbally Rd., Athy, Co. Kildare
059 863 1101
www.coursetown.com
€100+ per room, S/D. MC/V

With limited choices in or around Athy, this 200-year-old farmhouse is a highlight. Set just a few kilometers from town on rich farmland, the surrounding gardens with rare plants are a true delight. The proprietors, Iris and Jim Fox, will ensure that your stay is nothing less than magnificent.

The homemade victuals at breakfast are to die for, so don't be shy!

Barberstown Castle

Straffan, Co. Kildare
01 628 8157
www.barberstowncastle.ie
€250+ per room, S/D. MC/V

Located just far enough away from the constant animation of Dublin, the Barberstown Castle is a keen example of what upper-crust country living is all about. Constructed in the thirteenth century, the grounds and quietude make it an appealing escape. The castle's kitchen is also renowned in gourmet circles, so enjoy an evening meal, perhaps after a day of golfing at the nearby and top-notch K-Club.

Abbeylodge B&B

Dean Street, Kilkenny City
056 777 1866
www.abbeylodge.ie
€35+ per person

With its own literal corner on the Kilkenny tourist market, the Abbey Lodge B&B is a modernly decorated establishment with fine amenities. The spacious rooms have comfortable beds, small flat-screen televisions, and small yet elegant bathrooms. The breakfast will last you past midday. Prices here are lower than other B&Bs in Kilkenny and the location cannot be beat. Quiet with private, gated parking, it is a five-minute stroll from downtown. If the Abbeylodge is full, try their lovely sister guesthouse, the Bregagh House (056 772 2315, *www.bregaghhouse.com*).

Butler House

Patrick St., Kilkenny City

056 772 2828

www.butler.ie

€120–300 per person, S/D/T. MC/V

To truly live in the medieval aura of Kilkenny is to stay in the ever-popular Butler House. Built akin to the spirit of Kilkenny Castle, this guesthouse has marble fireplaces and much grand allure to bring satiable rest and relaxation. Nothing of luxury is spared in this immaculate establishment; from deluxe double rooms to extravagant suites, if you can spare more than one night en route, a minimum two-night stay would be highly recommended, as are the rooms overlooking the luxuriant seventeenth-century garden.

EcoBooley

Eamonn Looby, Ronga, Clogheen, Cahir, Co. Tipperary

052 65 191

www.ecobooley.com

€130+ weekend, €270–350 weekly; S/D/T.

This eco-lodge will truly make you feel welcome and removed at the same time. Opened as an ecological experiment, this small cottage is gaining in popularity. Located near the Tipperary Heritage Trail, the rustic feel and superb naturalness of it all make it a wonderful getaway location.

Cashel Palace Hotel

Main St., Cashel, Co. Tipperary

062 62 707

www.cashel-palace.ie

€175–450 per room, S/D/T. MC/V

This four-star palace hotel is nothing short of striking. Designed in the 1700s as a Queen Anne–style mansion, the hotel boasts twenty-three rooms of fine décor, along with a prize-winning restaurant to gratify inspired bon vivants. The establishment specializes in helping to arrange luxurious weddings and professional conferences.

Other Accommodations

Here are some other accommodations you might consider. (In the listings that follow, € = around 25 euros per person.)

- **€€€ Martinstown House. The Curragh, Co. Kildare.**
  045 44 1269
  www.martinstownhouse.com
- **€€ Kilkea Lodge Farm. Castledermot, Co. Kildare.**
  059 914 5112
  www.kilkealodgefarm.com
- **€ Rosquil House Guesthouse. Castlecomer Rd., Kilkenny City.**
  056 772 1419
  www.rosquilhouse.com
- **€€ Newlands Country House. Sevenhouses, Danesfort, Kilkenny City.**
  056 772 9171
  www.newlandscountryhouse.com

- € **Kilkenny Tourist Hostel. 35 Parliament St., Kilkenny City.**

  056 776 3541

  www.kilkennyhostel.ie

- € **Dunromin B&B. Dublin Rd. Kilkenny City.**

  056 776 1387

  www.dunrominkilkenny.com

- €€ **Kilmaneen Farmhouse. Ardfinnan, Newcastle, Co. Tipperary.**

  052 613 6231

  www.kilmaneen.com

- €€ **Inch House. Thurles, Co. Tipperary.**

  050 451 348,

  www.inchhouse.ie

- €€ **Silver Stream B&B. Goatenbridge, Ardfinnan, Co. Tipperary.**

  052 66 113.

- € **Cashel Holiday Hostel. Town Center, Cashel, Co. Tipperary.**

  062 62 330

  www.cashelhostel.com

- € **The Apple Farm (award-winning caravanning and camping). Moorstown, Cahir, Co. Tipperary.**

  052 744 1459

  www.theapplefarm.com

Restaurants and Pubs

Kildare, Kilkenny, and Tipperary have a conglomeration of restaurants, preeminent pubs, and even cookery schools offering tasty delights to appease the senses. Whether you are in the mood for an Irish hamburger or gourmet salmon, see the following options for some of the most highly recommended eateries in this part of the country. (In the restaurant listings that follow, € = around 25 euros per person.)

The Silken Thomas

The Square, Kildare

045 522 232

www.silkenthomas.com

€

Named after the heroics of Lord Thomas Fitzgerald, known as the Silken Thomas for his ritzy attire, this establishment's modern-day pub, restaurant, and en suite rooms allow the place to live up to its namesake as "the Complete Pub." A visit here means a whole great night's worth of entertainment, good food, and festive entertainment.

The Mill Restaurant and Café La Serre

Celbridge, Co. Kildare

01 630 3500

www.villageatlyons.com

€€€

The Irish and European Mill Restaurant has a rich, yet subtly elegant décor. The restaurant produces its delectable treasures with the highest-quality, local ingredients it can gather. For those who want to spend a little less, the Café La Serre is a nice option as well. Dining would not be complete without a visit to the Village at Lyons, which is a reconstruction effort of shops, bakeries, and artisans along the Georgian Canal.

Café Sol

William St., Kilkenny City

056 776 4987

www.cafesolkilkenny.com

€–€€

Reviewed as one of the best bistros serving vegetarian and Irish fusion in Ireland, the Café Sol lives up to its sunny endearments. It is open seven days a week for both lunch and dinner. The early-bird menu offers the best deal. The soups and gourmet sausages are worth their weight in gold.

Ristorante Rinuccini

1 The Parade, Kilkenny City

056 776 1575

www.rinuccini.com

€–€€

This Italianate showpiece serves wonderful lunch and dinner options by menu or à la carte. The lunch specials and early-bird menus mean you will save money on their already fairly priced cuisine. Additionally, they serve many items gluten-free. If you are in the mood for savory Salmone con Crosta di Pesto or what could be the best tiramisu in Europe, plan ahead and book reservations.

Fiacri Country House Restaurant & Cookery School

Boulerea, Knock, Roscrea, Co. Tipperary

050 543 017

www.fiacrihouse.com

€€–€€€

The seafood and sirloin steak truly put the Fiacri Country House Restaurant on the map. Flavorful mussels, prawns, fine smoked salmon, lean sirloin, and mouthwatering lamb are only some of the choices.

The Old Convent

Mount Anglesby, Clogheen, Co. Tipperary
052 65 565
www.theoldconvent.ie
€€

Winning more awards than they can name, Chef Dermot Gannon and his wife, Christine, run the Old Convent gourmet restaurant and guesthouse with superb fluidity. Served with deliberate excellence, you won't be rushed, and your taste buds will bask in the exquisiteness arranged before you. Book well ahead for both the restaurant and rooms.

Traveler's Tidbits

Here you will find the necessary information for Kildare, Kilkenny, and Tipperary. Tourist offices are located in each major area. The best websites for these areas are *www.heritageireland.ie, www.kilkenny.ie,* and *www.aherlow.com.*

Tourist offices operate during regular business hours.

AREA TOURIST OFFICES

Town	Address	Phone Number	In Operation
Kildare	Market House	045 521 240	All year
Kilkenny	Shee Alms House	056 775 1500	All year
Cashel	Heritage Center, Main St.	062 62 511	All year
Clonmel	Old St. Mary's Church	052 22 960	All year

Following is additional pertinent travel information. In the case of an emergency, dial 999 anywhere in the Republic of Ireland.

TRAVEL INFORMATION

Name	Address	Phone Number	Web Address
Garda (Police) Headquarters	Dominic Street, Kilkenny	056 772 2222	
St. Lukes Hospital	Freshford Rd., Kilkenny	056 775 1133	
Kilkenny Library (Internet)	6 John's Quay	056 779 4174	
Kilkenny Post Office	73 High Street	056 776 2327	
Genealogy Research (Kildare)	Newbridge, Co. Kildare	045 43 3602	*www.kildare .brsgenealogy .com*
Genealogy Research (Kilkenny)		Online database	*www.kilkenny .brsgenealogy .com*
Genealogy Research (North Tipperary)	The Governor's House, Kickham St., Nenagh, Co. Tipperary	067 33 850	*www .tipperarynorth .ie*

Note: See www.tipperarysouth.brsgenealogy.com for South Tipperary genealogical information.

County Cork

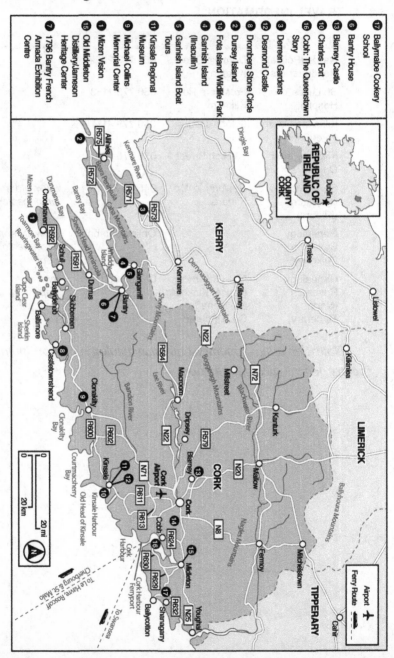

17 Ballymaloe Cookery School
6 Bantry House
13 Blarney Castle
10 Charles Fort
16 Cobh: The Queenstown Story
3 Derreen Gardens
12 Desmond Castle
2 Dursey Island
8 Dromberg Stone Circle
14 Fota Island Wildlife Park
4 Garinish Island (Ilnacullin)
5 Garinish Island Boat Tours
11 Kinsale Regional Museum
9 Michael Collins Memorial Center
1 Mizen Vision
15 Old Midleton Distillery/Jameson Heritage Center
7 1796 Bantry French Armada Exhibition Centre

CHAPTER 10

County Cork

Known throughout history in Ireland as a rebellious region, do not be surprised if you find Corkonians (as they are lovingly referred to) sporting T-shirts audaciously claiming Cork as its own independent country. While it has yet to separate from the Union, Cork is a booming metropolis waiting for its full recognition as the new Dublin. While smaller in size than its counterpart, its lively spirit, attractive artistic allure, and happening feel compete with Dublin's dynamic draw.

Getting Around County Cork

Getting to County Cork is easy enough by plane, train, bus, or ferry. Cork City is located 250km (160 miles) from Dublin and is 200km (130 miles) from Galway. You might save time (but not money) by flying into Shannon Airport, which is 120 (75 miles) away from Cork. It is the same distance from Waterford and only 85km (50 miles) from Killarney.

Flying

If you want to start your journeys from Cork, then Aer Arann (0818 210 210, *www.aerarann.com* or *www.cork-airport.com*)

flies in from both Dublin and Belfast. Aer Lingus (800 474 7424, *www.aerlingus.com*) has flights from London and other parts of Europe. British Airways (*www.ba.com*), Easy Jet, the budget Irish company Ryanair (*www.ryanair.com*), and bmi baby (*www.bmibaby.com*) all serve Cork as well. Getting from the airport to the city can be done on Bus Éireann (021 450 8188, *www.buseireann.ie*), which takes you to the Parnell Place Bus Station in Cork city center. They also service other towns and districts in County Cork. Taxis are also available and will cost about €15 for the trip.

Train

Irish Rail (01 836 6222, *www.irishrail.ie*) have trains from major towns and cities in Ireland, all arriving at Kent Station (021 450 6766), located on Lower Glanmire Road. The city center is a twenty-five-minute walk from here.

 Alert

If you are driving into Cork City from Waterford and coming along the coast on the N25 past Youghal, consider taking the Carrigaloe-Glenbrook Ferry, operated by the Cross River Ferries Service (021 481 1485), into the city. Doing so might save you a lot of time. Driving around the Cobh Harbor can be a time-consuming annoyance. The trip on the ferry is quick, convenient, and affordable. Plus, it runs year round.

Ferries

Brittany Ferries (021 427 7801, *www.brittany-ferries.com*) departs from Roscoff, France, to the Ringaskiddy Ferryport in Cork.

Cork City

Known in Ireland as the "second city," Cork City is, at its essence, abuzz with business, art, and culture. Known for its rebellious political history as the pedestal of the National Fenian movement, Corkonians hold their head high as a representation of Ireland's success. It is in fact the booming epicenter of commerce for Ireland's southwestern coastal corner.

Dissected by the River Lee into various subsections (called *quays*), the city gives way to a wide, natural harbor that once gave trading ships a direct entrance into the city.

Here are some of the best sights to check out while you are in Cork City:

Cork Butter Museum

The Cork Butter Museum (021 430 0600) invites travelers to learn about Ireland's deep-rooted history in butter exportation. Open Monday–Saturday, 10 A.M.–5 P.M. Admission €2.50/3.50.

St. Ann's Church

Arranged with limestone and sandstone façades, St. Ann's Church (021 450 5906, *www.shandonbells.org*) is one of Cork's most important landmarks. It houses the unreliable "four-faced liar" clock. A climb to the top means you might get to ring the bells. Open Monday–Saturday, 10 A.M.–4 P.M. Admission €5/6.

Crawford Municipal Art Gallery

A school of design turned gallery, the Crawford Art Gallery (021 490 7855, *www.crawfordartgallery.ie*) houses the lovely works of nineteenth- and twentieth-century Irish and international artists, including Paul Henry and Jack Yeats. Open Monday–Wednesday and Friday–Saturday, 9 A.M.–5 P.M.; Thursday, 9 A.M.–8 P.M. Admission free.

Cork City Gaol

Deservingly the most popular sight in Cork City, the Cork City Gaol (Cork City Jail) (021 430 5022, *www.corkcitygaol.com*) offers an audiovisual showing, along with tours taking travelers through the reconstructed cells. Located about one mile from the city center, take a stroll here to learn about what it would have been like as a prisoner in times past. It does an exceptional job of bringing to life the horrors of the correctional system of the day. In the same edifice, the former governor's house is now the Radio Museum Experience, depicting the history of radio in Ireland and the world. Open March–October: daily, 9:30 A.M.—5:00 P.M. November–February: daily, 10:00 A.M.–4:00 P.M. Admission €4–6/7.

 Essential

Even in its free-market fervor, Cork has retained its artistic flair with the Cork International Film Festival and the Cork Jazz Festival, both taking place in October. Be sure to book tickets ahead if you want to partake. Contact the Cork Opera House (021 427 0022, *www .corkoperahouse.ie*) for information.

Old English Market

The city of Cork's most astute attraction is the famous English Market, located near the pedestrian intersection of Oliver Plunkett Street and Grand Parade. Guidebooks and food-specialty television programs alike rave about it. From gourmet blood pudding to pig's head to splendid sun-dried tomatoes, this is an epicurean's dream. Open Monday–Saturday, 9 A.M.–6 P.M. Admission free.

Cork City Tours

You can hop on and off a Cork City Tour Bus (021 425 5100) that goes to the city's most interesting sights. Or, you might opt for the moderately popular Cork City Historic Walking Tours (*www* *.walkcork.ie*, April–October, 10 A.M., 2 P.M., 4 P.M. €5/10). Both tours start at the tourist information center, on Grand Parade.

Cobh

Southeast of Cork City, Cobh was the most significant port in Ireland for trade and a major port-of-call for travelers. The first steamship crossing of the Atlantic started in Cobh in 1838. Interestingly, it was also the departure point of more than 2.5 million emigrants who left Ireland as a result of the great famine (1844–48). Emigration lasted for nearly 100 years, during which time over 6 million Irish people fled their own country for work and a chance at a better life.

 Fact

Cobh was christened "Queenstown" following a visit by Queen Victoria in 1849. Because it was the world's largest natural harbor, it was one of the most important merchant stopover points on the globe. Its importance lead to the construction of notable naval bases and was a port-of-call for luxury liners, including the last stop of the *Titanic* before its doomed crossing.

To learn more about the history of the region, visit the Cobh Heritage Centre, which details "the Queenstown Story" (021 481 3591, *www.cobhheritage.com*). Located at the Cobh Railway Station, which can be accessed by taking the train from the Cork Train Station. Open May–October: daily, 9:30 A.M.—6:00 P.M. November–April: daily, 10:00 A.M.—5:00 P.M. Closed the week of Christmas. Admission €3–6/7.

The Titanic Trail (021 481 5211 or 087 276 7218, *www.titantic-trail* *.com*) is a popular daily walking tour exploring the history and heritage of the region. Join in at the Commodore Hotel, daily at 11 A.M., with an extra 2 P.M. session in the summertime. Times may vary from October to March. Admission €5/10–15.

North of the Great Island is Fota Island, which houses the Fota House and Gardens (021 481 5543, *www.fotahouse.com*, €3–5/6). The Fota Wildlife Park (021 481 2678, *www.fotawildlife.ie*), located between Cobh and the Cork City center off the N25, is a rewarding endeavor. Open Monday–Saturday, 10 A.M.–6 P.M. Admission €8.50/13. The family-friendly park, which lures sightseers to check out its plethora of exotic species, works to breed and reintroduce animals into their natural habitats.

Kinsale

In a vote, this small fishing village would undoubtedly top the list of Ireland's most picturesque towns. Its strategic location at the mouth of the Bandry River meant a rocky past with a myriad of controlling governments taxing its ports. Now harmonious in every sense and offering a variety of activities (yachting, golf, fishing, and sailing), the village boasts international regattas, along with a Festival of Fine Foods and a Jazz Festival in October. An enthralling Arts Festival takes place each July. The main sights of the city are the Desmond Castle, often called the "French Prison" (now a wine museum), Saint Multose Church, the Old Market House Museum, and Charles Fort, located outside of town on the road past Summercove.

Kinsale Ghost Tour

Spending a day and night in Kinsale would not be complete without showing up at the Tap Tavern for the now-famed Kinsale Ghost Tour (021 477 2240; for groups, 021 477 2263 or 087 948 0910 *www.kinsale.ie/ghost-tours.htm*). After enjoying a pint or two, buy your ticket and prepare for pure, unadulterated amusement. Hear the real and plausible histories behind the French Prison, the spooky St. Multose Church, and the sadly ironic tale of the White Lady who haunts Kinsale's upper avenues. Tours run each night during the summer, two nights per week in the lower seasons. No reservations needed. Departs Tap Tavern daily at 9 P.M. throughout the summer. Admission €10/15.

 Fact

A massive star-shaped fort, Charles Fort is located in Summercove. Built by Sir William Robinson in 1677, the building was used as a barracks. The parapets are dangerous to climb but offer stellar views of the Kinsale Harbor. If you are into archaeological exploration, drive down the road, across the river to a less-visited star fort called James Fort. A path known as the "Scilly Walk" connects the forts to Kinsale.

Historical Walk

If you cannot make the Ghost Tour, the Herlihy's Historical Stroll (021 477 2873 or 021 477 2234, *www.historicstrollkinsale.com*) is worthwhile. The tour highlights the town's medieval fortifications inside the walled town. Tours do not involve too much walking and leave daily at 11:15 A.M., March–November, from the Kinsale Tourist Office in the center, off of Pier Road. Admission €1–3.50/7.

Clonakilty

A nice escape from the hustle and bustle of Cork City, ebullient Clonakilty offers visitors a distinct western Cork experience. Set up first as a military camp in the latter 1500s, Clonakilty became famous for its fine linen in the 1800s. This market town still flourishes and offers visitors a nice base from which to explore the area. Here, you can visit the West Cork Regional Museum and the Lios-na-gCon Ringfort (*http://liosnagcon.com*). You can also access Inchydoney, an unspoiled nearby beach haven.

A visit to Clonakilty would not be complete without knowing a little about "the Big Fella," Michael Collins, who was born near the area. In short, Collins was the head of the military group representing the Irish Free State. In 1921, his forces beat the British, eventually leading to Ireland's freedom. Visitors can find many books about the rogue, who was able to outsmart and eliminate the British secret service in the Republic.

Things to See and Do

The magnetism of County Cork is undeniable. With so much to see and do, it would easily be possible to spend an entire vacation in this one county's grandeur. From Blarney to Bantry to ancient stone forts, Cork is a true highlight ne plus ultra of southern Ireland.

Blarney Stone, Castle, and Grounds

Many a traveler would agree that a visit to County Cork would not be complete without puckering up to kiss a certain Blarney Stone, located under a parapet atop the Blarney Castle (021 438 5252, *www .blarneycastle.ie*). Cormac Laidir MacCarthy built the castle circa 1446. The upper turret had three floors, the uppermost a private worship area. The castle was taken from the MacCarthy family and then later returned only to be taken again in the late 1600s. Finally, the Jefferyes families became its proprietors in 1688 and remain so today.

 Alert

One would have to be suspended by the ankles in order to fully reach the actual Blarney Stone. Due to potential danger, most visitors are leaned back and can kiss close enough to have some of the gift of gab rub off!

The well-groomed estate also has a fern garden and marked walks that can take up a couple of hours in the morning or afternoon. The Lake Walk, located on the grounds, will take you away from it all if you would like to enjoy the outskirts of the grounds in their splendor. The kids will enjoy the Witch's Kitchen and the Druids Cave as well. The Blarney House, a baronial mansion belonging to the Scottish Colthurst family, recently opened for guided visits from April to June. Castle open daily, 9:00 A.M.–5:30 P.M. Varied times in winter. Estate walks close earlier. Admission €4–8/10. Closed Christmas Eve and Day.

Bantry House

The famed mansion known as the Bantry House (027 50 047, *www.bantryhouse.ie*) has been in the White family's possession since the early 1700s. They were at one time titled the Earls of Bantry. Now they have opened the doors of their estate to visitors wanting to absorb the enthralling history behind the elegant manor.

 Essential

Located on the northern coast of the Beara Peninsula, the Anam Cara Writer's and Artist's Retreat (027 74 441, *www.anamcararetreat .com*) is a ruby in the rough, tucked away near the Kealincha River. The retreat is designed to inflate any artist's afflatus. The charming hosts recommend staying a week to ensure maximum benefit.

The house was first constructed with a southern-most façade; the northern bayside façade was constructed later. Along with a fabulous entrance hall, there is an extensive library with a rosewood grand piano on display, a loggia opening up to the famed Rose Garden, and antechambers. The most renowned rooms are the Gobelin Room, which houses the Gobelin tapestry, and the Rose Room, containing tapestries dedicated to Marie Antoinette upon her marriage to the dauphin of France. Open March–October, daily, 10 A.M.–6 P.M. Admission €5/10.

The Bantry House runs a bed-and-breakfast with en suite rooms in the east and west sides of the manor. Additionally, the house also rents its Gatelodge, a self-catering luxury cottage available for weekly rentals, perfect for four adults.

Drombeg Stone Circle

First established in the second century B.C., the Drombeg Stone Circle is one of the most impressive stone circular forts in all of Ireland. Just off Glandore Road near Clonakilty, the stone structure contains seventeen small pillars, sixteen of which are standing, and is approximately 30 feet in diameter. Interestingly, the place is thought to have been an altar used for human sacrifices. Nearby are two rounded huts, which are thought to be ancient hunting cabins.

 Fact

A cleverly constructed cooking hearth is viewable near the small stream, accessible from the huts by following the walkway. Upon heating the stones, the hunters would drop rocks into the water to boil it. Experiments re-enacting this cooking method have proved it to be an efficient manner in which to cook; the hot stones could boil water many times their volume and keep food hot for well over two hours.

Garinish Island (Ilnacullin)

The small island (18 hectares, or 40 acres) of Garnish should top any traveler's list. The island hosts an exotic garden, housing subtropical plants, from rhododendrons to Bonsai trees. Set up by the revered architect Harold Peto, the spot was created for the island's proprietor, Annan Bryce. From here, you can also take a boat to see the seals in Bantry Bay. The best way to get to the island is via Blue Pool Ferries (027 63 333) or Harbour Queen Ferries (087 234 5861). The *Lady Ellen* ferry (087 944 3784) also runs trips to the island and around it.

Cape Clear Island (Oileán Chléire)

If you truly want to get away on an island, consider the dream-like Clear Island, located on the outskirts of the Roaringwater Bay. The island is a bird-watching paradise, has a nice Clear Island Heritage Centre (028 39 119), and is home to Dunamore Castle, which can be reached by a trail from the harbor. The island has a Storytelling Festival (028 39 157) in late August and early September. There are a few quaint B&Bs from which to choose, along with a campsite (028 39 119) and hostel (028 41 968). Take the Naomh Ciarán Ferry (028 39 153, *www.capeclearferry.com*) to the island from Baltimore.

Accommodations

Depending upon what tops your list of sights to see or activities to do, Cork has a plenteous array of quality B&Bs, luxury hotels, self-catering cottages, and guesthouses. Because there is so much to see and do, it might be best to choose the top locations you would like to visit, and then choose a guesthouse, manor, B&B, or hotel to fit.

Glencairn Bed & Breakfast

Underwood, Rochestown, Co. Cork
021 489 2951 or 086 826 818
www.glencairnbb.ie
€45–90 per room; S/D/T

Located outside of Cork City, this is one of the most homey B&Bs you might stay in around all of Ireland. The owners will make sure all your needs are met. In the early spring or late fall, expect a blazing turf fire to welcome you into their humble abode. The smallish rooms might be considered cramped by the pessimistic, but they are full of charm and well maintained. The B&B is situated for easy access into Cork City and the charming Kinsale

Village, which is about thirty minutes away. Enjoy a full Irish breakfast in the B&B's newly added glass foyer.

South Reen Farm (Eco-Lodging)

Union Hall, Co. Cork (near Skibbereen)

028 33 258

www.southreenfarm.com

€700–1100 per week

The epitome of eco-friendly, self-catered lodging, the South Reen Farm retreat is a soothing escape set in a pastoral haven and organic farm. A small ramble through the garden and one encounters the Atlantic's heaving waves in the distance; the inlet protects swimmers. If halcyon moments top your list, the South Reen Farm should also.

Farran House

Farran, Co. Cork

021 733 1215 or 086 811 1244

www.farranhouse.com

€70–100+; S/D/Family. MC/V

Built in the 1700s, this flawlessly restored Italianate home sits in the Lee Valley, a short jaunt from the Kilcrea Abbey and medieval castle. The house is near several golf courses, and equestrian facilities and fishing venues are nearby as well. With its location, it makes an excellent middle ground from which to explore the interior of County Cork. The establishment has four rooms available; group bookings and families welcome. To get there, go 17km (11 miles) west of Cork City on the N22. It is just after Ballincollig.

Hagal Farm (Eco-Lodging)

Coomleigh West, Bantry Bay, Co. Cork

027 66 179

www.hagalholistichealth.com

€40–70 per person; €125+ per night sleeping six

Choosing between staying at the quaint B&B or the self-catering garden lodge will be the most stress you will experience at the Hagal Farm. The Hagal Farm offers top-notch service with a smile. Enjoy a wonderful breakfast and the choice of full board if reserved ahead. Enjoy a healing massage, reflexology treatment, or other types of therapy should you want to de-stress and get away from it all.

Hayfield Manor Hotel

Perrott Avenue, College Road, Cork City

021 484 5900

www.hayfieldmanor.ie

€200+; suites €500–1,000+; MC/V

This five-star establishment is perfect for those who really want to live it up while in southwestern Ireland. With marble bathrooms and spacious rooms, the Hayfield Manor Hotel is home to a premier spa, two top-notch restaurants, and has won too many awards to list. It is a great location for a variety of activities, including golf.

Other Accommodations

Here are some other accommodations you might consider. (In the listings that follow, € = around 25 euros per person.)

- **€€ Gougane Barra Hotel. Ballingeary.**
026 47 069
www.gouganebarrahotel.com
- **€€€€ Sheraton Fota Island Hotel. Fota Island.**
021 467 3000
www.sheraton.com/cork
- **€€–€€€ Rolf's Holiday Cottages. Baltimore.**
028 20 289
www.rolfsholidays.eu
- **€€€ Glengarriff Park Hotel. The Village, Glengarriff.**
027 63 000
http://glengarriffpark.com
- **€€ Lancaster Lodge. Lancaster Quay, Cork City.**
021 425 1125
www.lancasterlodge.com
- **€€ Jury's Cork Inn. Anderson's Quay, Cork City.**
021 494 3000
www.jurysdoyle.com
- **€€ Crawford House. Western Rd., Cork City.**
021 427 9000
www.crawfordguesthouse.com
- **€€€ Blindgate House. Kinsale.**
021 477 7858
www.blindgatehouse.com
- **€€€ Ballylickey Manor House. Bantry Bay.**
027 50 071
www.ballylickeymanorhouse.com
- **€ Blarney Caravan & Camping Park. Stone View, Blarney.**
021 451 6519
www.blarneycaravanpark.com

Restaurants and Pubs

Cork offers the epicureans some real treats. From cookery schools to some of Ireland's finest dining, travelers will find a unique experience with each meal. Cork City affords an amalgam of traditional and modern plates; here you will find a fusion vegetarian restaurant next to a pub serving Ireland's best burger. The English market is a highlight of Cork and a stroll here will allow you to see just how much emphasis the county as a whole puts on its dishes. (In the restaurant listings that follow, € = around 25 euros per person.)

Ballymaloe Cookery School

Shanagarry, Midleton, Co. Cork

021 464 6785

www.cookingisfun.ie

€110 half-day, €800+ week; MC/V

Located along the coast southeast of Cork City, the Ballymaloe Cookery School offers a plethora of short and long cookery classes. Located on their own organic farm, the family-run business includes award-winning chefs who have made their own BBC appearances. The cooking team is enthusiastic, fun, and most importantly, knowledgeable. If fine food and cooking are your passion, then book a course for your Ireland vacation before they fill up.

Café Paradiso
(Vegetarian Restaurant)

16 Lancaster Quay, Western Rd., Cork City

021 427 7939

www.cafeparadiso.ie

€

The well-located vegetarian restaurant was recommended by at least three stall owners in the English Market as one of the best vegetarian restaurants in Cork. For foodies who love anything vegetarian and organic, you will surely fall in love with this place. Service is friendly. Call ahead for groups larger than six.

Fishy Fishy Café

Kinsale, Co. Cork

021 470 0415

www.fishyfishy.ie

€–€€

This lovely little restaurant has gotten a lot of attention for its seafood cuisine. A tour guide jocularly commented that the Irish like to repeat themselves (notice "stop" or "yield" signs: There always seems to be two of them each intersection). It is the same with this restaurant. If you are not sure what they serve, they repeat it twice for further clarity. The Fishy Fishy Café tops the list for some of Ireland's finest cuisine, found in the little harbored heaven of Kinsale. No reservations taken.

O'Connor's Seafood Restaurant

The Square, Bantry

027 50 221

www.oconnorseafood.com

€€

While there are some nice dining experiences to be had in Bantry, O'Connor's Seafood Restaurant tops the list for its specialty cuisine. The early-bird specials, served from 6 P.M. to 7 P.M., are well worth it. The stupendous service and bountiful servings won't leave you with further cravings for at least twenty-four hours. They are closed Sunday and Monday nights in the winter months.

The Franciscan Well
Brew Pub
13 North Mall, Cork City

021 421 0130

www.franciscanwellbrewery.com

€

This brewery is a true delight among so many pubs from which to choose in Cork City. Brewing their own lager, ale, and even wheat beer, they pride themselves on using the freshest, most natural ingredients. The pub is a part of various beer-fests throughout the year.

Grapefruit Moon
Ballycotton, Co. Cork

021 464 6646

€

This fine dining, global-cuisine restaurant could have put Ballycotton on the map. The restaurant has no secrets: The freshest ingredients, the best chefs, and blue-ribbon service make it reason alone to venture off the beaten path.

Shopping in Cork

With so much to see (and buy!), Cork is a shopper's paradise. In Cork City, the main shopping boulevard for Corkonians and tourists alike is Patrick Street. The city also has a shopping center at Merchant's Quay, along with bookshops along Paul Street and MacCurtain Street.

Crafts of Ireland
Winthrop St., Cork City
021 427 5864

Located right off Patrick Street, this shop epitomizes Cork crafts. With weavings, ironwork, ceramics, and pure Irish works, this store is a must-shop.

Quills Woolen Market
Patrick St., Cork City
021 427 1717

While finding the perfect Irish tweed might prove next to impossible with all the choices at the Quills Woolen Market, do not let this stop you from visiting. Whether it is something handmade or factory produced, you will find it at this market, which has other shops throughout Ireland.

Traveler's Tidbits

Here you will find the necessary information for Cork. Tourist offices are located in nearly every town. The best websites to check out information for County Cork are *www.corkkerry.ie* and *www* *.cork-guide.com*. Beara Tourism (027 70 054, *www.bearatourism* *.com*) in Castletownbere offers some information on Beara and the environs.

In the following Tourist Office chart, "Seasonal" designates tourist offices generally open May through September. Tourist offices are generally open during regular business hours.

CORK TOURIST OFFICES

Town	Address	Phone Number	In Operation
Bantry	Old Courthouse	027 50 229	Seasonal
Blarney	Town Centre	021 438 1624	Seasonal
Clonakilty	Ashe St.	023 33 226	All year
Cork	Grand Parade	021 425 5100	All year
Glengarriff	Town Centre	027 63 084	Seasonal
Kinsale	Pier Rd.	021 477 2234	All year
Macroom	Castle Gates	026 43 280	Seasonal
Midleton	Jameson Centre	021 461 3701	Seasonal
Skibbereen	North St.	028 21 766	All year
Youghal	Market Square	024 20 170	Seasonal

Following is additional pertinent travel information. In the case of an emergency, dial 999 anywhere in the Republic of Ireland.

TRAVEL INFORMATION

Name	Address	Phone Number
Garda (Police) Headquarters	Anglesea St.	021 452 2000
Cork University Hospital	Wilton Rd.	021 454 6400
Bon Secours Hospital	College Rd.	021 454 2807
Cork Library	57 Grande Parade	021 492 4900
Wired World Internet	12A Washington St.	021 490 5695
Finishing Services Internet	Main St., Kinsale	021 477 3571
Cork Post Office	Oliver Plunkett St.	021 485 1042
Genealogy Research (Mallow Heritage Center)	27 Bank Place, Mallow	022 50 302

County Kerry

2 Blennerville Windmill	**10** Kerry Bog Village Museum
4 Carrigafoyle Castle	**5** Kerry Literary & Cultural Centre
9 Ceardlann Craft Village	**1** Kerry the Kingdom
13 Derrynane House National Historic Park	**17** Knockreer Estate
8 Eask Tower	**16** Muckross House & Gardens
6 Gallarus Oratory	**15** Seafari
18 Gap of Dunloe	**11** Skellig Experience
7 Ionad An Bhlascaoid Mhoir (The Basket Centre)	**12** Staigue Fort
14 Kenmare Druid Circle	**3** Tralee Steam Railway

CHAPTER 11

County Kerry

Christened "the Kingdom," County Kerry forms the south-western corner of the province known as Munster. With the finest in Irish serenity reflected in idyllically remote country corners, a trip to the region gives one a good sampling of what the whole Republic of Ireland has to offer. With its quaint and picturesque towns, it is no wonder that tourists flock here by the busloads. Head here in the off-season, or start your touring early, and explore the Beara and Dingle peninsulas to discover the true peace of this land.

Getting Around
County Kerry

Orientating oneself in Kerry is not that difficult. The central points for navigation along the coast, and the true draw of the county, are the various peninsulas jutting out to Ireland's (and Europe's) most western points. Those peninsulas are the Beara Peninsula (Ring of Beara), the Iveragh Peninsula (Ring of Kerry), and the Dingle Peninsula. The main cities or towns are Tralee (the capital), Killarney, Kenmare, and Dingle Town. For the Ring of Kerry, the most picturesque and less-crowded town of Kenmare makes a perfect base.

Flying

Flying into County Kerry can be done via the Kerry Airport (066 976 4644, *www.kerryairport.com*), which has flights to and from Dublin, Manchester, London Stansted and Luton, Frankfurt Hahn, and Lyon. The two carriers operating here most frequently are Ireland's Aer Arann (0818 210 210, *www.aerarann.com*), which has daily departures to Dublin, and Ireland's own budget airline carrier Ryanair (0818 30 3030, *www.ryanair.com*).

 Essential

You might also consider taking a horse-drawn carriage called a "Jaunting Car" (*www.killarneyjauntingcars.com*) driven by "Jarveys," which you can find at Kenmare Place at the center of town. Prices are negotiable for various excursions, priced from €20 to over €75. You can also find them near the Muckross House and Abbey.

Bus and CarIreland's national Bus Éireann (064 34 777, *www.buseireann.ie*) has services from Killarney into each of the various peninsulas and also to and from surrounding counties. Regular service includes a thirty-five-minute trip to Tralee, where you can then depart for Dingle Town. From Killarney, getting down to Kenmare (or vice versa) is easy enough.

From Killarney, buses also head to Cork, Galway, Dublin, Limerick, Waterford, and Rosslare. In the high tourist season, Bus Éireann is one of many running tours around the entire Ring of Kerry.

The best way to get around County Kerry is by car, especially if you want to get to the more remote sections of the peninsulas. The Beara and Dingle peninsulas offer some truly spectacular scenery, minus the buses and cars that throng the Ring of Kerry in the summer.

Train

Getting to Killarney can be done on the train from Cork and from Tralee. You can also get to Dublin from both places. The Killarney Railway Station (064 31 067, *www.irishrail.ie*) also serves Limerick and Galway.

Killarney

Droves of travelers head to southwest Ireland's premier tourist epicenter: Killarney. With hundreds of years of tourism under its belt, Killarney flourishes all year long. The marked "Tourist Trail" is a great way to see the city's highlights in under a couple of hours and starts at the town center car park, just off of Beech Road.

 Fact

A small farmer's market takes place each Wednesday morning outside the grocery store off of N71 in the center of Kenmare. Featuring locally grown produce, it is a perfect spot to grab provisions such as organic olives, fresh honeycomb, homemade desserts and breads, or various types of cheeses.

One of the main sights of Killarney is St. Mary's Cathedral (064 31 014), an impressive limestone edifice towering in true Gothic revival. The church, which is in the form of a cross, was started just before the famine in the 1840s. Farther along in town is the Famine Memorial, just at the tip of High Street.

Kenmare

Arguably the loveliest town in Kerry, Kenmare (or *Neidín*, meaning "small nest") is located at the tip of the Kenmare River (which is actually a bay) and the Sheen River. William Petty, one of the founders of the Royal Society, was granted the area of Kenmare by Oliver Cromwell, whom he worked under as his surveyor general. It was his progeny, the first Marquis of Landsdowne, who actually set it up as a town of stylish streets with two triangular sections forming the town's center.

The best places to see in Kenmare include:

Kenmare Heritage Centre and Druid Circle

Accessible from town, the Druid Circle is a fifteenth-century stone ring that was once a sacrificial altar. To learn more about it, visit the Heritage Centre (064 41 233) museum, located in the tourist office. Exhibit open July–August: Monday–Saturday, 9:00 A.M.–7:00 P.M. May–June and September: Monday–Saturday, 9:00 A.M.–5:30 P.M. Closed October–April. Admission €2/3.

Kenmare Lace and Design Centre

For those with a thing for lace, the Kenmare Lace and Design Centre (064 42 978), located above the tourist office, will truly please. With the passing down of the art, the Poor Clare Nuns became world famous for the craft. For nearly 100 years, the girls who learned the skill were able to fend off the famine. Some were even commissioned by British royalty. Open April–October: Monday–Saturday, 10:00 A.M.–5:30 P.M. November–March: Monday–Saturday, 10:00 A.M.–1:30 P.M. Admission free.

Tralee

Considered by many to be an unappealing alternative to spending your nights in Killarney or Kenmare, Tralee is admittedly more rugged. However, it does have its perks and a few sights that are worth exploring if you are passing through. The Kerry County Museum (066 712 7777) is noteworthy. It is a part of the visitor center (both open daily, admission €7/10) in Ashe Memorial Hall and also displays historical memorabilia. The best sights around Tralee include:

Blennerville Windmill

From Tralee, the Blennerville Windmill (066 712 1064) stands nearly 20 meters (66feet) in height and is one of a few that still functions. Open daily. Closed November–March. Admission €4/6.

Carrigafoyle Castle

Outside the town of Listowel, just west of Ballylongford, you will encounter Carrigafoyle Castle (meaning "rock of the chasm"). This fifteenth-century castle is a vaulted five-story stone fort with a spiral staircase leading to the top. At one time, the castle formed its own island and even had a small boat dock between the bawns. Open all year. Admission free.

 Essential

In Listowel, stop by the Kerry Literary and Cultural Centre (066 22 212, www.kerrywritersmuseum.com) at the Square, to learn about the impressive literary geniuses Kerry has churned out. Separate galleries are devoted to greats such as Brendan Kennelley, John Keane, and Bryan MacMahon. Each June a popular Writers' Week literary festival takes place.

Crag Cave

For kids and adults alike, Crag Cave (066 714 1244, www.cragcave.com) holds true to its self-labeled "Subterranean Magic" title. Formed of limestone, the cave was discovered only recently, in the mid-1980s. The thirty-minute tour includes visits to the "Kitchen and Crystal Gallery" caves displaying stalactites and stalagmites. Open mid-March–December: daily,

10 A.M.–6 P.M. January–February: Wednesday–Sunday, 10 A.M.–6 P.M. Admission €6/12.

Things to See and Do

The "Kingdom" of Kerry has lots to offer. From Killarney's sylvan edges to Dingle's cliff-side marvels, choices can be mixed and matched for all types of travelers.

Killarney National Park

Besides the Ring of Kerry, the Killarney National Park is Kerry's top tourist hotspot, especially for those who want to *see* rugged nature without having to necessarily *experience* it. The N71 road (connecting Killarney and Kenmare) cuts straight through the park, offering small pull-off areas giving way to spectacular views of the lakes dotting the horizon. The road takes about forty-five minutes to drive when traffic is flowing, but it can be gridlocked in July and August. On the road, you will come to the Ladies' View (where there is a café) and Moll's Gap viewpoints.

Getting to the entrance of the park is best achieved by parking at one of the lots off of the N71. One of the most central locations to stop is at the Torc Waterfall parking lot, which gives you access to color-coded trails on one side and roads leading to the Muckross Estate and Abbey on the other. Here, even with hail or high winds, you will find jarveys with Jaunting Cars waiting to take you for a spin.

To summit any of the local mountains (such as Carrantuohill, Ireland's tallest peak), you should consider going with a guide. Remember, the weather can change on a dime as you ascend, so be prepared with rain gear. It is recommended to start such an ascent off of the N72 at Cronin's Yard (064 34 936, *www.croninsyard.com*), which offers amenities such as toilets, a cozy tearoom, and some food items. The best guided tours are offered daily by Killarney Guided Walks (087 6394362, *www*

.killarneyguidedwalks.com). Visit the Muckross House's information center for maps.

Killarney Lakes and Inisfallen

Labeled an official "Area of Outstanding Natural Beauty" and an official UNESCO Biosphere Reserve, Killarney National Park has three main lakes. Those are the Lough Leane (called the "Lake of Learning"), the Upper Lake, and Muckross Lake. One of the most popular spots is the Meeting of the Waters, where all three lakes converge. The best view is from Dinis Island, which requires a boat hire.

Lough Leane claims the largest island in the park at Inisfallen (accessible by boat from Ross Castle), where the *Annals of Inisfallen* was composed. The island still retains some noteworthy monuments of early Christian architecture, including a monastery founded by a famous seventh-century monk, Saint Finian the Leper.

 Question

What is the Annals of Inisfallen?
The *Annals of Inisfallen* is thought to be a part of the greater compilation within the *Chronicle of Ireland*. The writings, compiled for over 300 years starting in the 1200s, are evidence of how the surrounding "Lake of Learning" received its appellation. Currently housed in the Bodleian Library in Oxford, the people and government of Killarney have demanded its return.

Gap of Dunloe

Located just outside the park's actual parameters is the impressive Gap of Dunloe. Ideal for viewing the surrounding Macgillycuddy's Reeks and Purple Mountain ranges, the touristy thing to do in summer is to take a harnessed horse trot through the valley. A much better way to experience the canyon is via bike. To make it a full day trip, rent a bike in Killarney Town and bike to Ross Castle. From there, take a boat for a tour of the lake and islets to Lord Brandon's Cottage, followed by biking through the Gap and back down to Killarney on the N72. Day trips and other excursions can be hired with Gap of Dunloe Tours (064 30 200, *www.gapofdunloetours.com*).

Ross Castle

Standing strong against Cromwellian forces, Ross Castle (064 35 851) was finally overtaken in part due to the fulfillment of a prophecy. The prophecy assured that the fortification would only be taken from the water by an armed ship. In 1652 when Ludlow brought boats to Lough Leanne in order to attack, the Irish forces relinquished their stronghold knowing that a fight from the water would bring their demise. A tower house built by a member of the O'Donoghue Ross remains, as do four smaller turrets at each corner. Entrance by guided tour. Open daily April–October, 9:30 A.M.–5:30 P.M. Admission €2.50–4/6.

Muckross House, Traditional Farm, and Abbey

The Muckross House (064 31 440, *www.muckross-house.ie*) sits at the forefront of the Killarney Lakes. The seigneury was constructed in 1843 and inspired by Victorian design. Left to the state in the 1930s, the mansion is now a sort of showpiece displaying local furniture and art originating from Irish and foreign lands. The surrounding gardens are immaculately kept. Walking, cycling, or taking a Jaunting Car around Muckross Lake is quite scenic. Estate open daily, July–August, 9:00 A.M.–7:00 P.M.; September–June, 9:00 A.M.–5:30 P.M. Closed during the Christmas period. Admission €3–5.50/7. Combination tickets available.

Muckross Traditional Farms

The Muckross Traditional Farms are a duplication of Kerry's farms of old. Especially fun for families, the place has done a masterful job of re-creating what farming was like before the advent of electricity and modern machinery. Families live and work here, kids and animals run amok, and the smell of homemade food truly sets the scene for all the senses. Visitors can also peek in on the carpenter and blacksmith shops. Open daily in May, 1 P.M.–6 P.M., and June–August, 10 A.M.–6 P.M. Saturday–Sunday only in April and September–October, 1 P.M.–6 P.M. Closed November–March. Admission €4–6/7.50.

 Alert

Moving father west in Kerry will bring you to greater Irish Gaelic–speaking areas. In farther-removed corners and especially Dingle, expect to find road and warning signs only in Irish. Inhabitants have raised complaints over the government's changing road signs to the made-up name *An Daingean* instead of what everyone knows as Dingle.

Muckross Abbey

The Muckross Abbey (or Friary) is 1.5k (1 mile) away and is of more historical significance than the manor. Founded in the 1440s, parts were constructed and inhabited intermittently. The impressive tower is as big as the church and the colonnade contains a yew tree at the center with variegated arcades at each side. Cromwellian forces burned a good portion of it in 1652. Open all year.

The Ring of Kerry

The magnetic draw of the Ring of Kerry (the Iveragh Peninsula) is its pure Irish beauty and historical significance. Showcased in travel documentaries and in articles for decades, it is Kerry's most renowned region. The outer extremity of the peninsula tends to go untouched by bigger vehicles and a route of biking or driving including the inner sanctums of the peninsula on uncluttered back roads is an otherworldly experience. It is the largest peninsula in southwest Ireland.

If you are driving alone, consider a counter-clockwise route, as you will be able to look out the window to view the scenery. If others are with you, a clockwise circuit will allow the passengers full views. No matter your route, review a map beforehand, start early, and keep in mind that buses have the right of way.

Along the N70, you will run into Sneem, a small town just west of Kenmare that has some nice spots to explore, but farther along is Staigue Fort. The circle fort exemplifies fort construction in Ireland and is possibly the best in the country. With walls 5 meters (18 feet) high and 4 meters (13 feet) thick, the fort is best appreciated after a quick visit to the exhibition hall, which accepts donations.

Continuing the route west outside Derrynane Town is the Derrynane House, which dates from the 1600s. Home to Daniel O'Connell, who sparked Ireland to fight for its rights without violence, the area is now a National Historic Park. Audiovisual shows are available that describe O'Connell's political struggles. Farther along is Cahersiveen, which has access to Valentia Island and the Skellig Islands (see below). Glenbeigh is the next town, where you can visit the Kerry Bog Village (066 976 9184, *www .kerrybogvillage.ie*), which re-creates the rural, austere mode of living in olden days. Finally, on the N72, is Killorglin Town, resting in one of Kerry's most delightful settings. The annual Puck Fair Festival (066 976 2366, *www.puckfair.ie*) takes place in August and fills the streets with theater, good food, and (strange enough) a live goat mounted on a pedestal at the town center, adorned with ribbons. Definitely book accommodations well in advance.

Alert

For a trip to the Skellig, bring a minimum of €50 per person cash for boat trips (and tip). ATMs are harder to locate in these regions. Bring wind- and waterproof wear, along with extra clothes. Pack a picnic lunch, but try not to eat too much before the initial crossing. Seasickness is common.

Skellig Islands

Accessible from Portmagee and Valentia (Oileán Dairbhre), the Skellig Islands (Oileán na Scealaga) are best experienced early in the day as laws restrict the numbers of visitors allowed. The best time to visit is between May and September, although boats start accepting clients at Easter. Book ahead if possible, but especially in July and August. Call up any number of operators, including local historian Des Lavelle (066 947 6124) in Portmagee or Eoin Walsh (066 947 6327 or 087 283 3522) on Valentia Island. Tours tend to last from 10 A.M. until 3 P.M. Ensure that your tour enables you to walk around Skellig Michael to see the seventh-century monastic sights and modern lighthouses.

 Fact

The Skellig Islands are an avid avifauna viewer's paradise. With Mother Carey's chickens flying about, kittiwakes, and puffins, the islands are a popular birder's destination. Notwithstanding, a trip to the islands might be one of the best adventures in all of Ireland.

A trip to the Skellig Islands is better appreciated after visiting the Skellig Experience (066 947 6306, *www.skelligexperience.com*), which details the life and times of the monks who once inhabited the islands. The exhibit also includes more detailed information regarding the area's wildlife.

Dingle Peninsula

The otherworldly delight of Dingle (An Daingean) makes you feel a million miles away from happening Killarney. Dingle is a place for those wanting refuge from the masses to truly experience the Gaeltacht way of life.

Dingle Town is home to nearly 2,000 inhabitants and its charming placidity make it quite popular in July and August. With a picturesque port, views of rolling hills and ridgelines, fun-loving locals, bookshops, cafés, quaint B&Bs, and a centrally located tourist shop, not much else to ask for remains.

 Essential

A bottle-full of fun comes from this bottlenose delight: Fungie the Dolphin. When the fishermen of Dingle started noticing a lone dolphin enjoying the company of people company more than his own kind, they nicknamed him Fungie. Now, you can even arrange to swim with the convivial ocean-dweller. Contact the Brosnan's (066 915 2626, *www.dingledolphin.com*) for gear and information.

Exploring the Dingle Peninsula can be done in a short amount of time. One noteworthy, yet hair-raising drive (only on a clear day) is through Conor's Pass, offering dazzling views of the peninsula and harbor. If you have time to spare, the eight- to ten-day walking tour along the 180km (290-mile) Dingle Way (*www.dingleway.net*) is stunning. Grab the *Dingle Way Map Guide* from the tourist office before setting out. The shorter 48km (30-mile) Pilgrim's Route connects the peninsula's sites and ends with an arduous climb up Mt. Brandon.

For those with less time, driving or biking the rewarding Slea Head (Ceann Sléibe) 40km (25-mile) route around the R559 proffers a greater amount of sights in less distance than anywhere else in the country. These include the Dunbeg Fort (An Aún Beag), the Slea Head cross, the village of Ballyferriter (Baile an Fheiréaraigh), the monastic settlement of Riasc (An Riasc), the drystone church of the Gallarus Oratory (Séipéilin Ghallrois), and the Kilmalkedar (Cill Maolchéadair) church and graveyard.

Blasket Islands

Accessible and viewable from Dunquin, the westernmost islands in Europe are the Blasket Islands (Na Blascaodaí). Great Blasket (An Blascaod Mór) was inhabited until 1953 and is worth a day's exploration. The Blasket Center (Ionad an Bhlascaoid Mhóir; 066 915 6444) offers a magnificent display of the area's rich past and is recommended before venturing out to sea.

Beara Peninsula (Ring of Beara)

Made up partially of County Kerry and Cork combined, the Beara Peninsula is a rarely explored gem that radiates with quaint villages and open heath. Known for its bootlegging past in the French Brandy trade, the Beara has stunning countryside. Most noteworthy is Healy Pass grafting its way through the Caha Mountains and Hungry Hill. For those serious about walking, the 196km (310-mile) Beara Way (*www.bearaway.net*) should suffice nicely. Additionally, the Beara Way Cycle Route beckons those who want to accomplish a truly rustic feat.

Accommodations

County Kerry offers accommodations to suit all budgets. Hospitality abounds and travelers will be hard-pressed to find a guesthouse,

B&B, or even hostel that does not have a welcoming host willing to share local knowledge.

Water's Edge B&B

Muxnaw, Kenmare
064 41 707
www.kenmare.eu/watersedge
€35–50 per person; S/D/T

Located just over the bridge on the edge of Kenmare, the Water's Edge B&B has spacious en suite rooms, comfortable beds, roomy bathrooms, and tranquility that is unmatched. The hostess, Noreen Cronin, will ensure you feel at home, provide a lovely breakfast, and give you information on the numerous activities available in the area. True to its namesake, Water's Edge has a wonderful view of the Bay of Kenmare. The center of Kenmare is a ten-minute stroll away and is a perfect place to unwind.

Pax Guest House

Upper John St., Dingle
066 915 1518
www.pax-house.com
€70/120-160 per room; S/D/T/F

With friendly hosts, amazing views, and an unsurpassed breakfast, the Pax House deserves its many awards. The host, John O'Farrell, is keen to help his guests explore the wealth of history, culture, and natural beauty exuding from this fine peninsula. His accomplished goal: to do it in four-star class and style. With a comfy lounge, dining room, and outdoor patio, the Pax Guest House soothes the soul.

Coolclogher House

Mill Road, Killarney

064 35 996

www.coolclogherhouse.com

€190–250 per room, S/D/T/F. MC/V

A mansion that sits on a grand estate, the Coolclogher House offers some of the best luxury accommodations in Killarney. Set apart from the hustle and bustle of the town center, this manor is a true escape. With tasteful furniture and art, along with views overlooking the tidy garden and Kerry mountains, rooms are available for singles and couples. Additionally, the whole house is available to rent to groups of around ten to twelve persons.

Sallyport House

Kenmare

064 42 066

www.sallyporthouse.com

€75–85 per person; S/D.

Located just a short walk along a riverside trail to Kenmare, and a short drive from Killarney, the Sallyport House is nothing short of exemplary. With period pieces decorating this Edwardian manor, the hosts are brimming with Irish hospitality, ensuring a pleasant stay.

Iskeroon

Ring of Kerry (between Waterville and Caherdaniel)

066 947 5119

www.iskeroon.com

€45–90 per room; S/D. MC/V

Reviewed umpteen times in some of the world's best travel literature, the Iskeroon continues to live up to its unsurpassed name and ideology. With B&B–style rooms, along with a self-catering studio available for longer-term rentals, it is located past the Scarriff Inn and down toward Bunavalla Pier.

Other Accommodations

Here are some other accommodations you might consider while in County Kerry. (In the listings that follow, € = around 25 euros per person.)

- **€ Abbey Court B&B. Killowen, Kilgarvan Rd., Kenmare.**
  064 664 2735
  www.abbeycourtkenmare.com
- **€ Oldchurch House B&B. Killowen, Kenmare.**
  064 42 054
  www.kenmare.net/oldchurch
- **€€ Sea Shore Farm Guesthouse. Kenmare.**
  064 41 270
  www.kenmare.eu/seashore
- **€ Driftwood B&B. Kenmare.**
  064 89 147
  www.driftwoodkenmare.com
- **€€€€ Glanleam (Guest House). Valentia Island.**
  066 947 6176
- **€€ Captain's House. The Mall, Dingle.**
  066 915 1079
- **€€€ Tahilla Cove Country House. Sneem.**
  064 45 204
  www.tahillacove.com

- **€ Peacock Farm Hostel. Gortdromakiery, Muckross, Killarney.**
  064 33 557
- **€ Portmagee Hostel. Portmagee, Ring of Kerry.**
  066 948 0018
  www.portmageehostel.com

Restaurants and Pubs

From quirky corner eateries to deluxe fine dining, County Kerry has it all. Award-winning establishments can be found from Beara to Dingle and if in doubt, simply ask a local for her personal recommendations. (In the restaurant listings that follow, € = around 25 euros per person.)

Lime Tree Restaurant
Shelburne St., Kenmare
064 41 225
www.limetreerestaurant.com
€€

Undoubtedly the premier casual restaurant in Kenmare, the Lime Tree Restaurant has received numerous awards for its fine cuisine, value, and jovial atmosphere. With locally sourced ingredients and fish from the region's clearest waters, highly recommended is the Chocolate Terrine.

The Chart House
The Mall, Dingle Town
066 915 2255
€€€

Arguably the best restaurant in Dingle, the informal Chart House restaurant serves classic meat dishes of Kerry lamb alongside mouthwatering fish fillets. Meals are prepared with the best local ingredients.

Gaby's Seafood Restaurant

27 High St., Killarney

064 32 519

www.gabysireland.com

€€€€

Gaby's Seafood Restaurant beckons gourmets to its appetizing menu. Serving seafood and steaks, gastronomes will surely enjoy the succulent dishes created by head chef Geert Maes and the rustic cabinlike backdrop while sipping some of the finest wines available. Reserve well in advance if traveling in summer.

The Laurels Restaurant and Bar

Main St., Killarney

064 31 149

www.thelaurelspub.com

€€

Run by the O'Leary family for nearly 100 years, this little pub has moderately priced burgers, pizza, Caesar salads, and a wonderful mashed-potato-and-onion creation. The Irish stew with homemade soda bread cannot be beat on a cold evening.

Shopping in Kerry

Travelers will be overwhelmed with shopping, especially in Killarney, where choices abound. Following are some of the best shops in Kerry.

Quills Woolen Market

1 High St., Killarney

064 32 277

This market wheels and deals in all the best hand-knitted sweaters around, as well as other fine, natural products.

Mucros Craft Centre

Muckross House, off of Muckross Rd.

064 31 440

If visiting the Muckross House, be sure to stop by the Mucros Craft Centre, where you can watch artists and artisans fabricating their goods. For those interested in pottery, the inviting studio will surely delight. Here you will also find representations of crafts from all over the Republic. This is a great one-stop shop if you'll only be visiting a small area of Ireland.

A.B. O'Connor Bookshop

Shelburne St., Kenmare

064 415 78

This shop has some great reads and also sells books pertaining to Kerry, the Ring of Kerry, along with maps and guides to keep you informed. Some of the books on sale are from local authors.

Brian de Staic

18 High St., Killarney

064 33 822

www.briandestaic.com

Never before have you seen Celtic jewelry like this! Admire the professionally handcrafted bijoux at Brian De Staic.

Pieces done in the ogham alphabet (old Irish) will bring noticeable looks from those back home.

Traveler's Tidbits

Here you will find the necessary information for Kerry. Tourist offices are located in nearly every town. The best websites to see information for County Kerry are *www.killarney.ie*, *www.kerrycoco.ie*, *www.corkkerry.ie*, *www.guidekillarney.com* (also a local magazine), *www.kerry-tourism.com*, and *www.dingle-peninsula.ie*.

In the following Tourist Office chart, "Seasonal" identifies tourist offices generally open May through September. Tourist offices are generally open during regular business hours.

COUNTY KERRY TOURIST OFFICES

Town	Address	Phone Number	In Operation
Killarney	Beech Rd.	064 31 633	All year
Tralee	Ash Memorial Hall	066 712 1288	All year
Listowel	St. John's Church	068 22 590	Seasonal
Dingle	The Quay	066 915 1188	All year
Killorglin	Iveragh Rd.	066 976 1451	Seasonal
Kenmare	Heritage Centre	064 41 233	Seasonal
Waterville	Town Centre	066 947 4646	Seasonal
Skelligs	Valentia Island	066 947 6306	Seasonal
Cahirsiveen	Church St.	066 947 2589	Seasonal

Following is additional pertinent travel information. In the case of an emergency, dial 999 anywhere in the Republic of Ireland.

TRAVEL INFORMATION

Name	Address	Phone Number
Killarney Garda (Police) Headquarters	New Rd.	064 31 222
Killarney District Hospital	St. Margaret's Rd.	064 31 076
Killarney Library	Rock Rd.	064 32 972
Killarney Post Office	New St.	064 31 051
Genealogy Research	*www.brsgenealogy.com*	022 50 302

CHAPTER 12

Counties Clare
and Limerick

B ecause of their prominent locations on the River Shannon
and their roles as important cities in the province of Munster,
both County Clare (An Chláir) and County Limerick (Luimnigh)
have played crucial parts in the history of western Ireland. County
Clare is referred to as "the banner county" because of its past history of toting various banderoles at social and political events.
Clare has world-famous cliffs, enchanting towns, and impressive
castles. Tucked south of Clare and fed directly by the River Shannon, County Limerick is redefining itself. New, opulent buildings,
boutiques, chic stores, and cafés are all attracting new business.
While it's not a major tourist destination, its environs contribute to
the Emerald Isle's mystique.

Getting Around
Clare and Limerick

The most populated and central town in County Clare is Ennis,
which is 235km (145 miles) from Dublin and 130km (80 miles)
from Cork. County Galway is close at only 65km (40 miles) away.
The city of Limerick is 200 km (120 miles) from Dublin, 100km
(40 miles) to the north of Cork, and only 100km (60 miles) from
Galway.

Flying

The Shannon Airport (061 71 2000, *www.shannonairport .com*) is located off of the Limerick-Ennis roadway (N18) and is 25km (15 miles) west of Limerick. European airlines serving the Shannon Airport include Ryanair (*www.ryanair.com*), Air-France (*www.airfrance.com*), British Airways (*www.ba.com*), and Thomson Fly (*http://flights.thomson.co.uk*). Flight companies originating in the United States that fly to Shannon Airport include American Airlines (*www.aa.com*), Continental (*www .continental.com*), Delta Airlines (*www.delta.com*), US Airways (*www.usairways.com*), United (*www.united.com*), and Aer Lingus (*www.aerlingus.com*).

 Essential

If you happen to be in Ireland in November, head down to the Ennis Trad Festival (*www.ennistradfestival.com*). The jovial and laid-back atmosphere of this traditional-music event makes it a unique and fun getaway. Enjoy concerts, open music sessions, traditional dance, and band competitions. Any other time of year, consider the Glór Irish Music Centre (065 684 3103, *www.glor.ie*) with similar events Monday through Saturday.

Bus and Rental Car

Bus Éireann (061 313 333 in Limerick, 061 474 311 in Clare, *www.buseireann.ie*) serves the Shannon Airport to Limerick Bus Station for €6 from 6:45 A.M. until midnight, Monday–Saturday (two to three departures per hour during peak times) and Sunday (one every two hours). They have routes to Limerick's Colbert Train Station, where you can get to other major cities. Bus Éireann also has direct bus service from the airport to Dublin, Cork, Waterford, Tralee, and Killarney.

Citylink (091 564163, *www.citylink.ie*) runs four buses per day from the Shannon Airport to Galway City (1.5 hours). JJ Kavanagh & Sons (0818 333 222, *www.jjkavanagh.ie*) also serves the Shannon Airport, Limerick, and the Dublin Airport.

Book a rental car in advance from any major company, including Avis (061 715 600, *www.avis.ie*), Budget (061 471 1361, *www .budget.ie*), Hertz (061 471 739, *www.hertz.ie*), and the national Irish Car Rentals (061 206088, *www.theicrgroup.com*). Taxis from the Shannon Airport to Limerick's city center cost €35 if arranged from the help desk.

Train

Irish Rail (1850 366 222, *www.irishrail.ie*) has departures to Cork, Tralee, Killarney, Ennis, Dublin Heuston Station, and Waterford from the Limerick Colbert Station (061 315 555) off of Parnell Street, or require a connection at the famed Limerick Junction in County Tipperary. The Ennis Rail Station (065 682 4177) in Clare, off of Station Road, provides transport to destinations throughout Clare and to Limerick.

Ennis

The most bustling city in Clare is Ennis (Inis), with nearly 20,000 inhabitants. The place to splurge on food and accommodations, you will find no shortage of trendy pubs and bars. From Ennis, travelers can reach nearly any part of Clare on public transport.

The Ennis Franciscan Friary (065 682 9100) is open daily Easter through October and is worthwhile if you are spending some time in town. Founded by Donchad Cairbreach O'Brien, who was the King of Thomond, the structure still holds a beautiful stained-glass window, which at one time contained blue stained glass. Another highlight on site is the MacMahon tomb, constructed in 1475 and amended in 1843. Panels delineate the events of Christ's crucifixion.

Additionally, at the tourist office, you can visit the Clare Heritage Museum (065 682 3382) off of Arthur's Row, which is open daily Tuesday through Saturday. It depicts the story and history of Clare over thousands of years.

Doolin and Lisdoonvarna

In Doolin, the epicenter of Ireland's traditional music, you will find wayfarers from far and wide. In fact, there are more hotels, hostels, and B&Bs than residential homes. The famous O'Connors Pub (065 707 4168) near the harbor, and McGann's (065 707 4133) have nightly sessions of Irish folk tunes. For those looking for something even more remote, the small town of Kilfenora (Cill Fhionnúrach) offers traditional music sessions, especially in the summer months. Lisdoonvarna (Lios Dún Bhearna) has more in the way of restaurants and amenities than Doolin. Lisdoonvarna is home to the Matchmaking Festival (065 707 4005, *www .matchmakerireland.com*) each September, made famous in the 1997 film *The Matchmaker*.

Getting to the Aran Islands

Getting to the Aran Islands, County Galway, from Doolin is possible on Doolin Ferry (065 707 5555 or 065 707 1710, *www .doolinferry.com*) or the more frequent Aran Doolin (065 707 4455, *www.doolinferries.com*) when the weather and tides are cooperating. You can call ahead to ensure departures, but oftentimes lines are not answered if boats are running. On fair-weather days, wait at the Doolin port before the 10 A.M. or 1 P.M. departures to hop on a boat. Bring cash to the islands for hotel, meals, and boat cost (€15 per person, one-way). Ferries run to Inisheer (the smallest island) first and to Inishmor (the biggest island) last. If boats are not running, you can count on departures from Galway City and Rossaveal (Ros an Mhíl), County Galway (Chapter 13). The crossing can be rough with significant swells at times, so if you get seasick, come prepared.

Kilrush and Scattery Island

A visit to the town of Kilrush (Cill Rois) and Kilrush Marina (065 905 2072, *www.kilrushcreekmarina.ie*) followed by a boat trip to Scattery Island make a pleasant trip in the southwest of Clare. Scattery, named after a monster that supposedly once inhabited the isle, is rich in history due to the numerous groups who have vied and died for it. The grounds contain the best round tower in Ireland, as well as the ruins of various medieval churches. The visitor center is open daily. Call Scattery Island Ferries (065 905 1327) for departure times.

 Fact

The fabled monster of Scattery was known as "the Cathach." Currently illustrated on the chapel of Kilrush, he was thought to be a sea serpent. At the arrival of Saint Senan, the monster became stupefied. Climbing the highest hill, Senan ordered the monster to flee. Cathach is said to have yielded to the commandment and retreated to Doolough Lake.

Limerick City

Limerick is depicted as poverty-stricken and dilapidated in the renowned Pulitzer Prize–winning memoir by Frank McCourt, *Angela's Ashes*, and the film released thereafter. While much has changed, the third-largest city in the Republic still possesses a rough aura. If driving, the one-way roads and national arteries, such as the N18, are frequently jammed.

The literary *Angela's Ashes* Walking Tours (061 32 7108) leads visitors around the sights appearing in the book. Tours depart daily at 2:30 P.M. from Arthur's Quay at the tourist information office. To do the tour yourself, check out the Limerick of *Angela's Ashes* (*http://homepages.iol.ie/~avondoyl/angelas1 .htm*) website.

The best sights in and around the city include:

The Hunt Museum and King John's Castle

The Hunt Museum (061 312 833, *www.huntmuseum.com*) offers visitors over 2,000 works to peruse. A child-friendly establishment with well-priced snacks and meals, it is open Monday–Saturday, 10 A.M.–5 P.M.; Sunday, 2 P.M.–5 P.M. Closed Good Friday, New Year's Day, Christmas Day, and December 26. Admission €4–6.25/7.75.

Farther afield, King John's Castle (061 411 201) off of Nicholas Street has little to offer save its medieval appeal. Additionally, the excavating work, which has unearthed jewelry and pottery, is partially explained in the courtyard, and the visitor center is decent enough with its audiovisual presentation.

St. Mary's Cathedral

The oldest edifice in Limerick, St. Mary's Cathedral (061 310 293) was founded by Domhnall Mór O'Brien and fully erected in the 1180s. The fifteenth century brought a lot of changes to the original structure. The tomb of "the Great Earl," known as Donal, can be found, as well as the impressive black-oak stalls, where the choir once stood, depicting angels, animals, and griffons. A climb to the belfry, added in the latter 1670s, is possible. Open Monday–Friday, 9:30 A.M.–4:30 P.M. Donations appreciated.

Limerick City Gallery of Art

For art and history lovers, the Limerick City Gallery of Art (061 310 633, *www.limerickcity.ie/LCGA*) possesses various Irish paintings, including a handful by Jack B. Yeats. In addition, the museum holds the National Collection of Contemporary Drawings and has concerts along with literary readings peppered throughout the year. Open Monday–Wednesday and Friday, 10 A.M.–6 P.M.; Thursday, 10 A.M.–7 P.M.; Saturday, 10 A.M.–5 P.M.; Sunday, 2 P.M.–5 P.M. Admission free.

Foynes Flying Boat Museum

Located 35km (22 miles) from Limerick City in Foynes, off of the N69 between Limerick and Tralee, the Foynes Flying Boat Museum (069 65 416, *www.foynesflyingboatmuseum.com*) was a major stopover for flights between the United States and Europe between 1939 and 1945. Try your hand at the B314 flight simulators for a thrilling experience. Aviation junkies will love the replica, which serves as a museum. Open daily: March, 10 A.M.–5 P.M.; April–October, 10 A.M.–6 P.M.; November 1–15, 10 A.M.–4 P.M. Closed November 16–March 30.

 Fact

The Pan-American luxury plane called the Yankee Clipper, also referred to as a "flying boat," was the first to land at Foynes. Complete with a Wright Twin Cyclone engine, the plane served the famous and influential. The "flying hotel," as it was later called, was used extensively during World War II. Famed passengers include Franklin D. Roosevelt and Winston Churchill.

Adare and Lough Gur, County Limerick

Adare is considered by many (and is advertised as) the "Prettiest Village in Ireland." Historical pundits might not agree due to its overly English influence, but the village has a lot of appeal nonetheless. Fully restored in the 1820s and 1830s, sites in town include the Trinitarian and Augustinian priories with the nearby Adare Castle, Desmond Castle on the River Maigue, and St. Nicholas Church with the Chantry Chapel. The Heritage Centre Tourist Office (see "Traveler's Tidbits" in this chapter) has exhibitions and guided tours.

Off the N20 between Limerick and Cork, located near Croom and Bruff, is the Lough Gur, home to a 5,000-year-old Neolithic settlement and the impressive Great Stone Circle. Over thirty ancient sites can be found around the shores of this lake. The burial mounds and prehistoric sites make up this archaeological reserve. The Lough Gur Visitor Centre (061 360 788) offers detailed insight into the tools, weapons, and livelihoods of the times. Open May–September, daily, 10 A.M.–6 P.M. Admission €3/5.

Things to See and Do

While Limerick does have much to explore, the natural beauty of County Clare dominates the list of things to see and do in Ireland's Shannon Region. From castles to limestone landscapes, along with Ireland's most impressive seaside cliffs, County Clare has a surfeit of activities to keep travelers out and about all day long.

 Essential

If you are visiting Bunratty from April through October, consider the Traditional Irish Night (061 360 788) rather than the banquet. With dancing and fine food and wine, followed by storytelling and music, you will have a true céilidh, a night of partying Irish style. Open nightly 7:00 P.M.–9:30 P.M. Admission €24.95–37.45/49.95.

Bunratty Castle and Folk Park, and Medieval Banquets, County Clare

The exquisitely refurbished Bunratty Castle and Folk Park (061 711200, *www.shannonheritage.com*) serve up a twice-nightly medieval banquet, a highlight in the Shannon Region. With fair maidens, court jesters, and the medievalism of it all, you will think that you have stepped into a time warp. Book well in advance for this four-course banquet. Dinner served twice nightly at 5:30 P.M. and 8:45 P.M. year round, lasting two and a half hours. Call 061 360 788 for reservations. Admission: free for children under five, €28.75 (ages six to nine), €43.25 (ages ten to twelve), and €57.50 (adults).

 Essential

Treat yourself to one of life's finer treats and head to the Wilde Irish Handmade Chocolate Factory Shop (061 922 080) in Tuamgraney, County Clare. To the west of Lough Derg where the R463 and R352 meet, this artisan shop creates masterpieces of organic and fair-trade products. With sixteen fudge varieties from super-dark to praline, it is a highlight for any exploring epicure.

Medieval banquets are also available from April to October at the Knappogue Castle (061 360 788; 6:30 P.M.) in Quinn, County Clare, or at the Dunguaire Castle (091 637 108; 5:30 P.M. and 8:45 P.M.) in Galway City, County Galway.

If you do not have time for a feast, then the Bunratty Castle and Folk Park is well worth a visit. Since the 1950s, restoration of the castle has brought back its former grandeur. It now holds what many believe is the best collection of fourteenth- to seventeenth-century furniture in the world (see *www.bunrattycollection.com*). Castle open daily 9 A.M.–4 P.M.

See ticket prices for Bunratty Castle Folk Park below.

The Bunratty Folk Park sits adjacent to the castle and is a replica of an Irish rural village in the 1800s. The hamlet consists of a handful of hired villagers explaining bygone days. Various cottages, the Ardcroney Church, farmhouses, a corn mill, and the new Bunratty Walled Garden all illustrate the rustic and agrarian livelihoods of long ago. Open daily. June–August, 9 A.M.–6 P.M.; September–May, 9 A.M.–5:30 P.M. Joint admission to castle and folk park is €9/14.

Cliffs of Moher, County Clare

If shrouded in misty fog, explore the visitor center and wait a few minutes (coastal weather can change quickly) for the skies to clear to view the awe-inspiring Cliffs of Moher (Aillte an Mhothair) (061 708 6141, *www.cliffsofmoher.ie*), located near Doolin, off of the R478. This exceptional landmark is one of Ireland's most treasured and visited natural wonders.

 Alert

Walking the trail beside the Cliffs of Moher used to be the *thing* to do. However, several mishaps over the years have led to locals explaining the inherent dangers of doing so. With wind picking up to record speeds in an instant, many travelers now walk alongside the road instead.

Soaring at over 200 meters (650 feet), the cliffs have been sculpted by gale-force winds and rain over millions of years. The rock is a combination of sandstone and black shale; its precipitous edges are home to various bird species, especially from April to July.

The Cliffs of Moher Visitor Experience is a massive, eco-friendly facility built into the hillside. This €30-million center offers some free sights, but you will have to pay to enter the Atlantic Edge Exhibition. With hands-on displays to explain the geological phenomenon, adults and kids can have fun while learning. The center also houses a restaurant, café, and shops. Open daily at 9 A.M.; closing hours vary throughout the year. Parking €8. Admission €2.50–3.50/4.

 Fact

While meandering in the Burren, do not fret if you spot a pond and notice it has disappeared hours later, especially if you are using them to navigate a walk. The ponds in low-lying areas, such as near Corfin, are where limestone becomes flooded and turloughs are formed, especially during rainy spells. They are created when water linked with area cave systems flood through holes and fissures, called *grykes*, at ground level. In the Burren, these can fill up and empty out quite quickly as water flows more easily through this terrain and is believed to be affected by the tide.

Taking the three-hour walk from Fisherstreet, Doolin, to the Cliffs of Moher is a possibility. A walk from the Cliffs of Moher south to Hag's Head point takes one hour. For cliff-side cruises and other package deals from Doolin contact O'Brien Cruises (065 707 555) or Cliffs of Moher Cruises (065 707 5949, *www.cliffs-of-moher-cruises.com*) from April through October.

The Burren, County Clare

One of the most magical landscapes in Ireland, the Burren (*Boireann*, meaning "rocky land") used to be the bottom of a tropical sea. Shaped by millions of years of rain, wind, erosion, and glaciers, the now-protected region of 16,000 hectares (40,000 acres) is a geologist's delight.

The Burren region was occupied as far back as the Neolithic period, and remains of megalithic tombs, such as the Poulnabrone

Dolmen, along with hundreds of ring forts can still be found. The rare and exotic flora of the Burren (including Alpine, Arctic, and Mediterranean species), which grow practically year round, make up 75 percent of Ireland's diverse plant species. The stunning region attracts naturalists from all over the world, especially in late spring when the area comes alive with its most vibrant displays. The fauna of the region is made up of foxes, badgers, hare, bats, red squirrels, stoats (short-tailed weasels), and plenty of butterflies, including the rare Burren green. The Burren Centre (065 708 8030) in Kilfenora off the R476 has all the information you need about this rich landscape. Open daily: March 15–May, 10 A.M.–5 P.M.; June–August, 10 A.M.–6 P.M. Closed November–March 14. Admission and tour €3.50–4.50/5.50.

Walking the Burren

A hike is a wonderful way to explore the region's true highlights. *The Burren: A Rambler's Guide & Map*, available in any of the region's tourist offices (Ballyvaughn recommended) is a handy resource. Green Roads, or ancient grass-walking paths, can be found throughout the area. One of the best circuit walks is the Caher Valley and Gleninagh Mountain Walk (reference book *Best Irish Walks* #44), which starts off south of the R477 opposite the Gleninagh Castle. The walk incorporates limestone fields, part of the Burren Way (a 42km/26-mile trail from Liscannor through Doolin to Ballyvaughan), and ends on a famed Green Road, called the "Old Road," circumnavigating Black Head pier.

Walking tours are available with the Heart of Burren Walks (065 708 9998 or 087 292 5487, *www.heartofburrenwalks.com*) led by expert guides, giving half- and full-day tours, with custom trips available. Burren Wild Walks (087 877 9565, *www.burrenwalks .com*) also offer daily and custom trips.

Here are the top five things to do near the Burren:

1. Visit Aillwee Caves and Birds of Prey Centre. The Aillwee Cave (065 707 7036, *www.aillweecave.ie*) was once used by the now-extinct Irish brown bears during hibernation periods. Great for the family, the cave is the only one open to tourists; professional spelunkers get to explore the hundreds of other chambers in the area. A café, tearoom, and craft shop have lovely local honey and cheeses for sale. Open daily, 10 A.M.–5:30 P.M.; until 6:30 P.M. July–August. Admission €8–13/15.

2. Marvel at The Glenisheen Wedge Tomb. Near the Aillwee Cave system, the Gleninsheen Wedge Tomb dates back to 3000 B.C. Located on private property, the tomb is a must-see. If the gate happens to be locked, search for anyone who might give you permission to visit.

3. Explore Corcomroe Cistercian Abbey. Known as "Saint Mary of the Fertile Rock," the Corcomroe Cistercian Abbey, near Bell Harbour, is a great example of what could have been a coenobium, most likely constructed by the son of Donal Mór O'Brien. A perfect example of what is hidden within the picturesque Burren, the formidable stonework and carvings are reason enough to venture here. Open daily.

4. Photograph the Poulnabrone Portal Tomb. Dating back to 2000 B.C., the Poulnabrone Tomb, weighing in at over five tons, is a wondrous architectural marvel just off the R480. The remains of ancient bodies were found during excavation in the mid-1980s. Get here early to beat the crowds. Open daily.

5. Indulge at the Burren Perfumery (*www.burrenperfumery .com*). With an audio-visual presentation discussing the flora of the Burren, the heavenly scents are what make this place worthwhile. The perfumery also houses a tea-

room with organic homemade food available. Open daily, with varying hours throughout the year. Admission free.

Dysert O'Dea, County Clare

Brimming with history and just south of Corofin and north of Ennis off of the R486, the Dysert O'Dea (065 683 7401, *www .dysertcastle.com*) is composed of a famous Romanesque gateway, round towers, and one of Ireland's finest high crosses. Originally founded by Saint Tola in the early 700s, it was later abandoned, quite possibly until the latter 1600s when the cross was erected. A history and archaeology trail of twenty-five sites makes a splendid stroll. Guided tours (one to three hours) are available by prior arrangement. Open May–September, daily, 10 A.M.–6 P.M. Free parking. Admission €2.50–3.50/4.

Accommodations

Finding a hotel with a view will not be a difficult task. For those wanting to splurge, castle hotels, guesthouses, farmhouses, and self-catering lodging are all available. In places such as Doolin, Lisdoonvarna, and Limerick City, hostels are a great way to live on the cheap and explore the surroundings.

Gregans Castle Hotel (Eco-Friendly)

Ballyvaughan, Co. Clare
065 707 7005
www.gregans.ie
€235+ per double room; suites €365-450;
S/D/T. MC/V

With a luxury five-star feel, the Gregans Castle Hotel is a four-star gem tucked in a quiet valley overlooking the rocky vista of the Burren. The rooms have a relaxed décor, the bathrooms are spacious, and the service is impeccable. The Haden family, who own and manage the establishment, are constantly researching and updating their hotel to become more ecologically friendly. If you can only choose one lavish hotel during your stay in all of the Shannon Region, make this your choice. Multinight stays available at a reduced rate. Check online for specials.

Mount Vernon

Mount Vernon, New Quay, Burren, Co. Clare
065 707 8126
€110+ per person; sea view add €30; MC/V

Aly Raftery and Mark Helmore, the hosts and owners of Mount Vernon, might have one of the best views in all of Ireland. Overlooking the Burren and the sea to Galway Bay, this Georgian villa has a lot of literary history exuding from its antique décor. Meals are available with a day's notice. The lovely town of Kinvara, not far from here, is worth exploring. Golf courses are nearby.

 Fact

Going green takes dedication on all levels. Becoming certified as an ecologically friendly hotel in Europe is quite difficult. Staff must undergo training. Owners and managers must implement costly measures viewed as investments for the future. For travelers, staying in these establishments means you are taking a step toward greener travel.

Rainbow Hostel and B&B

Doolin, Co. Clare

065 707 4415

www.rainbowhostel.net

€15–25 per person, hostel; €25+ per person,

B&B; S/D/T/F.

While there are many choices for accommodations in the popular town of Doolin, the Rainbow Hostel is a top choice for those on a budget. The hostel has a partner B&B next door. Offers en suite rooms, kitchen and laundry facilities, and the establishment is couple and family friendly. Go on a guided walk with Mattie Shannon (co-owner) to learn more about the archaeology and geology of the Burren landscape. Bikes available for rent. Free WiFi, but BYOL (bring your own laptop).

For a shoestring meal starting at 12:30 P.M. in Doolin, try the Stone Cutters Kitchen (065 707 5962) off the R478, which serves lots of goodies, including seafood chowder, fish cakes, and vegetarian soups.

Dooneen Lodge B&B

Caher Rd., Mungret, Co. Limerick

061 301 332

www.dooneenlodge.net

€35+ per person; S/D.

Located near Limerick, Adare, and a short drive to the Burren, the Dooneen Lodge B&B is gaining precedence as the friendliest B&B in the county (with the best breakfast). The informative website details the many activities available in the region. The hosts will be more than happy to help you plan various day trips as well.

Flemingstown House

Kilmallock, Co. Limerick

063 98 093

www.flemingstown.com

€50 per person; self-catering lodge available;

S/D/T/F. MC/V

Centrally located on a picturesque farm outside of Limerick, and not a far drive from Cashel, Killarney, or Cork, the Flemingstown House has already made a renowned name for itself. A trip to this 250-year-old farmhouse is an adventure in itself and merits at least two nights.

Other Accommodations

Here are some other accommodations you might consider while in County Clare or County Limerick. (In the listings that follow, € = around 25 euros per person.)

- **€€ The Old Ground Hotel & Pub.**
  Ennis, Co. Clare.
  065 682 8127
  www.flynnhotels.com/Old_Ground_Hotel/index.html
- **€€€€ Moy House. Lahinch, Co. Clare.**
  065 708 2500
  www.moyhouse.com
- **€ Sleepzone. Kincora Rd., Lisdoonvarna.**
  065 707 4036
  www.sleepzone.ie
- **€€€ Castle Oaks House. Castleconnell,**
  Co. Limerick.
  061 377 666
  www.castleoaks.ie

- €€€€€ **Glin Castle. Glin, Co. Limerick.**
06834173
www.glincastle.com
- € **Trainor's Hostel. Ballingarry Village, Co. Limerick.**
069 68 164
trainorhostel@eircom.net
- € **Cherry Blossom Budget Accommodation.**
Alexandra Terrace, O'Connell Ave., Limerick City.
061 469 449

Restaurants and Pubs

Like many of the coastal counties, travelers can expect to find superior seafood, especially at farther-removed peninsulas, around Lough Derg, and towns such as Killaloe, and Scarriff. The main thoroughfares in Ennis and Limerick City have assorted international dishes to offer. (In the restaurant listings that follow, € = around 25 euros per person.)

Kasturi

Carmody St., Ennis, Co. Clare
065 684 8060
€€

The Indian cuisine at Kasturi will surely fill the void for hot and spicy. With all the best choices, from chicken to vegetarian, this restaurant fills up quickly on the weekends. Lunch specials are a great way to save some money, but the atmosphere really comes to life at night.

The Roadside Tavern

Kincora Rd., Lisdoonvarna, Co. Clare
065 707 4084
www.roadsidetavern.ie
€

After a day exploring the seaside sweeps near the Cliffs of Moher and the town of Doolin, kick back at the Roadside Tavern. Run by the Curtin family and established in 1865, live music and all the pints you can handle are on tap seven nights a week. Try the special Irish stew made with Burren beef.

The Cherry Tree Restaurant

Lakeside, Ballina, Killaloe, Co. Clare
061 375 688
www.cherrytreerestaurant.ie
€€€

Located in Killaloe, just off the southern tip of where the Lough Derg becomes the River Shannon, the Cherry Tree Restaurant is an award-winning eatery with a lakeside vista. Specialties include everything from pan-fried fish to roasted duck.

The Green Onion Restaurant

Old Town Hall, Rutland St., Co. Limerick
061 400 710
€€

Great price. Great atmosphere. Great selection. This characterizes what the Green Onion has been maintaining with lively flair for years. Located just across from the Hunt Museum, the baked goat cheese specials are a must.

The Wild Geese

Rose Cottage, Adare, Co. Limerick

061 396 451

www.thewild-geese.com

€€€

At first glance, it is a little on the pricey side. But, once you have tasted the succulent baked salmon or Irish sirloin, cost will be the furthest thought on your mind. The early-bird menu is the best deal and dessert is not complete without trying one of the dessert wines on hand.

Traveler's Tidbits

Here you will find the necessary information for Counties Clare and Limerick. Tourist offices are located in nearly every town. The best websites to check out information are *www.visitlimerick.com*, *www.limerick.com*, *www.visitclare.net*, *www.shannonheritage.com*, and *www.shannonregiontourism.ie*.

In the following Tourist Office chart, "Seasonal" identifies tourist offices generally open May through September. Tourist offices are generally open during regular business hours.

CORK TOURIST OFFICES

Town	Address	Phone Number	In Operation
Adare	Heritage Center	098 45 384	All year
Limerick	Arthur's Quay	061 317 522	All year
Ennis	Arthur's Row	065 682 8366	All year
Shannon Airport	Airport Office	061 471 664	All year
Cliffs of Moher	Visitor Centre	065 708 1171	Seasonal
Kilrush	49 Francis St.	065 905 1577	Seasonal
Kilkee	O'Connell Sq.	065 905 6112	Seasonal

Following is additional pertinent travel information. In the case of an emergency, dial 999 anywhere in the Republic of Ireland.

TRAVEL INFORMATION

Name	Address	Phone Number
Garda (Police) Limerick	Henry St.	061 212 400
Limerick Hospital: St. John's	St. John's Sq.	061 46 2222
Ennis Hospital	Galway Rd.	065 682 4464
Limerick Library	57 Grande Parade	021 492 4900
Ennis De Valera Library (Ennis)	Harmony Row	065 682 1616
Limerick Post Office	39 Upper William St.	061 409 805
Ennis Post Office	Bank Place	065 682 8976
Clare Heritage Centre (Genealogy)	Church St., Corofin	065 683 7955

CHAPTER 13

County Galway

One can clearly hear the heartbeat of Ireland's west exude from County Galway (Gaillimh). While Galway City is the region's artistic nucleus, the craggy Aran Islands and boggy Connemara each offers its own window into Gaelic culture, language, tradition, and charm. Galway abounds in hill and trail walking, along with biking opportunities far and wide. Its coastline offers phenomenal postcard beaches; effortlessly travelers can extend themselves into areas unbeknownst and uncommon.

Getting Around County Galway

Galway City is County Galway's most booming and well-known town. Galway City is 220km (136 miles) from Dublin and easily accessible by train or bus. It is also 210km (130 miles) from Cork and 190km (120 miles) from Killarney.

Flying

The Galway Airport (091 755 569, *www.galwayairport.com*) is located in Carnmore, 8km (4 miles) outside of the city. Aer Arann (08 18 210 210 or 091 541 900, *www.aerarann.com*) serves a majority of the flights. Four flights per day (three on Sunday) connect

Dublin to Galway. Elsewhere in Europe from Galway, the airport serves Belfast, London Luton, Edinburgh, and Manchester. Another option is to fly into the international hub of Shannon Airport (90 km/55 miles south; see Chapter 12).

Getting from the airport to the city center is possible in a taxi (€20); free taxi phones are available inside the airport. Abbey Cabs (091 569 469) and Galway Taxis (091 561 111) are on call from Eyre Square. Inquire with your hotel or B&B to arrange a pickup/drop off. Only one bus per day departs from the Galway Rail Station to the airport at 12:50 P.M. and departs there at 1:25 P.M.

 Essential

Galway City traffic can be jam-packed, especially during rush hour and on weekends. The city center is pedestrian only, so driving is not feasible. Car parks are located on the edge of the city center. The cheapest one is Qpark (*www.qpark.ie*), which also offers even cheaper rates if your hotel has made a deal with them.

Bus and Car

Bus Éireann (091 562 000, *www.buseireann.ie*) has a travel center at Ceannt Station, southeast of Eyre Square, in Galway City. They operate several routes per day connecting to the Shannon Airport through Ennis and Galway from 7 A.M. to 9 P.M. Additionally, buses to the Galway suburb of Salthill and to Dublin leave from the Eyre Square Bus Station. Various other companies, including City Link (091 564 163 or 1 890 280 808, *www.citylink.ie*), depart from Galway to Dublin (6:30 A.M. to 5:30 P.M.) from the Galway Tourist Office. Buses also travel into Connemara and to Cleggan from the tourist office.

Train

Irish Rail (091 561 444, *www.irishrail.ie*) links Galway's Ceannt Station to Dublin's Heuston Station with various departures daily.

Those traveling elsewhere would use the Athlone Station to go into County Mayo or the Portarlington Station to go into the south of Ireland.

Galway City

Galway City is a booming mini-metropolis where medieval and Gaelic roots coalesce with modern art and hip university youth. It is best explored on a walking tour; the folks at Galway Tours (091 561 386 or 086 402 1819, *www.galwaytours.ie)* run superb tours daily departing from the fountain at Eyre Square, May–September, Monday–Friday, at 11 A.M. Private tours are available. For a more gory approach, try Galway Gothic Tours (0877 782 887, *www.legendtours.ie/gothic.php).*

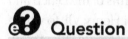 **Question**

Why does Eyre Square contain the JFK Memorial Park?
Following John F. Kennedy's visit to Galway, the city has maintained a special place in its heart for the beloved president. It was at Eyre Square where Kennedy exited his car to hug the mayor's mother. He stated thereafter that anyone from Galway was welcome in the White House. His untimely death devastated the city, and the park was subsequently given this honorific.

The following sections detail the best sights in Galway City.

Eyre Square

This central pedestrian zone has a few notable sights. In the front sits the seventeenth-century Browne Doorway taken from the remnants of a mansion off of Abbeygate Street. The Quincentennial Fountain is near the JFK bust marking the JFK Memorial Park in the backdrop.

Collegiate Church of St. Nicholas

Known as the Church of St. Nicholas of Myra (091 564 648, *www.stnicholas.ie*), this gem off of Market Street is Galway's oldest house of worship and is currently presided over by the Church of Ireland. Christopher Columbus supposedly prayed here in 1477 before further attempts at his around-the-world ventures. Eerily marked is the spot where Mayor Lynch in the early 1490s hanged his son before banishing himself to a reclusive life. Guided tours are available except on Sunday. Church open daily, January–February, 9 A.M.–5 P.M.; March–December, 9 A.M.–7 P.M. Donations appreciated.

Lynch Castle

Located in what is now the AIB (Allied Irish Bank), Lynch Castle was home to Galway's most prominent "tribes," or families. The outer façade of the sixteenth-century mansion still portrays Irish gargoyles in their full glory. Moreover, the coat of arms of the Lynch and Fitzgerald families are adorned with the crest of Henry VII, to whom they were loyal. Located on Abbeygate Street Lower and Shop Street. Open during the bank's regular business hours. Admission free.

 Fact

Just below the King's Crest on the outside of Lynch Castle is a figure of a monkey holding a baby. This statuette is an accolade to the tree-bound creature that saved a toddler within the structure from imminent peril. A walking tour of the city delves further into this and other legends of Galway.

Spanish Arch

Located across the Wolfe Tone Bridge, the Spanish Arch was a portal that Spanish merchant fleets used to enter with goods, namely brandy. It is one of the only parts of the city's medieval walls that still stand. Other remnants of the city's fortified partition can be seen throughout the city's pubs and inside the main shopping mall off of Eyre Square.

 Essential

A river cruise along the Lough Corrib offers a stunning view of Galway City. With a melding of history, nature, and lore, the tours are offered daily by Corrib Princess (091 592 447, *www.corribprincess .ie*) in ninety-minute sessions. Celtic Boat Safaris (087 981 1579) offers single and multiday guided excursions and adventures.

Galway City Museum

Galway City Museum (091 532 460, *www.galwaycitymuseum .ie*) proudly displays some of the key artifacts and documents depicting the city's past. For War of Independence researchers, it houses interesting memorabilia and photographs. The elegant Galway Hooker boat replica is a must-see, as are the various exhibitions on hand. Open June–September, daily, 10 A.M.–5 P.M.; October–May, Tuesday–Saturday, 10 A.M.–5 P.M. Admission €2.50/5.

Galway Cathedral

The Galway Cathedral, completed in the 1960s, is actually denominated the Cathedral of Our Lady Assumed into Heaven and St. Nicholas (091 563 577, *www.galwaycathedral.org*). Local artisans completed the structure in local limestone and marble. The mosaics, statues, and central dome are all designed for elegant simplicity. The website displays some of the music and organ recitals. Located next to the Salmon Weir Bridge and University and Gaol Road. Open daily, 8 A.M.–6 P.M. Donations appreciated.

Nora Barnacle House

This nineteenth-century private museum located in Bowling Green is known as the Nora Barnacle House (091 564 743, *www*

.norabarnacle.com). The residence of James Joyce's wife, the small house displays handwritten letters between the two, along with photographs, furniture, and other noteworthy items. Best to call or e-mail ahead.

Galway is known for its festivals and offers plenty throughout the year. Reserve accommodations ahead for these time periods. The best festivals are:

1. **Galway International Oyster Festival.** From Dublin to Westport and from Blarney to the Burren, you will hear locals talk about the Galway International Oyster Festival (091 587 992, *www.galwayoysterfest.com*). The event takes place during the last week of September each year.

2. **Galway Horse Races.** The Galway Horse Races (091 753 870, *www.galwayraces.com*) take place in July or early August each year. Each day has a different theme, and closed-circuit television broadcasts the event throughout the grounds.

3. **Galway Film Fleadh.** For an art-filled summer season at one of Ireland's largest film festivals, the Galway Film Fleadh (091 751 655, *www.galwayfilmfleadh.com*) comes highly recommended.

4. **Galway Arts Festival.** For the finest sampling of Ireland's most dramatic, musical, and comedic renderings, the Galway Arts Festival (091 509 700, *www.galwayartsfestival.ie*) lasts two weeks in mid-July each year.

Things to See and Do

County Galway is a chock-a-block of sights, sounds, and history. While Galway City is west Ireland's most happening town, regions such as Connemara, Joyce Country, and the Aran Islands all offer visitors a unique blend of tradition and steady progress.

Connemara

A majority of County Galway's interior is made up of the vastness that is Connemara (*www.connemara.ie*), which also includes the Connemara National Park. The Connemara region extends west of Galway to the Atlantic, and the boggy interior gives way northward to rolling hills and dome-topped mountains known as the Twelve Bens.

Moving west from Galway City along the R336, R343, and R340, you will encounter the small fishing hamlets of Spiddal (An Spidéal), Carraroe (An Cheathrú), and others around Mace Head.

The most splendid town in the area is Roundstone (Cloch na Rón; *www.roundstone.ie*) near Bertraghboy Bay. This vibrant, artsy hangout is full in the summer, but getting away is easy by walking, fishing, or sailing. The Roundstone Arts Week (*www.roundstoneartsweek.net*) takes place at the end of June each year.

Exploring Connemara

To the north along the N59, the town of Oughterard (Uachtar Árd) offers the county's best fishing, as well as the Glengowla Mines (091 552 360, open March–November, daily, 10 A.M.–6 P.M.). The Aughnanure Castle (091 552 214; open April–October, daily, 9:30 A.M.–6 P.M.) is a six-story gem with two defensive walls (called *badhun*) that was a ruling hub of the O'Flaherty clan. Additionally, the Quiet Man Bridge, made famous in the John Wayne film *The Quiet Man*, is a great spot for photos if you can beat the tour buses.

Clifden: A Base for Exploration

Connemara's capital town is Clifden (An Clochán). Bustling in comparison to the aforementioned villages, it has its own allure. Walking or biking the Sky Road is one way to appreciate the landscape; other walks are outlined at the Connemara Walking Centre (095 21 379) off of Market Street, which also offers the Michael Gibbons Walking Ireland Tours, specializing in archaeological and historical outings. Or, contact Connemara Safari (095 21 071, *www.walkingconnemara.com*) for longer excursions and island hopping adventures. West Ireland Cycling (091 588 830, *www .westirelandcycling.com*) off of Upper Dominic Street in Galway City offer unique cycling packages.

Alert

Walking in Connemara leaves hikers exposed to the elements. Bring proper hiking boots, socks, a warm hat, and a long-sleeve wind/rain jacket. If kids are along, carry energy snacks: trailmix and bottled water are available at the grocer in Letterfrack. During spring, summer, and fall, bring insect repellent with you everywhere in Connemara, as the annoying pests known as midges proliferate.

Killary Adventure Center

A company gaining notable recognition over the years, the Killary Adventure Centre (095 43 411, *www.killaryadventure.com*) offers innumerable activities for kids and adults alike. Located just outside of Leenane, they also have an on-site hostel (dorm €20–25 per person) and B&B (€35–50 per person). From kayaking to bungee jumping to tranquil guided walks, this is a great place to meet fellow travelers and to get your adrenaline pumping. Private groups welcome. Half-day/full-day activities: €40 per person/€85 per person.

Connemara National Park

Located on the edge of Letterfrack, the Connemara National Park (095 41 054, *www.connemaranationalpark.ie*) has a superb visitor center that gives way to gravel and board-walked nature trails through the boggy terrain. Four of Connemara's Twelve Bens are contained within its 2,000-hectare (5,000-acre) boundaries.

Before venturing out on one of the three well-marked trails, check out the visitor center to read up on the flora and fauna of the region; the film you can watch there is a noteworthy addition. The vistas from the upper parameters afford awe-inspiring views of Kylemore Abbey and Lough, as well as Ballynakill Harbour. Park open all year. Visitor Centre open April–May and September to mid-October, 10 A.M.–5:30 P.M.; June, 10 A.M.–6:30 P.M.; July–August, 9:30 A.M.–6:30 P.M. Admission free.

Kylemore Abbey

The Gothically inspired Kylemore Abbey (095 411 146, *www .kylemoreabbey.com*) jumps out quite unexpectedly on the drive between Leenane and Letterfrack. Beckoning further exploration, the Kylemore (meaning "big wood") estate is made up of an abbey, neo-Gothic cathedral, Victorian garden, and a lone mausoleum with a story all its own.

The castle was converted to an abbey in the 1920s; fourteen nuns currently live, worship, and run a convent school for girls here. While a good portion of the abbey is closed to visitors, five impressive rooms display part of its lavish interior and the chapel makes a nice photo stop. The well-done visitor center runs buses to and from the gardens. A restaurant and pottery shop are also on hand. In 2010, the convent school was closed; the rest of the estate has thus far remained unaffected. Open all year, 9:00 A.M.–5:30 P.M. Garden closed November to mid-March. Admission €7/12.

Inishbofin

Truly removed Inishbofin (Inis Bó Finne; *www.inishbofin.com*) has a placid, surreal ambiance. Located about 10km (6 miles) off of Connemara's northwest tip, the island is inhabited by 200 humble Irish souls making up five different villages. The island boasts amazing beaches, with scuba diving and snorkeling available. Excellent two- or three-hour walks can be had around the western or northern sides; bicycle rentals are also available at the main pier. Inishbofin is accessible from the town of Cleggan. Ferries run all year on varying schedules, so visit the website for specifics. Island Discovery (095 45 819/894, *www.inishbofinislanddiscovery.com*) and Inishbofin Ferries (095 45 806/903/831) offer service from Cleggan. The *Dun Aengus* mail boat departs Cleggan Monday–Saturday at 11:30 A.M. Purchase tickets for the *Dun Aengus* at the Spar Grocery Store in Cleggan. City Link (*www .citylink.ie*) buses connect Galway, Clifden, Letterfrack, and Cleggan.

Alert

Those looking to get off the beaten path certainly will be able to do so. However, careful research should be done beforehand. The middle regions of Ireland are composed mostly of heath and bog land. This mushy terrain with bog pits (akin to quicksand), accompanied by extreme temperature variations, can ruin any outing for the underprepared.

Aran Islands

The Aran Islands (*www.aranislands.ie*) are composed of three main islands: the largest, Inishmor (Árainn), the medium-sized Inishmaan (Inis Meáin), and the smaller yet more populated Inisheer (Inis Oírr). The tranquil islands top the list for travelers looking to get away, to historically explore, and to hear the chiming of Gaelic amongst the steadfast Irish islanders.

Historically, each island has played an important role in Celtic history. The islands are so removed and desolate that Christian monks could not resist settling there. They began occupying the islands and building beehive stone huts as early as the fifth century. Later inhabitants perpetuated their existence with sustenance farming techniques that turned the Burren-like terrain into arable land. The thousands of kilometers of renowned stone wall help to not only mark plots, but also to keep the wind from uprooting precious crops. The best sights and activities on each island are outlined in the following sections.

Inishmor

Most tourists arrive to the main port of Kilronan in Inishmor. The tourist office and Aran Heritage Centre (099 61 355) are great points from which to begin exploring. Numerous sights are accessible by walking, cycling, or hiring a driver or pony trap. The islands are hilly, so only the fit should consider walking or cycling. The famed 2,000-year old Dún Aengus fort is the most popular site; lined with stone spikes to ward off enemies, it sits on the edge of a 90-meter (300-foot) cliff face. While a great photo spot, parents should be aware that the sheer drop has no protective barrier, so keep an eye on children. The more-deserted but as-impressive Dún Dúchathair, known as the Black Fort, is a thirty-minute walk from Dún Aengus. The Clochán na Carraige, with surrounding Na Seacht Teampaill (the seven churches), is the island's most famous scattering of monuments.

 Essential

The friendly farmers and fishermen on Inishmor work during the tourist season giving guided visits. One way to see the best sights on the island is to hire a driver and guide. Contact Bertie Faherty, who runs Dún Aonghas Tours (087 237 9707 or 099 61 329, *www.dunaonghastours.com*). Arrange all Sunday transportation beforehand.

Inishmaan

The least-visited island, Inishmaan is not as developed as the other two isles. While the friendly locals love tourists, an adventure here is truly a step back in time. The most-frequented sights include the Teach Synge cottage, where writer J. M. Synge spent his summers, and the Dún Chonchuir, the oval-shaped fort in the center of the island.

Inisheer

Inisheer (*www.inisoirr-island.com*) is a true gem. It is located just 10km (6 miles) from the coastline of Doolin, County Clare. Navigating the island by bike is a great way to visit such sites as O'Brien's Castle, a fifteenth-century inner stronghold, and the Teampall Chaomháin, known as the Church of St. Kevin, which bestows its greatest appeal at sunset. A 10km (6-mile) marked walk begins behind the beach and in front of the soccer field.

Getting to and from the Aran Islands

Flying to the Aran Islands is feasible from the Connemara Airport in Minna, near Inverin (*Indreabhán*). Aer Arann (091 593 034, *www.aerarannislands.ie*) has one-way, roundtrip, and scenic flights available daily. Prices are €25/37/45 roundtrip.

Aran Island Ferries (091 568 903 or 091 572 273, *www.aranislandferries.com*) depart from Rossaveal. Timetable departures vary according to the season. Ferry crossings to Inishmore (or to Inishmaan or Inisheer) from Rossaveal are €13/25 and a bus transfer (one hour) there from Galway City is €2.50/3.50/4.

 Alert

> Getting to the port at Rossaveal (Ros an Mhíl) is slightly tricky. Drive the N59 to R336 south. At Casla, a sign for Ros an Mhíl points west. Upon turning, keep your eyes open for a sign with a small boat symbol on it. Continue past the Spar Grocery to the dock. Bring sufficient cash to the islands; banks are virtually nonexistent.

Aran Direct (091 506 786 or 091 566 535, *www.arandirect.com*) also operates ferries to the islands, providing a direct route from Galway City (with offices at 124 Eyre Square or 29 Forster Street) and transfers via bus (€4/6/7) to Rossaveal (one hour) and then to the islands. Newly scheduled departures on the high-speed catamaran christened the *Aran Princess* are detailed on the website. Prices from Rossaveal are €15/20/25 roundtrip.

Aran Island Hopping

Traveling intra-islands can be tricky. Both ferry companies operate direct-only routes to each of the islands from Rossaveal.

In theory, this means returning to Rossaveal to go onward to other islands. However, Doolin Ferries (065 707 4455/466, *www .doolinferries.com*) does travel intra-island according to demand and weather (see Chapter 12, which outlines departures from Doolin to the Aran Islands). They tend to depart from the Inishmore dock at 11 A.M. and will stop at other islands on their way back to Doolin, County Clare. Price is €15 one way.

Cars are not transported to the islands, nor are rentals an option. Mainland parking is available at the Rossaveal pier for €10 per day. Make sure to book plane or ferry tickets in advance if you plan to travel during the summer months. Check *www.aranislands .ie* for a listing of festivals and events.

Accommodations

County Galway abounds in quaint bed-and-breakfasts, castles, and welcoming guesthouses that will make choosing a place harder than actually finding one. Accommodations in Connemara and the Aran Islands should be reserved sooner than later, especially in summer. Castles, mansions, and other luxury accommodations often advertise rates up to 50 percent off during off-season months.

Tara House B&B

138 Lower Salthill, Galway City
091 527 966
www.tarahouse.ie
€80–100 per room, €45–60 single; S/D/T/F.

The Tara House B&B stands alone among B&Bs available in Galway City. Warmth emanates from the hosts, Anna and Michael Doherty. The Irish hospitality and atmosphere, along with the careful attention to detail make this a top pick. The tastefully decorated en suite rooms have all the amenities. Contact the hosts directly for the best family rates.

Hotel Meyrick

Eyre Square, Galway City

091 564 041

www.hotelmeyrick.ie

€150+ per room; suites €200+; S/D/T/F. MC/V.

This revamped railway station turned hotel dates back to 1845. The mahogany rooms, the on-site health spa, and backdrop of live piano instrumentation make any stay luxurious.

Seamist House

Market Hill, Clifden, Connemara

095 21 441

www.connemara.net/seamist

€35–50+ per person; S/D.

The Seamist House is located in vibrant Clifden and the renovated stone dwelling enhances its tranquil setting. The proprietor, Sheila Griffin, will ensure that your stay is nothing short of excellent and comfortable.

Kilmurvey House

Inishmor, Aran Islands

099 61 218

www.kilmurveyhouse.com

€55+ per person; S/D/T/F.

The Kilmurvey House deserves all the recent flattery it has received both online and off. Bursting with Irish character, the spacious interior and well-decorated rooms are a haven after a day of exploring. The hosts, Treasa and Bertie Joyce, have excellent dinner options at €40+ per person available if arranged in advance (not always available in the off-season).

Radharc an Chlair B&B

Inisheer, Aran Islands

099 750 19

€40+ per person; S/D.

Located uphill from O'Brien's Castle and a twenty-minute walk from the pier, the proprietor Breed Paul will whole-heartedly welcome you to the Radharc an Chlair. The rooms are small, cozy, and sufficient.

Other Accommodations

Here are some other accommodations you might consider while in County Galway. (In the listings that follow, € = around 25 euros per person.)

- **€€ Petra House B&B. 29 College Rd., Galway City.**
  091 566 580
  www.galway.net/pages/petra-house
- **€€ Bayberry House B&B. Off Threadneedle Rd., Galway City.**
  091 525 171/212
  www.bayberryhouse.com
- **€€€ The Quay House. Beach Rd., Clifden.**
  095 21 369
  www.thequayhouse.com
- **€€€ Renvyle House Hotel and Restaurant. Renvyle, Connemara.**
  095 43 511
  www.renvyle.com
- **€€ Man of Aran Cottage. Inishmore, Aran Islands.**
  099 61 301
  www.manofarancottage.com

- **€€ An Dún Guesthouse. Inishmaan, Aran Islands.**
  099 73 047
  www.inismeainaccommodation.com
- **€€ Tigh Searraigh B&B. Inisheer, Aran Islands.**
  099 75 024
  radharcnamara@hotmail.com
- **€€ Lios Einne B&B. Inisheer, Aran Islands.**
  099 75 025
  barbaraconneely@mail.com
- **€€ Murray's Doonmore Hotel. Inishbofin Island.**
  095 45 804/814
  www.doonmorehotel.com

Restaurants and Pubs

Galway is home to west Ireland's most famous restaurants, liveliest pubs, and rocking clubs. For reviews on everything up and coming, read over the Galway City Pub Guide (*www.galwaycitypubguide.com*). (In the restaurant listings that follow, € = around 25 euros per person.)

Nimmo's Restaurant and Wine Bar

Spanish Arch, Long Walk, Galway City
091 561 114
www.nimmos.ie
€€

Located in the tourist-frequented Spanish Arch area, Nimmo's Restaurant and Wine Bar is setting a new precedent with its prestigious gourmet offerings for both lunch and dinner, including sea bass, salamis, roast Irish lamb leg, and sweet trifles to please the palate. Cultural, social, and private events are held in its upper annex.

Ristorante Da Roberta

169 Upper Salthill, Galway City

091 585 808

€

If your B&B is located in Salthill, the Ristorante Da Roberta is a perfect place to fill up before heading to the nearby O'Connor's Famous Pub for some fine Irish tunes.

Currarevagh House

Oughterard, Connemara

091 552 312

www.currarevagh.com

€€€€

Prestigious and ideally situated overlooking the Lough Corrib, the Currarevagh House not only offers luxury accommodations, but a cookery school as well. They also arrange fishing and golf outings, along with swimming, hiking, tennis, and croquet. Those not staying at the mansion are still welcome to dine in the award-winning restaurant with a five-course menu on offer daily.

Teach Nan Phaidi

Kilmurvey, Inishmore, Aran Islands

099 61 119

€

The Teach Nan Phaidi is a thatched-roof haven among havens. Open from lunchtime until late afternoon, the atmosphere is picture perfect. Organic soups, sandwiches, and daily specials range from €10 to 20. For supper options, head over to the Pier House or Bay View restaurants overlooking the harbor.

Pubs

Pubs and clubs proliferate the Galway City center. Some of the best pubs and bars include: McSwiggan's (091 568 917, *www.mcswiggans.com*), Busker Brownes (091 563 377, *www .buskerbrownes.com*), and the Front Door/Sonny's (91 563 757, *www.frontdoorpub.com*). Live music at the Róisín Dubh (91 586 540, *www.roisindubh.net*) is especially appealing.

Traveler's Tidbits

Here you will find the necessary information for County Galway. The best websites to check out information are *www.galway.net* and *www.goconnemara.com*. For information about East Galway, visit Galway East (*www.galwayeast.com*) online.

In the following Tourist Office chart, "Seasonal" identifies tourist offices generally open May through September. Tourist offices are open during regular business hours.

GALWAY TOURIST OFFICES

Town	Address	Phone Number	In Operation
Discover Ireland Center	Forster St., Galway City	091 537 700	All year
Salthill Tourist Office	Promenade, Galway City	091 520 500	Seasonal
Oughterard Tourist Office	Town Centre, Oughterard	091 552 808	All year
Clifden Tourist Office	Galway Rd., Clifden	095 21 163	Seasonal
Aran Islands Tourist Office	Kilronan, Inishmor	099 61 263	All year

Following is other pertinent travel information. In the case of an emergency, dial 999 anywhere in the Republic of Ireland.

TRAVEL INFORMATION

Name	Address	Phone Number
Garda (Police) Galway City	Mill St.	091 563 161
University College Hospital	Newcastle Rd., Galway City	091 580 580
Galway City Library (Internet)	Hynes Building, Augustine St.	091 561 666
Squareyes Internet Café	Forster St., Galway City	091 500 688 www.squareyes.com
Galway City Post Office	Eglinton St.	091 562 051
Galway Family Historical Society (Genealogy)	Liosbaun Estate, Taum Rd.	091 756 737

CHAPTER 14

Counties Mayo, Sligo, and Roscommon

S easoned travelers to Ireland might opt for Counties Mayo, Sligo, and Roscommon because they offer delights unfrequented by the masses. Once the natural wonders of the lower west—the Ring of Kerry, Connemara, the Cliffs of Moher, and the Burren—are admired, the contrasting allure of the Irish hinterlands can be fully appreciated.

Getting Around Mayo, Sligo, and Roscommon

Getting to central towns is easy on public transport, but the best way to explore Ireland's upper- and central-west regions is by car.

County Mayo's largest town, Ballina, is 250km (155 miles) from Dublin, 100km (60 miles) north of Galway City, and 60km (37 miles) southwest of Sligo Town. County Roscommon borders both Mayo and Sligo and is 150km (90 miles) northwest of Dublin and only 80km (50 miles) from Galway City.

Flying and Driving

Located halfway between Galway and Sligo on the N17 in Charlestown, County Mayo, is the Ireland West Airport Knock (094 936 8100, *www.irelandwestairport.com*). Formerly the Knock International Airport, Ryanair (0818 303 303, *www.ryanair.com*), bmi baby (1890 340 122, *www.bmibaby.com*), Aer Lingus (0818 365000 or 1 516 622 4022 U.S., *www.aerlingus.com*), and Aer Arann (08 18 210 210, *www.aerarann.com*) serve several destinations throughout Europe from here. Sligo Airport (071 916 8280, *www.sligoairport.com*) in Strandhill connects only to and from Dublin.

All national and international car rental companies are located at the Ireland West Airport Knock. This includes Avis (094 9367707, *www.avis.ie*), Budget (090 662 4668, *www.budget.ie*), and Hertz (094 9367333, *www.hertz.ie*), which also has a counter at the Sligo Airport.

 Essential

Because County Mayo was so shaken by the Great Potato Famine, many left for better lives in the United States. If you are researching your family roots in Mayo, visit the Mayo North (096 31 809, www.mayoroots.com) or South Mayo (094 954 1214, www.mayo .irishroots.net) Heritage Centres. The North Heritage Centre sits on Lough Conn in Castlehill with an on-site museum and Enniscoe Gardens.

Getting to and from the Ireland West Airport Knock is possible via taxi or bus. Call Seán McCann (087 251 3370) or Colm Horkan (087 2532 044) for taxi service before or upon arrival. Additionally, Bus Éireann (096 71 800, *www.buseireann.ie*) connects the airport and Charlestown (twenty-five minutes), where other buses and the railway connect.

Bus

Bus Éireann connects Dublin to Roscommon (Boyle, Roscommon Town), Mayo (Ballina, Westport, Castlebar, Cong), and Sligo (Drumcliff, Strandhill, Sligo Town), among other towns in each. Express services connect Galway City to various towns in Mayo as well. Traveling from Westport, one can travel to Achill Island, Ballina, and into Sligo or over to Roscommon.

Train

Irish Rail (850 366 222, *www.irishrail.ie*) connects Dublin's Connolly Station to Carrick-on-Shannon (County Leitrum), Boyle (Roscommon), and Sligo Town (on Lord Edward Street). The Dublin Heuston Station serves Roscommon, Ballina, Castlebar, and Westport. Traveling from Galway City to Roscommon and farther west into the regions of County Mayo is also an option.

County Mayo

County Mayo (Maigh Eo) receives less hype than County Galway. Mayo's appeal is its historical resilience, its hidden corners, and its raw, wild landscape of bog, mountain, and meadow. The Great Potato Famine hit Mayo the hardest and while it is still recovering in some ways, those exploring Ireland's wilder wonders will not be disappointed.

One of Mayo's treasures is the town of Cong (Conga), which sits cushioned between Lough Mask and Lough Corrib. Not far from the luxurious grounds of Ashford Castle the town is worth exploring for its clear tourist draw; the film *The Quiet Man* (1951), starring John Wayne, was filmed here. A backdrop of rivers, streams, and forests lends itself to further exploration.

Sitting off the Clew Bay and undeniably Mayo's most adorable town is Westport (Cathair na Mairt). The town's population hovers at around 6,000 inhabitants and walking to the Westport Quay Harbor makes a worthwhile jaunt.

Westport House and Gardens

The Westport House and Gardens (098 25 430, *www .westporthouse.ie*) is a spectacular mansion overlooking Clew Bay. With gardens and an amusement park feel, a trip here makes a fun family outing. Attractions on hand for kids include a small zoo, pedal boats, and a train. Killary Adventure Company (see Chapter 13) has opened a branch here offering activities including kayaking, a climbing wall, laser tag, and archery. Westport House and Gardens is open daily from the end of March to September, 11:30 A.M.–5:30 P.M., Sunday only in October. Westport Attractions are open daily June–August, 11:30 A.M.–5:30 P.M.; Sunday only in May. Admission to House and Gardens €7.50/9/12. Admission to House, Gardens, and Attractions €16.50/18/21.

 Fact

James Wyatt laid out Westport, one of the first and only "planned" towns in Ireland. His design includes an octagonal mall and the main tree-lined thoroughfare along the River Carrowbeg. Famed architect Richard Castle worked on the impressive Westport House before Wyatt added his own touch.

Land of Poetry: County Sligo

County Sligo (Sligeach) is recognized as the childhood home of William Butler Yeats (1865–1939) and his brother, the painter Jack Yeats (1871–1957). References to Sligo's pastoral sanctums appear in both of their works.

A majority of monuments in Sligo Town are in remembrance of the Yeats. The best Yeats sights (all with free admission) in Sligo Town are outlined in the following sections.

The Model Arts and Niland Gallery (071 914 1405, *www .modelart.ie*) holds over fifty of Jack's paintings and works by Sean Keating, Estella Solomons, Paul Henry, Charles Lamb, and others. The newly redeveloped building and museum will commission and showcase even more projects throughout the year. Open Tuesday–Saturday, 10:30 A.M.–5:30 P.M.; Sunday, 11:00 A.M. –4:00 P.M.

Yeats Building and Sligo Art Gallery

Near Hyde Bridge and the engraved bronze W. B. Yeats statue is the Yeats Building housing the Sligo Art Gallery (071 914 5847, *www.sligoartgallery.com*). A true artist's haven, the Yeats International Summer School that takes place here is part of the Yeats Festival (071 914 2693, *www.yeats-sligo.com*) held from late July to mid-August each year. Open Monday–Saturday, 10 A.M.–5 P.M.

Sligo County Museum and Yeats Room

Located on Stephen Street in a former Presbyterian Church, the Sligo County Museum (071 914 1623), which is a part of the town library, contains the notable Yeats Room. Inside visitors can peruse manuscripts, photographs, and a copy of W. B.'s Nobel Prize from 1923. Open Tuesday–Saturday, 10 A.M.–noon and 2 P.M.–5 P.M.

Historical voyagers spending time in town should pass by the derelict Sligo Abbey (071 914 6406) off of Abbey Street. Constructed by Maurice Fitzgerald in 1253, it has over the years nearly burned down twice. However, the resilient structure still portrays magnificent lancet windows, along with an ornately carved altar. Open mid-March to the end of October, daily, 10:00 A.M.–6:00 P.M.; November–December, Friday–Sunday, 9:30 A.M.–4:30 P.M.

County Roscommon

Roscommon (Ros Comáin) does have a remote and landlocked attraction to it. If traveling on the train from Dublin, you'll be able to see all the bog land. Further exploration into the heart of the county reveals some real treasures; there are over 5,000 ancient ruins.

Roscommon Town is a busy commercial area, but worth a quick visit. The Roscommon Museum (090 662 5613, open June–September, Monday–Friday, 10 A.M.–3 P.M.), the quadrangular Norman Castle (1269), and the Dominican Priory can easily take up two hours.

 Alert

The supposedly haunted Boyle Abbey (071 966 2604) was founded in the 1160s. Considered one of the best-preserved priories of its kind in Ireland, Cromwell's men destroyed much of the place, but the gatehouse (now a visitor center) succinctly details the events. Open daily 10 A.M.–6 P.M., April–October. Admission €1/1.50/2.00.

While in County Roscommon be sure to check out Strokestown Village and its Park House, Gardens, and Famine Museum. The pleasant village of Strokestown (Béal na mBuillí) offers some interesting (and educational) attractions, including a raw look back at tragic times accurately portrayed in the Famine Museum. It is connected to the Strokestown Park House (071 963 3013, *www.strokestownpark.ie*). The estate has the longest herbaceous border in Britain and Ireland, according to the *Guinness Book of World Records*. Open mid-March to the end of October, daily, 10:00 A.M.–5:30 P.M. Guided tours available Monday–Friday, 11:30 A.M., 2:00 P.M., and 4:00 P.M.; Saturday–Sunday, 5:00 P.M. only. Call for other openings. Combined admission to House, Gardens, and Museum €6/12/13. Separate tickets and group rates available.

Things to See and Do

The draw of Mayo, Sligo, and Roscommon is the astounding number of activities to keep any type of traveler occupied. Tourists seeking open spaces dotted with loughs, stunning coastlines, and quaint towns will be enticed by Mayo. Travelers attempting to uncover the rural poetic muse of Yeats will be drawn to Sligo, while the ever-popular Lough Key Forest Park, for example, in Roscommon would appeal to an outdoorsy type of family.

Croagh Patrick and Coffin Ship Sculpture, County Mayo

Near Westport, Croagh Patrick (*www.croagh-patrick.com*; known as "the Reek" by the thousands who climb it on the last Sunday in July, called "Reek Sunday") sits over Clew Bay at 750 meters (2,461 feet). The mountain is not overcrowded during other times of the year. Ireland's pious Saint Patrick fasted here for Lent in 441 for forty days and nights. Only able-bodied hikers ready for the grueling two-hour trek need attempt it. Always come prepared for weather changes and hike with rain gear. The Croagh Patrick Visitor Centre (098 64 114) marks the trailhead. Open daily, April–May, 10 A.M.–6 P.M.; June–August, 10 A.M.–7 P.M.; September–October, 11 A.M.–5 P.M. Call or e-mail for November–March hours.

Doo Lough Valley, County Mayo

Better experienced than described, the Doo Lough Valley is akin to Glendalough (County Wicklow) for its absolute splendor. Spreading out from the R335 between Westport and Leenane and east of the Mweelrea Mountains, the Doo Lough (Black Lake) Pass has its own sorrowful tale. Known as the "Famine Walk," over 200 souls perished on the roundtrip journey between Loisburgh and Delphi after being denied food from their landlord. The picturesque valley is most assuredly worth a slow drive, as is staying in Delphi (County Galway) a day or two to salmon fish and explore the lake's environs.

 Essential

Cast completely in bronze, the Coffin Ship National Famine Memorial sculpture on site is a replica of the ramshackle ships used to transport Irish emigrants during the Great Famine. Common on board was the spread of the deadly "Famine Fever," a type of typhus spread through lice. The ghostlike skeletons that appear to be floating eerily around the ship leave a lasting imprint on the mind.

Mayo's Islands: Achill, Clare, and Inishturk

With its broad west side overlooking the Atlantic, County Mayo has three superb islands beckoning exploration. The first, Achill Island (An Caol, *www.achill-island.com*) is actually connected to the mainland via a bridge. With a far-removed feeling similar to the Dingle Peninsula (County Kerry), the island boasts five Blue Flag beaches, along with an array of mountains and staggering cliffs. A visit to the Deserted Village at Slievemore containing empty stone cottages and a graveyard are a showcase to the hard times of west Ireland's past. Keep an eye out for the various works of famed painter Robert Henri, who lived on the island and shared his work with the locals. Paintings appear in guesthouses, restaurants, and petrol stations. The Achill Tourism website (*www.achilltourism.com*) offers insight into the island's events, festivals, and accommodations.

Clare Island (*www.clareisland.info*) is an ideal spot in Clew Bay for walking and rambling. Mount Knockmore sits perched in the center of the isle, rising to 460 meters (1,510 feet). The Cistercian abbey and Grace O'Malley's castle are monumental hotspots. A Yoga Retreat Center (98 25 412, *www.yogaretreats.ie*) promotes *stretching* your visit to the island for healing, rest, and relaxation.

Ferries depart Roonagh Quay, west of Louisbourgh, and take about fifteen minutes one way. For daily departures visit the Clare Island Ferry Company (086 851 5003, *www.clareislandferry.com*) or O'Malley Ferries (098 25 045 or 086 600 0204, *www.omalleyferries.com*).

 Essential

> Art and activity amalgamate on the 90km (56-mile) North Mayo Sculpture Trail (Tír Sáile; 098 45 107,1*claggan@eircom.net*) that starts on the R314 from Ballina and ends in Blacksod Point. A descriptive book of the same name is available at the local tourist office.

Inishturk Island (*www.inishturkisland.com*) is the island of choice for travelers seeking true solitude. In the off-peak season, you might be the only one on the "Wild Boar Island." Exploring the back roads and visiting the bird sanctuaries along its cliffs make a fascinating day. Fishing and scuba diving are available in summer. Located just about 15km (9 miles) off of Mayo's coast, ferries depart from Roonagh Quay at 11:00 A.M. and 6:30 P.M. Contact the Inishturk Ferry (098 45 541 or 086 202 9670, *patrickheanue@vodaphone.ie*) for details. Private hire available.

Céide Fields, County Mayo

The collection of unearthed 5,000-year-old stone walls of Céide Fields are an archaeological dream. Discovered by Patrick Caulfield and later examined by his archaeologist son Seamus, the place has become one of the world's foremost preserved Stone Age discoveries (all thanks to the bog). On site are megalithic tombs, houses, and various remnants that open a window into ancient days. To get the most out of a visit, take a guided tour from the well-designed Visitor Centre (096 43 325). Located off the R314 west of Ballycastle. Open daily: mid-March–May and November–October, 10 A.M.–5 P.M.; June–September, 10 A.M.–6 P.M. Admission €2.50/3.50.

 Fact

W. B. Yeats dedicated a poem about the tiny island of Innisfree in his 1893 *The Rose* collection. Inspired by the island's beautiful solitude, he forever endeared the place as a peaceful escape from urban life. In true irony, the *Rose of Innisfree* Tour Boat (071 9164557, *www.roseofinnisfree.com*) has daily departures (along with food and poetry recitals) from Parke's Castle on the northeast edge.

Driving Yeats Country, County Sligo

With Lough Gill at its center, a drive, bike, or walk around Yeats Country will bring you close to the poet's pastoral muse. With hiking trails circumnavigating the entire lake and grounds, packing a picnic lunch and heading out for a few hours makes a splendid outing.

From the N4, turn right onto the R287 until arriving at Donney Rock. Park the car and take the somewhat vertiginous trail down to the Dooney Rock lookout to enjoy the beautiful and awe-inspiring panoramas of the lake. Trails also extend out from this point.

Rounding pass Innisfree and onto the R288, Parke's Castle (071 916 4149, open daily, mid-March–October, 10 A.M.–6 P.M. Admission €2/3) is actually in County Leitrum. The fortified manor was built in 1609 for Englishman Robert Parke. It has been painstakingly restored to its former glory.

The R288 becomes the R286, which takes you up the N16 and continues up to beautiful Lough Glencar with its waterfall, accessible from a path. The small road continues around Glencar's northern edge to the N15.

 Essential

> A vicariously nostalgic treat is a visit to the peninsula of Rosses Point. The young Yeats brothers spent much of their summers at their uncle's Elsinore House, a small estate originally built by pirate John "Black" Jack. The picture-perfect locale inspired many of Jack's paintings, including *The Metal Man*, *White Shower*, and *The Graveyard Wall*.

Overlooking Drumcliff Bay is the former home of the Gore-Booth family, the Lissadell House and Gardens (071 916 3150, *www.lissadellhouse.com*). Yeats, a close friend of the family, spent many a night in this massive manor and even depicted the famous Gore-Booth sisters in poetic verse. The family is revered here for their willingness to help the Irish locals during the Great Famine. Additionally, it is the birthplace of Constance Markievicz, who was elected to the British House of Commons. Tours available. Open daily, 10:30 A.M.–6:00 P.M.; October–mid-March, 10:30 A.M.–5:00 P.M. Admission to House and Gardens €6/12.

Farther along is W. B. Yeats's grave in the Drumcliff church-
yard off of the N15 toward Donegal, which includes a notable high
cross and monastic ruins. A pint (and a good meal) in honor of
the great poet can be had at the Yeats Tavern (071 916 3117) on
Bridge Street.

Rambling up Knocknarea and Ben Bulben

For climbers, the 328 meter (1,074-foot) Knocknarea (Cnoc
na Rí) to the west of Sligo Town awaits the fit for a one-hour
workout. The pinnacle affords views of Ben Bulben and Rosses
Point. Continuing north on the N15, the mighty 526-meter (1,726-
foot) Ben Bulben (Binn Ghulbain) is a large glacier-etched rock
formation jutting abruptly into the sky. A view from its upper vantage point (on a clear day) is in all likelihood the best-kept vista
in Ireland.

 Alert

For those turning Yeats Country into "adventure country," a ramble
up Ben Bulben is quite a feat. Only experienced climbers should
go up the north side slope, which is not only steep, but gets hit
with nasty winds and storms from the Atlantic. A much safer climb
is up the south side of the slope, which is smoother and has better
paths.

Carrowmore Megalithic Cemetery, County Sligo

The timeless allure of cemeteries, cairns, dolmens, and tombs
come to life with a visit to the Carrowmore Megalithic Cemetery
(071 916 1534). The site is Ireland's largest Stone Age cemetery and
Europe's second biggest. While some of the ruins date back nearly
5,000 years, the stone rings and passage tombs once numbered
in the hundreds. A discovery at the end of the 1990s unearthed

a grave that was later carbon tested at over 7,000 years old. All of this and more is handsomely presented and detailed in the visitor center. Guided tours available. Located outside Carrowmore toward Church Hill. Open daily, 9:30 A.M.–6:30 P.M. Closed October–April. Admission €2/3.

 Essential

The Suck Valley Way (090 666 3602. *www.suckvalley.com*) in Roscommon is a national marked way covering 75km (47 miles). It follows the River Suck and passes through the astutely dubbed "Nine Friendly Villages." Bring along fishing string and a hook (and obtain a fishing license) to enjoy the river's perch and pike.

Eagles Flying Irish Raptor Research Center, County Sligo

A cool activity for any type of traveler, the Eagles Flying Irish Raptor Research Centre (071 918 9310, *www.eaglesflying.com*) offers two stupendous birds of prey shows daily. With these trained birds swooping to and fro, the hour-long demonstration is an educational and mesmerizing encounter with close calls for all! Located on the road to Temple House in Portinch, Ballymote. Research Centre open April to early November, daily, 10:30 A.M.–12:30 P.M. and 2:30 P.M.–4:30 P.M. Eagles Flying show daily at 11:00 A.M. and 3:00 P.M.

Arigna Mining Experience, County Roscommon

Fun for the entire family, the Arigna Mining Experience (071 964 6466, *www.arignaminingexperience.ie*) was Ireland's last fully functioning coal mine until the 1990s. After closing, locals wanted to keep its memory alive. Exhibitions detailing the mine's history are discussed by ex-miners who make wonderful local guides.

Located in north Roscommon in the Arigna Valley. Open daily, 10 A.M.–5 P.M. Admission €6/8/10.

Lough Key Forest Park, County Roscommon

Just near Lough Key and its thirty-two islands is the Lough Key Forest Park (071 966 2363, *www.loughkey.ie*). Ideal for a family outing; trail walking, monuments, and picnic areas are just some of the appealing attractions. Do not be surprised if you spot deer, hedgehogs, or otters. A twelfth-century abbey sits on Trinity Island; a nineteenth-century castle sits on Castle Island. Rowboats and motorboat rentals are available. Pony trap rides through the park will please the kids. Camping (071 966 2212, May–August) is available, as is an adventure playground and visitor center with various activities.

Accommodations

Castles and country houses top the list for places to stay in Counties Mayo, Sligo, and Roscommon. Because of the region's expansive natural beauty, these removed and esteemed establishments help bring you closer to the sublimity that has attracted and inspired legendary artists and poets alike.

Ashford Castle

Cong, Co. Mayo
094 954 6003, 1800 346 7007 (US)
www.ashford.ie
€200–500+ per room; suites €500–800+;
S/D/F. MC/V

Pristine. Picturesque. Perfect. Ashford Castle encapsulates *everything* that one would expect in Ireland's premier resort. Overlooking the deeply reflective waters of the Lough Corrib, the thirteenth-century castle was built originally for the De Burgo family before the Guinness family became its proprietors. To enter Ashford is to enter an Irish fairy tale. With its oak paneling, revered art, stunningly decorated rooms with the finest amenities, casual and fine dining, and two bars, along with a spa, sauna, and gym it is a dream come true. A nine-hole golf course, tennis courts, boating, fishing, archery, clay pigeon shooting, falconry, and horseback riding are all extracurricular pursuits on hand. Splurge here to enjoy what celebrities such as Mel Gibson, Barbra Streisand, Woody Allen, and Ronald Reagan have all discovered. Access is limited to guests only; if you wish to explore the lavish grounds make a reservation for tea and explore afterward.

Stella Maris
Country House

Ballycastle, Co. Mayo
096 43 322
www.stellamarisireland.com
€200–250+ per room;
S/D/F. MC/V

Constructed in 1853, the Stella Maris (or "Star of the Sea") sits tranquilly on Bunatrahir Bay. Built originally for the British Coast Guard, the manor became a convent before World War I. Now owned and operated by Chef Frances Kelly, the estate offers beautiful rooms and award-winning dining using local and organic produce. Open April–October.

Temple House
Ballymote, Co. Sligo
071 918 3329
www.templehouse.ie
€90+ per person;
S/D/T/F. MC/V

Located near Ballinacarrow, the renowned 1,000-acre estate of Temple House is a Georgian gem perfectly positioned to explore the often-overlooked region between Ireland's west and northwest. The value for the stay here is noteworthy and the homey and historical feel of the place is apparent.

Tree Tops B&B
Cleveragh Rd., Sligo Town
071 916 0160
treetops@iol.ie
€40+ per person; S/D

Superbly located and well priced, the Tree Tops B&B makes a wonderful spot to rest in Sligo Town. For cleanliness, comfort, and pure Irish wonderfulness, this quaint home is a top choice for travelers seeking a truly local home-away-from-home experience.

Lough Key House B&B
Boyle, Co. Roscommon
071 966 2161
www.loughkeyhouse.com
€45+ per person;
S/D/F. MC/V

Ideally situated to explore the Lough Key Forest Park, the Lough Key House B&B is an Irish gem in its cozy comforts, hospitality, and wonderful breakfasts. Aged and refined, this 200-year-old Georgian period manor is set among the Curlew Mountains.

Castlecoote House

Castlecoote, Co. Roscommon

090 666 3794

www.castlecootehouse.com

€115–190+ per room;

S/D/F. MC/V.

The Castlecoote House is a restored Georgian mansion built on what used to be a sixteenth-century castle. The estate overlooks the River Suck, intersecting the Suck Valley Way. The MacGeraghty clan settled the estate, but the exact history has yet to surface completely.

Other Accommodations

Here are some other accommodations you might consider while in Counties Mayo, Sligo, and Rosscommon. (In the listings that follow, € = around 25 euros per person.)

- €€ **The Garden Gates, Castlebar,**
  Co. Mayo,
  094 902 3110
  www.westportgardengates.com
- € **Old Mill Holiday Hostel, James St.,**
  Westport, Co. Mayo,
  098 27 045
  www.oldmillhostel.com
- €€€ **Ardmore County House Hotel,**
  The Quay, Westport, Co. Mayo,
  098 25 994
  www.ardmorecountryhouse.com

- €€ **Atlantic Breeze B&B, Pollagh Keel,**
  Achill Island, Co. Mayo,
  098 43 189
- €€ **Michaeleen's Manor, Quay Rd., Lisloughrey,**
  Cong, Co. Mayo,
  094 954 6089
  www.congbb.com
- €€ **Urlar House, Drumcliff, Co. Sligo,**
  071 916 3110
- € **Harbour House Hostel, Finisklin Rd.,**
  Sligo Town,
  071 917 1547
  www.harbourhousehostel.com
- €€ **Lisadorn B&B, Donegal Rd.,**
  Sligo Town,
  071 44 283
- € **Willowbrook Hostel and Camping Park,**
  Willowbrook, Kiltybanks, Ballaghderreen,
  Co. Roscommon,
  094 986 1307
  www.willowbrookpark.com
- €€ **Lough Key Caravan and Camping Park,**
  Lough Key, Co. Roscommon
  071 966 2212,
  www.loughkey.ie

Restaurants and Pubs

Dining options become more local as you move away from the bigger towns in rural Ireland. This is especially true in Sligo and Roscommon. The largest county of the three, Mayo is brimming with dining selections; Ballina, Westport, and Castlebar offer traditional and modern Irish fare, while the coastal regions and islands have delectable seafood. During the summer and peak holiday times, make reservations for dinner as early as possible. (In the restaurant listings that follow, € = around 25 euros per person.)

The Lemon Peel

The Octagon, Westport, Co. Mayo
098 26 929
€€

The Lemon Peel is a modern and stylish bistro serving up tasty modern-Irish concoctions using local produce. The host and chef, Robbie McMenamin, does a grand job of not only cooking, but of greeting his patrons. Serious about its food, the Lemon Peel is both gourmet and free-spirited.

Café Rua

Spencer St., Castlebar, Co. Mayo
094 928 6072
www.caferua.com
€€

The Café Rua offers a delectable set menu that, while slightly on the pricy side, does match its notoriety as one of the Castlebar-Westport region's best traditional dining venues. Numerous epicures concede that the slow-roasted pork belly ribs are a favorite.

Achill Cliff House and Restaurant

Keel, Achill Island, Co. Mayo
098 43 400
www.achillcliff.com
€€

A hotel and a restaurant, the Achill Cliff House is held in high esteem for its wonderful selection of fresh seafood and traditional dishes. From mussels to Atlantic salmon and roast leg of Achill lamb, the oceanic and meaty delights are served with a smile. Hotel rooms are simple but clean and comfortable.

The Silver Apple

Lord Edward Street, Strandhill Rd., Sligo Town
071 914 6770
€€

The Silver Apple is a French-inspired dining establishment with flawless décor and an appetizing menu. With a well-thought out children's menu, do not be shy about bringing them along. The extensive wine selection means a perfect accompaniment of ruby Bordeaux or sweet Banyuls.

Coach Lane at Donaghy's

1-2 Lord Edward Street, Sligo Town
071 916 2417
€€

An international mélange of flavor with a focus on seafood, the Coach Lane also has pub grub, French, and Italian cuisine. The place gets packed on weekends, making for an animated atmosphere. Reserve ahead to avoid disappointment.

Jackson's Restaurant and Guesthouse

Market Sq., Roscommon Town

090 663 4140

www.jacksons.ie

€€

Award-winning chef Geraldine Garvin ensures that each plate is prepared and presented as an artistic master-piece. Dishes are categorized as vegetarian and pasta, meat and poultry, and fish. Superb and stimulating for the taste buds is the honey-roasted half duckling. Kiddy dishes are offered and prepared with the same idea that freshness and the use of in-season local produce makes the meal. The guesthouse has spacious rooms great for families.

Traveler's Tidbits

Here you will find the necessary information for Mayo, Sligo, and Roscommon. The best websites to check out information are *www.mayo-ireland.ie*, *www.mayo.ie*, *www.sligotown.net*, and for upper Roscommon, visit *www.kinghouse.ie*.

On the following page is the Tourist Office chart; "Seasonal" identifies tourist offices generally open May through September. Tourist offices are open during regular business hours.

MAYO, SLIGO, AND ROSSCOMMON TOURIST OFFICES

Town	Address	Phone Number	In Operation
Achill Tourist Office	Achill Sound, Co. Mayo	098 45 384	Seasonal
Ballina Tourist Office	Cathedral Rd., Co. Mayo	096 70 848	Seasonal
Castlebar Tourist Office	Linenhall St., Co. Mayo	094 902 1207	Seasonal
Westport Tourist Office	James' St., Co. Mayo	098 25 711	All year
Sligo Tourist Office	Temple St., Co. Sligo	071 916 1201	All year
Boyle Tourist Office	King House, Co. Roscommon	071 966 2145	Seasonal

Below is other pertinent travel information. In the case of an emergency, dial 999 anywhere in the Republic of Ireland.

TRAVEL INFORMATION

Name	Address	Phone Number	Web Address
Sligo Hospital	The Mall, Sligo Town	071 917 111	
Mayo General Hospital	Westport Rd., Castlebar, Co. Mayo	094 902 1733	
Roscommon General Hospital	Roscommon Drive, Roscommon Town	09 032 6200	
Mayo County Library	The Crescent, Westport, Co. Mayo.	098 25 747	www .mayolibrary.ie
Sligo Central Library	Stephen Street, Sligo Town	071 9111675	www .sligolibrary.ie
Roscommon Library	Abbey St., Roscommon Town	090 663 7274	
Westport Post Office	North Mall, Westport, Co. Mayo	098 25 219	

Name	Address	Phone Number	Web Address
Sligo Post Office	Lower Knox St., Sligo Town		
Boyle Post Office	Knockvicar, Boyle, Co. Roscommon	071 966 7006	
Mayo North Heritage Centre	Enniscoe, Castlehill, Ballina, Co. Mayo	096 31 809	*www .mayoroots .com*
South Mayo Family History Research Centre	Main St., Ballinrobe	094 954 1214	
Sligo Heritage and Genealogy Centre	Temple St., Co. Sligo	071 914 3728	
Roscommon Heritage and Genealogy Company	Church St., Strokestown, Co. Roscommon	071 963 3380	

County Donegal

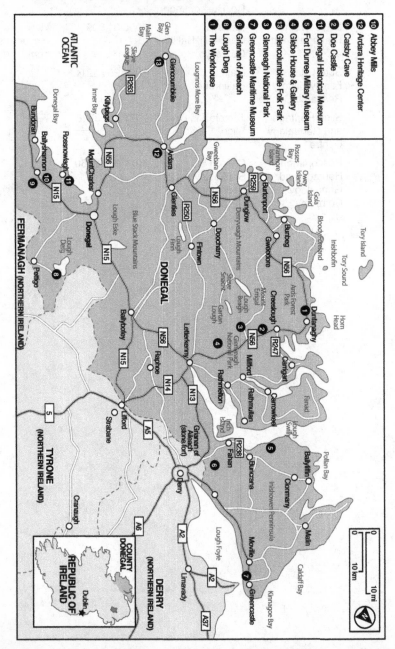

1. The Workhouse
2. Lough Derg
3. Grianan of Aileach
4. Greencastle Maritime Museum
5. Glenveagh National Park
6. Glencolumbkille Folk Park
7. Glebe House & Gallery
8. Fort Dunree Military Museum
9. Donegal Historical Museum
10. Doe Castle
11. Catsby Cave
12. Ardara Heritage Center
13. Abbey Mills

CHAPTER 15

The Northwest Corner: County Donegal

C ounty Donegal is a refreshing, one-of-a-kind county that is only now being fully explored and appreciated by travelers. If you are searching for a unique destination in a remote corner that exudes everything Ireland, this is it. Donegal is an exquisite example of what embodies Ireland as a whole: history, culture, warm hearts, stunning landscapes, and mouth-watering cuisine. It is a county removed, yet a special locale that once visited, beckons return. It is worth as many days as one can devote, especially to appreciate its hidden treasures.

Getting Around County Donegal

In Donegal, dramatic landscapes, stunning cliffs, sandy beaches, and a rugged countryside give way to traditional towns and a multitude of peninsulas jutting off into numerous bays. While Donegal Town, Ardara, or Killybegs (or Kilcar) are great points to explore the south and west of the county, Gweedore and Bunbeg are prime locations to explore Glenveagh National Park, the Rosses, and even Tory Island.

Flying and Bus

Donegal has its own airport (0 74 954 8284, *www.donegalairport* *.com*), located in Carrickfinn, Kincasslagh. It is an hour from Donegal Town, which can be accessed using Bus Éireann (074 912 1309, *www.buseireann.ie*), which also goes to Galway, Sligo, and up north to Derry and to Dublin. Currently, there are no trains to or from County Donegal.

Donegal Town

Donegal is the name of the county as well as the name of the main city, which is more of a town than anything else. Locals and area guides alike therefore refer to it as "Donegal Town." The area flourishes in its own beauty, and tourism is an ever-growing sphere. Donegal Town itself is worth a morning or an afternoon stroll; the town center is not large by any means. It is, however, filled to the brim with local shops. An excellent lunch can be had at one of the many local pubs catering to both denizens and tourists alike. This is also a great place to stock up on any provisions for your explorations through the southern and western regions of the county.

Donegal Town's main attraction is Donegal Castle (described later in "Things to See and Do"). Just follow the signs from the center of town to discover an exquisitely restored ruin bringing deserved pride to the town's inhabitants.

 Essential

Parking in Donegal town is tight. The best parking is beside the tourist information office next to the river. But, this is likely to be full in summer. The parking area most likely to have spaces is the one next to the church as you come into town off the N15. Keep spare change available for the parking meters.

Glencolmcille

Saint Columba, or the Glen of St. Colmcille, gives Glencolmcille its name. This grassy valley gives a distinct contrast to the boggy areas around it. From Killybegs or Kilcar, the area is easily reachable. The town affords Stone Age ruins, along with the renowned St. Columba Church, north of the village of Cashel. If you want to explore more of Donegal's unique place in Irish history, try the Folk Village Museum and Heritage Centre (074 973 0017) in Cashel, near the beach. Be sure to stock up on fudge, marmalade, and curious local wines! Consider taking your stock to one of the fine local beaches, such as those near Doonalt or Malinbeg. Open daily April–September. Admission is €2.50/4.

Arranmore Island

With a small population and spectacular scenery to boot, Arranmore Island (Árainn Mhór) is one of Donegal's most famed locales to glimpse impressive sea caves and enjoy sandy beaches. The enjoyable Arranmore Way walk circumnavigates the island and offers nice views of the Green Island, a bird retreat. Visit the Arranmore Ferry (074 952 0532, *www.arranmoreferry.com*) office for more information about getting to the island. Ferries leave from Burtonport Pier, a few miles from Dungloe, which is off the N56.

Tory Island

With an interesting history of resistance to move to the "mainland," the inhabitants of Tory Island are artists, weavers, drivers, restaurant owners, and B&B owners. Some are still fishermen. Although the island is only a slight distance off the northwest coast of Donegal, east of Bloody Foreland Head, the residents maintain a unique presence, more reserved, yet equally dignified, when compared to their Irish counterparts. Irish is spoken by most of the islanders on a day-to-day basis, but everyone speaks English as well. The island has become famous for its idiosyncratic art form known as "naive art." The island offers bird watching, the Tory School of Primitive Painters, and ceilidhs, which are music and dancing sessions of old. To get there, see *www.toryislandferry.com*.

Fact

Surprisingly, Tory Island has its own monarch. Elected to the post in the mid-1990s, Patsy Dan Rogers has served as the official King of Tory for over a decade. While his post is anything but demanding, he does earn a small salary from his so-called subjects and still meets and greets travelers. He is an internationally renowned painter and a fun-loving storyteller. Read about him and see some of his artwork at *http://patsydanrodgers.littleireland.ie.*

Rossnowlagh

In the last few years the secret tranquility that is Rossnowlagh (Ross Neamblach) has been made known. This beach spot is an ideal location to simply forget about it all for a couple of days. The area has several B&Bs, beachside bungalows, and hotels scattered throughout, especially closer to the touristy town of Bundoran, located nearly ten miles south. The beach of Rossnowlagh is a stunning example of other "Blue Flag" beaches that you can find dotted all around Donegal.

 Fact

A "Blue Flag" is an international marker applied to beaches in over thirty countries. A beach or marina is labeled so after it has met the strict criteria of the nonprofit Foundation for Environmental Education (FEE). Upon review, the beach is tested in accordance to water quality, high environmental standards, and certain safety provisions.

Other Blue Flag beaches in Donegal can be found (moving north along the coast) in Bundoran, Murvagh, inside Rintra Bay, Gweebarra Bay, Kincasslagh, Sheephaven Bay, Portsalon, along Glengad Head in Inishowen Peninsula, and Inishowen Head.

In the summer months, these beaches can be brimming with European holidaymakers, so book your accommodation ahead.

In Rossnowlagh, you can also visit the Donegal Historical Society Museum (071 985 2133) with surrounding gardens and forest. The museum and its collection, which is located in a friary, is quite small, but worthwhile if you want to view Stone Age equipment, local artifacts, and Irish instruments. Open daily, 10 A.M.–8 P.M. Donations accepted.

Ballyshannon

The bustling small town of Ballyshannon (Béal Átha Seanaidh) is better than Bundoran to base yourself for exploring south of Donegal Town. Set atop the River Erne, the town is still a gem, even if you are simply passing through. The real draw to the town, besides the quaint Georgian architecture lining the streets, is the grave of the acclaimed poet William Allingham (1824–89) at St. Anne's Church. Follow the signs from Main Street.

Additionally, just a drive outside of town, Assaroe Abbey (071 985 8966) still has its mill in working order and is now a noteworthy interpretative center. Follow the road signs to Abbey Mills (071 985 1580). Open June–September, Monday–Saturday, 11 A.M.–7 P.M.; October–May, Sunday only, 3 P.M.–7 P.M.

Horn Head

Located near Dunfanaghy, which boasts the Killyhoey and Marbe Hill Beaches, Horn Head (Corrán Binne) reveals some fascinating aspects of Donegal County. It is teeming with birdlife, awe-inspiring coastal panoramas and, on a good day, offers views all the way to Scotland. Near here is the Ads Forest Park, offering marked trails, perfect for an afternoon picnic. A drive to the Doe Castle is advantageous for historical buffs. Wrecked sailors of the Spanish Armada used it as refuge in 1588. Thereafter, the castle changed hands between the feuding MacSweeney's and eventually was overtaken by the Irish. Cromwellian forces took it by surprise in 1650. It was inhabited until the mid-1800s before it was deserted. It is located only nine miles from Dunfanaghy.

Things to See and Do

Abounding in activities, majestic landscapes, and historic sights, County Donegal offers everything for any type of traveler. Donegal Castle gives a glimpse into the history of the region, while the name alone of the Blue Stack Mountains brings about visions of a fairy-tale world. Revel in one of Ireland's best-kept secrets and enjoy the loughs, castles, and sylvan backdrop that make Donegal so decidedly special.

Donegal Castle

The word *Donegal* is an Irish transliteration of *Dun na nGall*, which actually means "fort of the foreigners." *Gall* most likely refers to the Norse invaders who conquered the area before anyone else came along. The castle overlooks the River Eske. Explore this fun site with a guided or self-guided tour. When you first enter it, it seems drab. Climb the stairs, past the *garderobe*, or toilet, and behold an exquisite refabrication of times past. Located on Castle Street. Open March–October, daily, 10 A.M.–5 P.M. Closed November–March. Admission €1.50–2.50/3.50.

Lough Eske and the Blue Stack Mountains

The wonderful Lough Eske, located just northeast of Donegal, used to be a happening fishing lake. Since the fishing is not what it once was, locals and tourists now use it as a wonderful picnic, walking, or cycling spot. While the lake is probably skipped for those excited about the Slieve League cliffs, you might consider spending a relaxing afternoon strolling around the area. The backdrop of the Blue Stack Mountains and the tree-lined road around the lough make it an appreciable half-day trip. If you have a bike, you can head out of Donegal Town that way. Lough Eske is only 7 km (4.5 miles) away.

Alert

While cycling or driving outside of town, follow signs for the N56 to Killybegs, followed by signs to Harvey's Point Country Hotel. Instead of stopping here, head straight down the small, tree-lined lane. The road runs along Lough Eske up into a minor back road. Ask the tourist office in Donegal Town if you are interested in going deeper into the Blue Stack Mountains on a guided or self-guided walk.

In the Lough Eske area, you will find the Wildwood Crafts Studio, displaying photos, crafts, and art from the area. You will also find the Rhu Gorse B&B and the Eas Dun Lodge B&B.

Venturing Through Donegal Bay

Donegal Bay encompasses everything that is Donegal. The Slieve League Mountains and the smaller towns and villages such as Glencolmcille embody Gaelic history, culture, and especially music. It is not until you visit that you truly appreciate what makes this area so extraordinary. One of the best ways to explore is by driving, although biking is also an excellent option. Rentals are available in both Donegal Town and in Ardara, which is a better point to start a cycling excursion. One of the prettiest roads to drive is the R263 to Glencolmcille, to Malin Beg and then up through the Glengesh Pass, in the middle of the peninsula, which connects to Ardara. If biking, consider the Stravally and Port roads. Port is a wonderfully empty farm village area with imposing views of the Atlantic. You can purchase the topographical OS Map #10 in the tourist office, which details the area.

Grianán of Aileach

An ancient ring fort supposedly constructed by the gods, Grianán of Aileach (Grianán Ailigh) stands almost as a portal to the Inishowen Peninsula. With prominent views of Lough Foyle and Swilly, the 77-feet-diameter circular fort was thought to be a place of worship before it was controlled by the royal O'Neill sept of Aileach. Murtogh O'Brien, king of Munster in the year 1101, tore down the fortification. Reconstruction of the fort began again in 1870, so historians are not quite sure if it looks the same as it once did. This, accompanied with the inviting church on the premises, makes it one of Donegal's most engaging monuments today. The fort is accessible 19km (12 miles) south of Buncrana off of the N13. Open daily, 10 A.M.–6 P.M. Admission free.

Glenveagh National Park and Castle

John George Adair from County Laois was not popular after evicting 244 tenants off his land in 1861 so that he could have an unspoiled view of the surrounding valley. Following his death, the property switched hands a few times. What remains today are the 16,000 hectares that make up Glenveagh National Park (Páirc Naisiúnta Gleann Bheatha) and Glenveagh Castle with surrounding gardens and the dark, glacial Lough Veagh.

Getting to the Glenveagh National Park can be slightly tricky. If you are heading from the Gweedore or Derrybeg region, head south on the R257, taking the R258 back road (optional), followed by a right-hand turn on N56 toward Letterkenny. Look for a brown sign where the N56 and the R251 split.

Ample parking is available at the visitor center. The impressive center has a tearoom and restaurant if you would like to eat there. Food is reasonable, averaging €12 for a main dish.

For those wanting to visit the Glenveagh Castle, buy your bus ticket inside the visitor center. The bus leaves from just outside the visitor center and takes ten minutes to get to the castle. The park also encourages walking to the castle, which is 4 km (2.5

miles) away. There is a gravel path along the road overlooking the river, which is lovely to walk. Plenty of families push their toddlers hitched in strollers along this route.

Additionally, the park has other trails available for walking. The visitor center asks that all walkers report first before taking off. Routes vary in length, from forty-five minutes to more than two hours. During your walk, you might spot a herd of red deer or the reintroduced golden eagle, which was once extinct in Ireland. Since its return, it has begun to flourish.

Each marked way has its perks. Most are quite hilly at the start and then straighten out before returning back toward the visitor center or castle. Guided nature walks of various levels are available in the summer. A six-hour hill walk takes place each month and is offered six months of the year. Call 074 913 7090 to reserve ahead of time. Glenveagh Castle requires a guided tour in order to see it in its full glory. The tours take place at different intervals according to season, but they only take groups of twenty persons or less with each session. So, once you arrive on the minibus, pay the minimal entrance fee and get your name on the list. You might have to wait up to one hour. If you are required to wait, enjoy the tearoom and splendid exotic garden. The park is open daily year round. Visitor Centre open Febuary–November, daily, 10 A.M.–6 P.M. Admission free. Glenvaugh Castle open April–October, daily, 10 A.M.–6 P.M. Admission €1.50/3.

Drive Inishowen Peninsula

The northernmost peninsula in Ireland is blessed with castles, staggering cliffs, and views of the sea that have to be experienced firsthand. The Inishowen Peninsula, which translates to "Island of Eoghain," is named after one of the sons of the once high king of Ireland who was based at the fort temple of Grianán of Aileach, the ring fort described in the previous section. Driving times can vary on the peninsula, especially if it is a high-travel season or a weekend with nice weather. Either way, it is best to make it a day trip in order to see all the sights. The length of the tour is 160km to 200km (100+ miles), depending upon the various options listed.

Inishowen Tour Route

The route around the Inishowen Peninsula can actually start at the Grianán of Aileach and follow the R238 along the west side to Buncrana, known for its beaches and the rebuilt Buncrana Castle and O'Doherty's Keep. It was burned by the English then rebuilt and used as a manor.

Continue northwest on the back road toward Dunree Head, which displays the Dunree Fort, and onward to the Gap of Mamore, rendering wonderful views of the seascape of Lough Swilly.

After Dunaff Head, Ballyliffin on the R238 is the next destination before Doagh Isle. The small islet is home to the spine-chilling Ireland Haunted House and educational Doagh Famine Village (086 846 4749, *www.doaghfaminevillage.com*).

 Fact

The northernmost point in Ireland is Malin Head, a cape off the Inishowen Peninsula. Getting there is easy enough by following the R242 from Malin to Ballyhillin, which can be done during your day trip here.

Next, take the R242 to Malin Head. Here is a great spot for bird watching, photo snapping, and a coffee break. Following, head back on the R238 to Greencastle, a fishing port and natural gate to Lough Foyle, which was founded in 1305 by Richard de Burgo, who was often referred to as the Red Earl of Ulster because of his rosy cheeks. Then, the final leg of the journey continues on the R241 and R238 toward Muff.

This tour can also be done in the opposite direction. As a note, if you are driving alone, you might consider driving counterclockwise in order to get the best view out your own window.

Accommodations

Because the locals are so splendid, consider staying at any one of the quaint B&Bs available in Donegal. Having that extra hospitality will mean a lot after a day full of exploration. Additionally, choices range from self-catering lodges to luxury spas.

Donegal Manor

Clar Road, Donegal Town, Co. Donegal
074 972 5222
www.donegalmanor.com
€70–120+ per room; S/D/F. MC/V

Exploring the town of Donegal can be done in a relatively short amount of time. However, staying at the Donegal Manor makes one want to take as long as possible. This exquisite four-star accommodation sits on a lovely estate, yet is easily reachable from Donegal Town. The wonderful service sets this comfortable and spotless hotel apart from all the rest. During the off-season, you will get excellent mid-week rates by contacting them ahead of time with your reservation. The manor has a capacious family room. Overall, this guesthouse offers amazing amenities, including a baby-sitting service. With perfect ratings on reviews, if you are heading to the northern reaches of the Republic, this is a must stay! To locate the manor, take the N15 toward Ballybofey.

Inishduff House

Largymore, Kilcar, Co. Donegal
074 9738 542
www.inishduffhouse.com
€60-100+ per room. S/D/T

If you are heading to the Slieve League Mountains and Cliffs, and searching for a quaint B&B with wonderful service, then the Inishduff House is an ideal choice. With one of the best views overlooking the ocean and the small Inishduff Island, this B&B is located just outside of Killybegs and will delight even the pickiest B&B occupant with its simple yet spotless rooms. Single, double, and even triple rooms are available. Ms. Ethna Diver, the proprietor, can suggest the best sights to see and the best restaurants to try. Getting there can be a tad tricky. Follow the signs through Killybegs, and go up the coastal road R263. You will pass the expensive, yet delicious, Kitty Kelly's restaurant, the affordable, simple Blue Haven restaurant, and eventually come to the Inishduff B&B.

Teac Jack

Gweedore, County Donegal
074 953 1173
www.teacjack.com
€40+ per person. S/D/T/F. MC/V

For those who want a location that puts them close to the Glenveagh National Park, this small hotel is the place. Its simple rooms are comfortable enough and its full Irish breakfast will give you an ample day's energy. Throughout the busy season and on weekends, expect excellent Irish and country live music blaring from the restaurant and pub down below. The locals who frequent this area are talkative and fun-loving. This hotel is great for younger couples, families with teenagers, and the like. Seniors or others searching for deluxe comfort, fine amenities, and anything posh should consider elsewhere. This establishment thrives on its attractions, pub, and local popularity, not necessarily its rooms. It serves as a great stopover, along with tasty bacon cheeseburgers with a pint! To get there, take the R257 west of Gweedore, past Derrybeg.

Frewin House

Ramelton, Co. Donegal

074 915 1246

www.frewinhouse.com

€70–90+, 500€+ weekly cottage. S/D. MC/V

This painstakingly restored Victorian house is a diamond in the rough surrounds that make northern Donegal so attractive. The house sits on wooded grounds near the small town of Ramelton, which sits along the River Lennon. Frewin is located near beaches, golf courses, and wonderful walking areas. The house also has a luxury cottage available for multiday rentals. Do not tell, but the prices are amazing! To get here, take the R245 north from Letterkenny to Ramelton.

Other Accommodations

Here are some other accommodations you might consider while in County Donegal. (In the restaurant listings that follow, € = around 25 euros per person.)

- **€€€ Ballyliffin Lodge and Spa. Ballyliffin.**
  074 937 8985
  www.ballyliffinlodge.com
- **€€€ Harvey's Point County Hotel. Lough Eske, Donegal Town.**
  074 972 2208
  www.harveyspoint.com
- **€€€ Castle Grove County House Hotel. Letterkenny.**
  074 915 1118
  www.castlegrove.com

- **€€€ An Chúirt Gweedore Court Hotel and Earagail Health Club. Gaoth Dobair.**
  074 953 2900
  www.gweedorecourthotel.com
- **€€ Arasaín Bhalor. Falcarragh**
  074 916 2787
  www.arasainbhalor.com
- **€€ Heron's Cove. Ballyshannon.**
  071 982 2070
  www.heronscove.ie
- **€ Errigal Youth Hostel. Dunlewey, Gweedore.**
  074 953 1180
  www.errigalhostel.com

Restaurants and Pubs

In recent years, Ireland has been creating unique fusion cuisine combining recipes of old with modern delicacies. If you think all you will have to eat in Ireland is potatoes, you will be pleasantly surprised. Donegal is one of Ireland's best-kept food havens. It has some of the finest seafood in the entire country; the chowder cannot be beat. (In the restaurant listings that follow, € = around 25 euros per person.)

McGrory's of Culdaff
Culdaff, Inishowen Peninsula
074 937 9104
www.mcgrorys.ie
€€

This hotel, pub, and restaurant serves up some of Donegal's finest cuisine. Not only can you order superior food, but it also has a homey hotel on its upper floors.

Smuggler's Creek

Ballyshannon, Rosnowlagh

071 985 2366

€€€

Overlooking the Rosnowlagh Bay, this seafood restaurant serves the local catch in scrumptious dishes. If you want to splurge on one restaurant in Donegal, this should be the one. Reviews suggest the rooms are not what they once were.

Kealy's Seafood Bar

Greencastle (Harbor)

074 938 1010

€€€

This award-winning restaurant also serves local produce, along with organic vegetables.

Weeping Elm

Rathmullan

074 915 8188

www.rathmullanhouse.com

€€€€

Serving breakfast, lunch, and exquisite gourmet dinners, the Weeping Elm is a restaurant under the Rathmullan House, which is a fine country house in itself. The restaurant, however, serves a unique variety of dishes inspired by the chef. Call ahead for reservations.

Mannies Bar and Restaurant
Convoy, near Donegal Town

€

The welcoming owners and staff of Mannies Bar and Restaurant will make your meal. With live music every week and good ol' pub food to boot, Mannies will take you back in time, all for a great price. The restaurant is twenty-five minutes from Donegal Town on the Convoy Road.

Shopping in County Donegal

Donegal is known for its tweeds, hand-woven sweaters, paintings, and even glass. The Donegal Craft Village, on the Ballyshannon Road outside of Donegal Town, has the largest array of choices available. Most prices are set, but if you are buying more than one item at a local vendor's shop, you might be able to bargain.

Some of the best shopping in Donegal can be had in Ardara; as the handloom weaving capital of Donegal, it is no surprise. The area is widely known for its fine selection of tweeds and hand-knitted products, namely sweaters, scarves, and caps. Larger shops line the main street, while smaller shops can be found throughout the town center and perimeter.

Traveler's Tidbits

Here you will find the necessary information for Donegal. From the location of the post office to the hospital, you are covered. In the following Tourist Office chart, "Seasonal" identifies tourist offices generally open May through September. Tourist offices are generally open during regular business hours.

DONEGAL TOURIST OFFICES

Town	Address	Phone Number	In Operation
Bundoran	The Bridge	071 984 1350	Seasonal
Donegal Town	The Quay	074 972 1148	All year
Dungloe	The Quay	074 952 1297	Seasonal
Inishowen Tourism Society	Cardonagh, Inishowen	074 937 4933	All year
Letterkenny	Neil T. Blaney Rd.	074 912 1160	All year

Following is other pertinent travel information. In the case of an emergency, dial 999 anywhere in the Republic of Ireland.

TRAVEL INFORMATION

Name	Address	Phone Number
Garda (Police) Headquarters	Quay Street	074 972 1021
Donegal Hospital	Upper Main St.	074 972 1019
Donegal Cyber Café	Castle St.	074 972 2933
Donegal Post Office	Tirconnail St.	074 972 1007
Donegal Ancestry	Ramelton, Letterkenny	074 915 1266

Note: See www.donegalancestry.com for more information about genealogical research.

CHAPTER 16

Northern Ireland: Counties Fermanagh, Tyrone, and Derry

Shrouded in myth, legend, and geological phenomena, Northern Ireland offers much in the way of outdoor and family activities. County Fermanagh's lakes are an ever-popular getaway for tourists and Irish alike; a boat ride to its ancient isles makes an unforgettable day out. County Tyrone's main claim to fame is its fun and educational Ulster American Folk Park, while Derry (or Londonderry) is steeped in rugged history. County Antrim boasts the most-visited cliffs at the Giant's Causeway and the fairy-tale Glens of Antrim.

History of Derry/Londonderry

While Northern Ireland is bundled with history, legend, and lore, that of Derry/Londonderry (Daire for "Oak Grove") is one of its most remarkable counties. Saint Columba was the first to settle the place as a cloister, but later exiled himself to Iona in Scotland. As the town began sprouting from the banks of the Foyne River and becoming one of Northern Ireland's most venerable spots, it was quite attractive to marauders.

By the early 1600s, the English under King James I began occupying a greater amount of the territory by ensuring that loyal

Protestants from England and Scotland settled there. As the Irish were pushed to less-desirable corners, their anguish and resentment toward the English crown grew.

Seen as an opportune venture, companies from London invested time, money, and people into constructing a massive wall surrounding the city. The barrier proved useful in the famed 1688 Siege of Derry when the Earl of Antrim surrounded and attempted to capture the fortified town. After bombarding and starving the inhabitants for over three months, he withdrew. It was then that the city earned its nickname, the "Maiden City," in reference to its unbreached ramparts.

 Fact

Both *Derry* and *Londonderry* refer to the county and the main city. Officially, the correct title is Londonderry, but numerous maps, books, tourist office materials, and the Republic of Ireland refer to it as *Derry*. The name game is still an issue and was based originally on political views of Unionists (loyal to the English Crown) and Nationalists (loyal to the Republic of Ireland).

The saddest, yet most decisive, moment in Northern Ireland's history occurred quite recently in the "Bloody Sunday" massacre of 1972. After decades of maltreatment, minority Catholics in the area of Bogside began a peaceful civil rights march. They had no permit to proceed, so a British battalion arrived on the scene. Claiming they were fired upon first by snipers, the British troops fired at the crowd, massacring fourteen. This sparked national and international outcry and more years of strife known as the "Troubles" in Northern Ireland.

Today, Derry is a peaceful place that has its sights set on moving forward. Museums and monuments offer a glimpse into its troubled past.

Getting Around Northern Ireland

Northern Ireland is accessible from various points in the Republic. The most common route traveled in the east is from Dublin to Belfast, while County Derry is easily accessible from Donegal. Derry is 100km (60 miles) from the popular town of Enniskillen and 120km (75 miles) from Belfast. It is 230km (140 miles) from Dublin.

 Question

Where can I see the Murals of Bogside?
The vivid murals along Rossville Street and Lecky Road in Bogside bring Derry's past struggles to life. Accessible from outside the Butcher's Gate in Derry, you will encounter murals designated The *Hunger Strikers*, *The Rioter*, *Operation Motorman*, the *Death of Innocence*, and off of Lecky Road, the *Bloody Sunday* illustration, among others.

Flying

Bypassing Belfast and accessing farther-removed counties in Northern Ireland is possible by flying into the City of Derry Airport (028 7181 0784, *www.cityofderryairport.com*). Aer Arann (*www.aerarann.com*) operates flights throughout Northern Ireland and the Republic. Other cities served outside of Ireland include London, Bristol, Glasgow, and Liverpool by RyanAir (054 156 9569 UK, *www.ryanair.com*) and British Airways (034 522 2111 UK, *www.ba.com*).

Taking a taxi from the airport into Derry city costs about £14 and takes approximately fifteen minutes. Getting to Derry from either of the Belfast airports is feasible with Airporter (028 7126 9996, *www.airporter.co.uk*).

Bus

Operating all throughout Northern Ireland is Ulsterbus (028 7126 2261, *www.translink.co.uk*), which has services to Derry, Omagh, and Enniskellen, among other routes. In Derry, the bus station is on Foyle Street. From here, Ulsterbus's Goldline Bus 212 connects Derry to Belfast in just under two hours, while Bus 274 links to Dublin in four hours.

 Alert

> The currency in Northern Ireland is the pound sterling (£), used in the United Kingdom. The country code for Northern Ireland is 0044 (+44) and the area code is (0)28. The country code plus only "28" is used if calling from outside Northern Ireland's borders. Road signs and speed limits are labeled in miles, so keep an eye on your speedometer.

Train

One of the most convenient ways to get around is on Northern Ireland Railways (028 9089 9411, *www.nirailways.co.uk*). Services join Derry to Portrush, continue southeast to Antrim and over to Belfast and proceed through Lurgan and Portadown to Newry. From Belfast, you can travel south to Dublin's Connolly or Pearse stations. If originating in Dublin, purchase tickets with Irish Rail (01 836 6222 in Republic, *www.irishrail.ie*) to go into Northern Ireland.

Enniskillen, County Fermanagh

Brimming with waterways and canals, a majority of County Fermanagh's sights are along its lakelands, made up of Upper and Lower Lake Erne. Craggy hills cut by glaciers give way to plains and bog land in the surrounding landscape. Among caves, dolomite bluffs, and escarpments, the popular town of Enniskillen (Inis Ceithleann) sits as a literal bridge between land and lake.

For travelers wanting to truly explore the lakelands, Enniskillen makes the perfect base. The town is quaint, the pubs mesmerizing, the locals proud yet humble. The central road in town changes its name no less than six times in its 1.6km (1-mile) stretch.

Following are the best places to check out while in and around Enniskillen.

Enniskillen Castle and Museums

One of the most famed sites about town is Enniskillen Castle and Museums (028 6632 5000, *www.enniskillencastle.co.uk*). Throughout the 1500s and 1600s, the castle changed hands multiple times. The museums are dedicated to the area's history; great memorabilia makes up the Inniskilling Fusiliers Museum (*www.inniskilling.com*), which houses honorary medals, guns, uniforms, and more from various eras, including World War I. Open all year Monday, 2 P.M.– 5 P.M., and Tuesday–Friday, 10 A.M.–5 P.M.; May–September, 2 P.M.–5 P.M. on Saturday; July–August, 2 P.M.–5 P.M. on Sunday. Admission £2/3.

Castle Coole

The coolest Neoclassical castle in Ireland is Castle Coole (028 6632 2690), now under the care of the National Trust (*www .nationaltrust.org.uk*). The mansion has furnishings from the late eighteenth and early nineteenth centuries, accompanied by original portraits, paintings, and the ornate ballroom and brilliant State Bedroom designed for King George IV. Located 2.4km (1.5 miles) outside of Enniskillen off of the A4. Grounds open daily, 10 A.M.– 4 P.M. Castle open 1 P.M.–6 P.M. on Sunday in April and September; daily, 1 P.M.–6 P.M.; and every day except Thursday, 1 P.M.–6 P.M.,

May–August. Also open Easter weekend. Castle admission £2/5, parking £2.

Belleek Pottery

Northwest of Enniskillen and on the upper tip of Lower Lough Erne, the village of Belleek (Beal Leice) would sit picturesque but unpronounced if it were not for its pottery. The porcelain is known as Parian ware for its attempt to match the allure of Ancient Greece's fine, white marble. On location are a visitor center (028 6865 9300, *www.belleek.ie*), restaurant, museum, audiovisual presentation, and showroom. Days and hours of operation vary throughout the year. Closed December 24 to the first Monday in January. Guided visit £2/3/4.

County Tyrone

The largest and most admired county in Northern Ireland, County Tyrone has some worthwhile historical sites and grand hiking opportunities into the Sperrin Mountains. For outdoor activities and local events check out Sperrins Tourism Limited (*www.sperrinstourism.com*). A good point for further exploration is Tyrone's most-populated town of Omagh (An Ómaigh).

 Fact

For history buffs, the Tullaghoge Fort between Stewartstown and Cookstown was the inaugural site of each of the O'Neill kings. The ceremony was solidified with the newly appointed king throwing his shoe over his head, indicating how he would honorably follow in his forefather's footsteps. A throne blessed by Saint Patrick once sat here, but was later destroyed by an envoy of Elizabeth I.

The village of Gortin also makes a fitting starting point for walking in the region, including some of the surrounding Sperrin peaks. Gortin's lakes are in proximity for an afternoon stroll, as is the Gortin Glen Forest Park, just 10km (6 miles) north of Omagh. The An Creagan Visitor Centre (028 8076 1112, *www.an-creagan .com*) allows sightseers to learn more about the area's history, culture, and environment.

Beaghmore Stone Circles

At the An Creagan Visitor Centre, you can also learn about Tyrone's Beaghmore Stone Circles, which are located off of the A505 outside of Cookstown. It was during the cutting, drying, and collecting of peat in the area in the 1940s that locals discovered these now world-famous ruins. Archaeologists believe the site was constructed around 2000 B.C. and was used to keep track of sun and moon patterns. Open daily. Admission free.

Tyrone Crystal

Another good stopping point in Tyrone is Dungannon Town, which was once the throne of the O'Neill bloodline that ruled the area from the eleventh century until the sixteenth. The town is home to one of Ireland's oldest crystal factories known as Tyrone Crystal (028 8772 5335, *www.tyronecrystal.com*). Factory Shop open Monday–Saturday, 9 A.M.–5 P.M. Factory tours: Monday–Friday, 11 A.M., noon, and 2 P.M. Admission £3/5.

Inside Derry's Walls

Much more manageable than Belfast, the city and county of Derry make a nice transitional point from Donegal into Northern Ireland. While signs indicating the movement into another "country" are nonexistent, the change is sensed more than seen.

The best way to see the city is to walk on top of the encompassing wall, which takes less than an hour. Originally, each section of the wall had its own entrance gate. The main entrance points are Magazine Gate, Butcher's Gate, Bishop's Gate, New Gate, Ferryquay Gate, and Shipquay Gate. Walking tours are operated by Derry's Irish Tour Guides (028 7127 1996, *www .irishtourguides.com*).

Following are the most worthwhile sites while walking the Derry Walls.

The Craft Village

This mini-hamlet dubbed the Craft Village (028 7126 0329) was erected to provide an economic stimulus to Derry's center. It was officially opened less than twenty years ago and contains wonderful artisans' boutiques. Open daily.

Tower Museum

Just outside the Craft Village is the Tower Museum (028 7137 2411). The museum hosts a variety of award-winning exhibitions. The most fascinating display is the Armada shipwreck called *La Trinidad Valencera*. Wrecked in the latter 1500s, a scuba club from Donegal discovered the ship in the 1970s. Presented are artifacts including cannons, pottery, wooden utensils, coins, and much more. The museum also hosts the refurbished Story of Derry, where the city's history is recounted with audiovisual presentations. Open July–August, Monday–Saturday, 10 A.M.–5 P.M.; Sunday 2 P.M–5 P.M.; September-June, Tuesday–Saturday, 10 A.M.–5 P.M. Admission £4.

 Fact

The Chapter House of St. Columb's Cathedral has some interesting tidbits from the Siege of Derry, including a hollow cannonball fired into the city containing the terms of surrender by James II. "No surrender" was their famed reply. This powerful phrase has been the Loyalists' slogan ever since.

St. Columb's Cathedral

One of Derry's oldest buildings, St. Columb's Cathedral (028 7126 7313, *www.stcolumbscathedral.org*) was completed in 1633. The central cloister and prominent tower are original, while the spire and chancel were added in the later nineteenth century. Open April–September, Monday–Saturday, 9 A.M.–5 P.M.; October–March, Monday–Saturday, 9 A.M.–1 P.M. and 2 P.M.–4 P.M. Admission £2.

The Glens of County Antrim

Appropriately titled with its stunning valleys and unforgettable coastline, County Antrim's periphery is the stuff of legends. Lush and rolling, nine hollows giving way to the sea make up the plateau between Cushendun and Glenarm, known as the Glens of Antrim (Gleannta Aontroma).

 Essential

> The lofty Torr Head Scenic Road, located just east of Ballycastle, connects to Cushendun. Worthwhile for its scenery, the precarious route travels past Fair Head, approaches Murlough Bay, Torr Head, and Runabay Head. A 5km (3-mile) marked circuitous walk begins at Fair Head, accessible from Coolanlough. Torr Head, which affords views of Scotland on a clear day, has a deserted coastguard station worth exploring.

Along the Glens, Cushendun is the most quaint and picture-perfect seaside hamlet. Spending an afternoon walking one of the coastal walks, or simply enjoying a picnic on its sandy strand, is heavenly.

At the Glens' interior is the village and region of Glenariff, the prettiest of all the valleys. The town gives way to the Glenariff Forest Park (028 2955 6000, *www.forestserviceni.gov.uk*) containing the Waterfall Walkway and the roaring Ess-na-Larach Waterfall, among other less-crowded trails.

Things to See and Do

Keeping busy in these diverse counties will not be an issue. For families or couples, a boat cruise along the lakes of Fermanagh, a visit to the Marble Arch Caves, and a trip to the Ulster American Folk Park could easily take up three days. Following, a trip to the Giant's Causeway and its geological phenomenon will truly show travelers what Northern Ireland has to offer.

Both the Upper and Lower Lough Erne have plenty of sites to see. In the summer, much of the region has a resort feel, although getting off the beaten path is not difficult. The Upper Lough Erne is actually southeast of Lower Lough Erne. Its waters embrace a complex network of 100 islands linked with waterways. This is a fishing and birding paradise (see Chapter 20); grebes, kingfishers, whooper swans, and goldeneye are commonly spotted.

Lower Lough Erne

The Lower Lough Erne is where most visitors spend their time. Starting in Enniskellen and working your way counter-clockwise around the lake is one way to enjoy the sights. The B82, the A47, and the A46 circumnavigate the lake; cycling, walking, driving, or hiring a boat makes an immensely enjoyable journey. The Fermanagh Lakelands website (*www.fermanaghlakelands.com*) amasses various activities and operators in the region.

Cruising the Lower Lough Erne is another good way to see the historical sights. The well-established Erne Tours (028 6632 2882, *www.ernetoursltd.com*) in Enniskellen offers cruises along the lake from May through September; the Saturday evening cruise is followed by a three-course dinner at the Killyhevlin Hotel. Following are the top five things to see en route along the Lower Lough Erne.

Devenish Island

Called the "Ox Island," Devenish Island is a holy island due to the monastic settlement that was established here in the sixth century. Access to the island is possible by hiring a boat or taking a waterbus from Enniskillen.

Castle Archdale Country Park and Castle Caldwell Forest Park

Brimming with walking trails and a few cycling routes, the Castle Archdale County Park (028 6862 1588, *www.ni-environment.gov.uk*) offers bike and boat rentals, pony trekking, and has an informative Countryside Centre explaining the flora and fauna of the region. Encountered later is the Castle Caldwell Forest Park (after Boa Island), which is worth a visit for the Fiddle Stone entrance and bird-watching prospects.

White Island

From the small harbor at the Castle Archdale Country Park, access to White Island is provided on a fifteen-minute ferry ride and departs on the hour. The island is an eye-opening monastic settlement; a twelfth-century chapel holds six Celtic stone figures, most likely from the ninth century. A libidinous *sheela-na-gig* statue is also on site.

Boa Island

Accessible off of the 447, this remote gem holds the creepy Janus Stone (with entwined oval heads) and Lusty Man effigies in the Caldragh Cemetery. The path is signposted off of the bridge on the west side of the isle.

Cliffs of Magho

Along the A46 at the Lough Navar Forest Park (with forest drive) and the Cliffs of Magho are wonderful areas to amble about. Walking to the top edge of the 200-meter (650-feet) limestone plateau is not for the meek, but the views afforded from this perched point are stunning. Continuing onward along the route brings the circuitous journey to a close at Tully Castle on the water's edge and farther along at Monea Castle, which sits inland.

Marble Arch Caves, County Fermanagh

The Marble Arch Caves (028 6634 8855, *www.marblearchcaves .net*) is a UNESCO International Geopark located off the A4 and A32, 5km (3 miles) from the Florence Court Estate. They are one of Europe's most renowned underground networks of rivers, secret bowers, and deep caverns. Open daily, 10:00 A.M.–6:00 P.M. (last tour begins at 4:30 P.M.), mid-March to June and September, and until 6:30 P.M. (last tour begins at 5:00 P.M.) July–August. Advanced bookings highly recommended. Admission £5/5.25/8 or £18 per family.

 Alert

During periods of inclement weather, call before heading out to the Marble Arch Caves to ensure that tours are still running. Prepare yourself for a bit of walking once inside. Wear comfortable hiking shoes or boots and bring a warm sweater or jacket along. The caves are not handicapped accessible.

Ulster American Folk Park, County Tyrone

Located close to Derry in County Tyrone, the Ulster American Folk Park (028 8224 3292, *www.folkpark.com*) opens a timeless door into the former lives of Ulster. The park is dedicated to the inhabitants of the region who left their homelands in the eighteenth and nineteenth centuries. Many of the 300,000-plus individuals who emigrated from these lands ended up in the United States. The Exhibition Hall tells this story and holds some timeless historical pieces as well. Located 10km outside of Omagh on the A5. Open April–September, Monday–Saturday, 10:30 A.M.–6:30 P.M., Sunday, 11:00 A.M.–6:30 P.M.; October–March, Monday–Friday, 10:30 A.M.–5:00 P.M. Admission (including 10 percent charity donation) £3.40/5.40 or £10.80–15.20 per family.

 Fact

The saga behind the mythical formation of the Giant's Causeway truly reveals the Irish gift for storytelling. In short, Ireland's Finn Mac-Cool wanted to battle Scotland's Benandonner. Finn realized just how gargantuan his rival was upon espying him. Finn's wife convinced her hubby to dress as a baby. When Benandonner saw the enormous infant and realized how colossal the father must be, he dashed home.

Giant's Causeway, Co. Antrim

One of the top undertakings in Northern Ireland is a visit to the jaw-dropping UNESCO World Heritage Site known as the Giant's Causeway (028 2073 1855, *www.giantscausewaycentre.com*). Learning about and viewing the geology behind the place is an educational experience like no other: the basaltic columns seen today are the marvelous aftermath of volcanic eruptions over 60 million years ago. Open daily, September–June, 10 A.M.–5 P.M.; July–August, 10 A.M.–6 P.M. Admission free, but car parking is £5. Minibus roundtrip tour £2.

North Antrim Coast, County Antrim

The northern regions of the Antrim coastline stretch from Portstewart to Ballycastle, making up Northern Ireland's most revered and spectacular seaboard. A drive east or west along the A2, the B146, and the B15 will take travelers to the panoramic vistas afforded from the seaside.

 Essential

> The Carrick-a-Rede Rope Bridge (028 2076 9839) in Ballintoy is not for the acrophobic. The rope bridge, 20 meters (66-feet) long and 1-meter (1-yard) wide, hanging over a 23-meter (75-feet) chasm, links the mainland with Carrick-a-Rede Island. Its main use is by salmon fisherman dropping their nets for a catch each spring. Open daily March–October. Admission £2/2.70/3.70.

Beyond the famed surfing town of Portrush, the impressive ruins of the once-mighty Dunluce Castle (028 2073 1938; open daily, admission £2) stands on a stack of black basalt. Dating from the sixteenth century (with towers possibly from the fourteenth), the castle has been in and out of the MacDonnell family's hands for hundreds of years. Built on the literal edge of the cliffside, part of the quarters fell to the sea in the latter 1630s. On the other side of the Giant's Causeway, the scant remains of Dunseverick Castle are not nearly as impressive. The spot is so revered because it was linked to the roads from Tara (see Chapter 7) and was visited by Saint Patrick.

Old Bushmills Distillery

In Bushmills proper, a visit to the Old Bushmills Distillery (028 2073 3218, *www.bushmills.com*) is a potentially inebriating affair. Visitors here will be able to enjoy a firsthand presentation of the distilling process of this world-famous whiskey. Children under eight are allowed on site but cannot partake in the factory tours, offered every half hour. Open November–February: Monday–Friday, 9:30 A.M.–3:30 P.M.; Saturday–Sunday, 12:30–3:30 P.M. March–October: Monday–Saturday, 9:15 A.M.–5:00 P.M.; Sunday, noon–4:00 P.M. Closed from December 23 until after the New Year. Gift shop and restaurant on site. Tour admission £3/5/9.

Accommodations

Eco-friendly cottages top the list for accommodations in Northern Ireland. These lodges set among the Fermanagh Lakelands are a divine getaway, while quaint B&Bs and fine budget accommodations ensure your stay will be both magical and affordable.

Innish Beg Cottages (Eco-Friendly)

Innishbeg, Blaney, Enniskillen, Co. Fermanagh

028 6864 1525

www.innishbegcottages.com

£120–240 weekends, £190–660 weekly. D/F and Groups.

Located amidst Lower Lough Erne, the Innish Beg Cottages are individual eco-friendly cottages that can sleep medium-sized groups. With an on-site Spa and Yoga Centre, visitors can enjoy a day out bird watching, hiking, cycling, fishing, or swimming before returning for some ultimate pampering.

Little Crom Cottages (Eco-Friendly)

29 Clones Rd., Newtownbutler, Co. Fermanagh

028 6773 8074

www.littlecromcottages.com

£175+ weekends, £550 + weekly S/D/F.

With two self-catering and eco-friendly cottages to choose from, the spacious cottages are of simple elegance; a night relaxing next to the wood-burning stove adds to the sylvan and homey appeal of the place.

The Omagh Hostel (Eco-Friendly)

Omagh, Co. Tyrone

028 8224 1973

www.omaghhostel.co.uk

£12.50 bunk or £25–30 single or double room; S/D/T/F.

The first hostel in Northern Ireland to receive the prestigious EU Flower Ecolabel, the Omagh Hostel is setting a standard hard to beat in County Tyrone. Shared and private rooms available.

Stangmore Town House

24 Killyman Rd., Dungannon, Co. Tyrone

028 8772 5600

www.stangmoretownhouse.com

£65–80 per room; S/D.

Well run and well priced, the Stangmore Town House is in the heart of Dungannon. With a restaurant and pub, you can enjoy a night dining on locally inspired meals while chatting with the locals.

Caw Cottage

1 Caw Park, Limavady Rd., Derry

028 7131 3915

www.cawcottage.com

£35–98 per room; S/D.

As advertised, the Caw Cottage is a lovely B&B along the River Foyle. A warm welcome, a hardy breakfast, and local information about what to see and do is guaranteed.

Valley View Country House and B&B

6a Ballyclough Rd., Bushmills, Co. Antrim

028 2074 1608

www.valleyviewbushmills.com

£30–40 + per person; S/D

The Valley View Country House and B&B is a quaint and tranquil establishment only a short drive from Antrim's best sites. The proprietor, Valerie McFall, will share her helpful knowledge of the area. Her rooms are decorated with light colors, have great amenities, steaming showers, televisions, and the best comforters around.

Crockatinney Guest House

80 Whitepark Rd., Ballycastle, Co. Antrim

028 2076 8801

www.crockatinney.ndo.co.uk

www.crockatinneycottages.com

£45–60 per room, S/D/F; £300

self-catering cottage, per three nights.

The Crockatinney Guest House is perfectly situated outside beautiful Ballycastle. Following a harty breakfast, a trip about town and further afield to the Giant's Causeway and the Glens of Antrim make wonderful day trips. The upstairs rooms offer the best views.

Other Accommodations

Some excellent hostel accommodations in Northern Ireland include the following. (In the listings that follow, £ = around 25 pounds per person.)

- **£ The Bridges Hostel. Belmore St., Enniskillen, Co. Fermanagh.**
  028 6634 0110

- £ Residential Centre Hostel. Camphill Rd.,
  Omagh, Co. Tyrone.
  028 8224 0918
- £ Derry City Independent Hostel. 44
  Great James St., Derry.
  028 7137 7989
  www.derry-hostel.co.uk
- £ Causeway Coast Independent Hostel.
  4 Victoria Terrace, Portstewart, County Derry.
  028 7083 3789
- £ Mill Rest Youth Hostel. 49 Main St., Bushmills,
  Co. Antrim.
  028 2073 1222
- £ Whitepark Bay Youth Hostel. 157 Whitepark Rd.,
  Ballinoty, Ballycastle, Co. Antrim.
  028 2073 1745

Restaurants and Pubs

The restaurants of Northern Ireland fare well on the local and
organic scene. And the pubs are every bit as welcoming and
friendly as any in the Republic. (In the restaurant listing that follow,
£ = around 25 pounds per person.)

Oscar's Restaurant and Pub
29 Belmore St., Enniskillen, Co. Fermanagh
028 6632 7037
££

Offering the region's best classic and modern Irish cuisine, seafood, and Italian delights, a trip to Oscar's is a
literal, literary affair. Named for its reverence to Oscar
Wilde, the casual dining experience fused with great

service make it a good and affordable eatery to grab a bite.

Vanilla

Castle St., Omagh, Co. Tyrone
028 8225 7733
££

A wonderful atmosphere and rotating menu, the service is superb and helpful on recommendations. For weekend dinners, consider reserving ahead as the place will not stay a secret for long.

Halo Pantry and Grill

5 Market Street, Derry
028 7127 1567
££

Brimming with natural light and mesmerizing dishes, the Halo Pantry and Grill offers seasonal delights and wonderful sweet courses; chocolates, jams, and more are available for take away. Without exaggeration, the Halo (as locals describe it) is the most favored restaurant in Derry.

The Exchange Restaurant and Wine Bar

Exchange House, Queens Quay, Derry
028 7127 3990
www.exchangerestaurant.com
££

A bustling eatery with energetic staff, The Exchange Restaurant and Wine Bar makes for a fine meal out. The choices of wines are phenomenal, while the food's focus is a savory and stylistic presentation that is definitely worth the wait.

Bushmills Inn Restaurant

9 Dunluce Rd., Bushmills, Co. Antrim

028-2073-3000

www.bushmillsinn.com

$$

Superbly situated close to the Old Bushmills Distillery and a short drive from the Giant's Causeway, the award-winning Bushmills Inn Restaurant was refurbished from seventeenth-century stables and a wine cellar. Featuring a balanced fusion of classic and modern Irish delights, the pan-fried peppered beef filet is stellar, as is a swig of the local malted spirit, Old Bushmills Whiskey.

Traveler's Tidbits

Here you will find the necessary information for Northern Ireland. The best websites to check out information are *www.discovernorthernireland.com*, *www.northantrim.com*, and *www.derryvisitor.com*.

Tourist offices operate during regular business hours.

NORTHERN IRELAND TOURIST OFFICES

Town	Address	Phone Number	In Operation
Derry Tourist Office	44 Foyle St., Derry	028 7126 7284	All year
Omagh Tourist Office	Strule Arts Centre, Townhall Sq., Omagh, Co. Tyrone	028 8224 7831	All year
Enniskillen Tourist Office	Wellington Rd., Enniskillen, Co. Fermanagh	028 6632 3110	All year
Antrim Tourist Office	16 High St., Antrim	028 9442 8331	All year
Ballycastle Tourist Office	7 Mary St., Ballycastle, Co. Antrim	028 2076 2024	All year

Following is other pertinent travel information. In the case of an emergency, dial 112 or 999 anywhere in Northern Ireland. For the police, request the Police Service of Northern Ireland (PSNI).

TRAVEL INFORMATION

Name	Address	Phone Number
Derry Hospital	Glenshane Rd., Derry	028 7134 5171
Central Library	35 Foyle St., Derry	028 7127 2300
Derry Post Office	3 Custom House St., Derry	028 7136 2563
Genealogy Centre	Shipquay St., Derry, County Derry	028 7126 9792 www.irishgenealogy.ie

Belfast Center

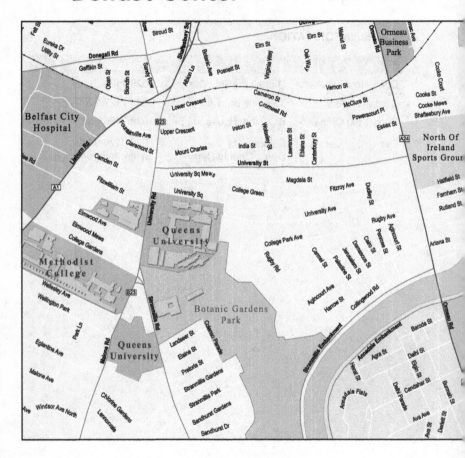

CHAPTER 17

Belfast and Beyond

Perfect for the multifaceted traveler, Belfast, County Down, and County Armagh offer an assorted mélange of activities for both independent and family vacationers. No longer only for the intrepid, Belfast has become a key point of interest for those interested in its whirlwind history. County Armagh and its central city offer splendid scenery and unspoiled Georgian charm. Ultimately, Northern Ireland's sylvan delights are best experienced with a visit to the Mountains of Mourne in County Down.

Getting Around Belfast, Down, and Armagh

Although driving in Belfast's city center can be nightmarish, several parking garages on the outskirts of the metropolitan area offer decent rates making it worthwhile and more convenient to park and hop on a bus. Driving to Belfast from Dublin (170km/105 miles) is easy enough along the N1, and depending on the time of day, takes around two to three hours. County Armagh and its central town of the same name take only an hour from Belfast.

Flying into Belfast

Belfast International Airport (028 9448 4848, *www.belfastairport .com*) is served by British Airways (1 800 403 0882 U.S., *www.ba.com*),

EasyJet (0871 244 2366 UK, *www.easyjet.com*), Aer Lingus (0870 8765000 NI, 1 800 474 7424 U.S., *www.aerlingus.com*), bmibaby (0871 224 0224, *www.bmibaby.com*), Continental Airlines (0129 377 6464, *www.continental.com/uk*), flyglobespan (08705 561 522, *www.flyglobespan.com*), and Jet2 (0871 226 1 737, *www.jet2.com*). The Airport Express bus connects the Belfast International Airport with the Europa Bus Centre. A taxi to the center costs approximately £30.

 Essential

If you are traveling in Ireland or Northern Ireland in the summer months, consider booking your train and bus tickets ahead of time. You will often find excellent deals online, especially in Northern Ireland, with day-passes giving you an opportunity to explore various regions within a twenty-four-hour period. Family passes offer good discounts as well.

The second airport in Belfast is the Belfast City Airport (028 9093 9093, *www.belfastcityairport.com*), which offers flights with Aer Arann (08005872324, *www.aerarann.com*) to Cork. Flybe (0871 700 2000, *www.flybe.com*) has extensive flights in and out of the city and various destinations in England and Scotland. BMI (0870 6070 555, *www.flybmi.com*) connects to London-Heathrow. For flights to and from Derry, check out the City of Derry Airport (028 7181 0784, *www.cityofderryairport.com*). The Airport Express bus from the Belfast City Airport links to the Europa Bus Centre. A taxi costs about £10. Airporter (0 28 71 269996, *www.airporter.co.uk*) links both airports to Derry.

Bus

Connecting to other areas in Northern Ireland or into the Republic can be done with Ulsterbus (028 9066 6630, *www*

.translink.co.uk). Two main bus stations operate in Belfast. The first is the Europe Bus Centre (028 9066 6630; behind the Europa Hotel near the Great Victoria Street Station). It is the point from which buses head to Derry and serve the west and south. The second is the Laganside Bus Centre (with the same phone number as Europa; off of Oxford Street), which has services throughout the day into Country Antrim and County Down, among other districts to the north and east. In Armagh City, the Bus Centre is off of Lonsdale Road and connects to the Europa Bus Centre in Belfast. Access from Armagh to Derry is best done through Dungannon.

Train and Ferry

From Dublin's Connolly Station, you can travel to Belfast's Central Station on Irish Rail (01850 3666 222, *www.irishrail.ie*) or reciprocally on Northern Ireland Railways (028 9024 6485, *www.nirailways.co.uk*). The Central Station thereafter connects to all North Ireland destinations, except for Derry, Larne, Portadown, and Bangor, which are associated with the Great Victoria Street Station (028 9043 4424), adjacent to the Europa Bus Centre.

 Alert

Parking outside of Belfast is recommended and cheaper. Templepatrick is one possible free spot. Following, hop on the Airport Bus 300 (roundtrip tickets are cheaper), which runs directly into the center of the city. Have change available. Don't leave your car in any open or free lots overnight. When in doubt, talk to your accommodation host as to the best method of transportation and parking.

Arriving or departing Belfast and its locality by ferry is also a viable option. Stenaline (028 9074 7747, *www.stenaline.co.uk*) sails to Scotland and elsewhere, as does P&O Ferry (0870 242 4777, *www.poirishsea.com*), and Norfolkline Irish Sea Ferries (0870 600 4321, *www.norfolkline-ferries.co.uk*) travels to England.

Belfast's City Center

Exploring Belfast's city center in a day will allow you to see a majority of the sites. Beyond the surface, this relatively young urban area has an expansive history and culture that is best worth savoring slowly. Belfast City Sightseeing (028 9045 9035, *www .belfastcitysightseeing.com*) offers a hop-on and hop-off busing option. For those with energy to spare, they also offer walking tours. Both types depart from the city center at Castle Place.

The most prominent sites to see in Belfast's city center include:

 Question

Why is the *Titanic* so revered in Belfast?
Belfast became one of the world's foremost shipbuilding yards. The *Titanic* was engineered and constructed here. At its launch in 1912, it was the biggest luxury liner in the world. Proud in their innovation, the sinking of the gargantuan vessel affected a part of the city's soul. More can be learned at the Ulster Folk and Transport Museum.

Belfast Cathedral/St. Anne's Cathedral

The Belfast Cathedral (028 9033 2328, *www.belfastcathedral .org*), also known as St. Anne's Cathedral, off of Donegal Street, is a relatively new marvel. The cornerstones of the expansive foundation were put in place in 1899, but parts of the building are still in the works. Worth seeing are the ten columns in the nave depicting scenes of Belfast and the striking mosaics made of hundreds of thousands of pieces of glass. Open Monday–Friday, 10 A.M.–4 P.M. Donations appreciated.

City Hall

A true indicator of Belfast's speedy rise in the revolutionary world, City Hall (028 9027 0456) is an impressive Renaissance structure of Portland stone, stained glass, granite, and marble. On the outside are statues dedicated to prominent folks, including Queen Victoria, the Marquis of Dufferin (1826–1902), and a memorial to those lost on the *Titanic* voyage. Being renovated and restored, the building is now laid out thematically, including: the History of City Hall, Belfast during World Wars I and II, the *Titanic*, former Lord Mayors, and gifts presented to the city. The lavish interior is best viewed on a guided tour. Call ahead to reserve places. Guided tours Monday–Friday, 11 A.M., 2 P.M., 3 P.M.; Saturday, 2 P.M. and 3 P.M. Admission free.

Grand Opera House

The Grand Opera House (028 9024 1919, *www.goh.co.uk*) is another of Belfast's Victorian gems. Bombed repeatedly over the years, the interior has been refurbished to its original luster. Various shows run throughout the year, so check the website and book in advance if interested. The smaller Baby Grand theater was added in 2006, as was Luciano's café bar and restaurant. Guided tours Wednesday–Saturday, 11 A.M. Admission £3; with lunch, £6/8.

 Fact

Housing contemporary visual arts and overseen by the Arts Council of Northern Ireland, the Ormeau Baths Gallery (028 9032 1402, *www.ormeaubaths.co.uk*) was once a Victorian bathhouse. The well-lit and open-spaced hall is located off of Dublin Road from the city center. It promotes exhibitions by Irish and international artists. An excellent bookshop houses limited-edition titles. Open Tuesday–Saturday, 10:00 A.M.–5:30 P.M. Admission free.

W5

Representing Whowhatwherewhenwhy, the W5 (028 9046 7700, *www.w5Online.co.uk*) is located in the Odyssey Centre. The thematically displayed areas meld art, discovery, and science. From problem solving to animation creation, it is a wonderful place to bring the kids. Days and hours of operation vary throughout the year. Closed December 24–26. Admission £4.90/5.40/6.80, family £20.

County Armagh

Saint Patrick favored County Armagh to become the religious epicenter of Ireland. What was a purely pagan region became the domain of Ireland's first stone church and later a hub of religious learning in Europe. Now it is the ministerial seat of the Anglican and Roman Catholic archbishops of Armagh. Tourists to the region note the rustic beauty of its countryside and the Georgian majestic dignity of its capital.

In town, the Armagh Public Library (028 3752 3142, *www .armaghrobinsonlibrary.org*) houses some impressive books and maps dealing with religion, philosophy, medicine, and travel dating back over 500 years. Coveted is a first edition and signed printing of *Gulliver's Travels*. Open Monday–Friday, 10 A.M.– 4 P.M.

Just off the city center is the Armagh Astronomy Centre and Planetarium (028 3752 3689, *www.armaghplanet.com*), which is worth an hour or two if you have kids along. Located off of College Hill, the Astropark offers a learning center and planetarium, along with a weather station and nature trail. Open Monday–Friday, 2 P.M.–5 P.M. Admission £5/6.

County Down

County Down is one region in Northern Ireland that should not be overlooked. Having much to offer passersby, this lush and fertile region below Belfast is home to the splendid Mourne Mountains and surrounded by charming villages and towns.

Following are a handful of small towns worth exploration in County Down.

Hillsborough

This attractive burb boasts Hillsborough Castle (028 9268 2244), which happens to be a luxurious Georgian mansion and the official residence of the king or queen of England when dropping by Northern Ireland. Additionally, Hillsborough is a haven for oyster lovers; the yearly festival takes place in late August each year.

Banbridge

An additional inviting town is that of Banbridge on the edge of the Bann Valley. Once world famous in the linen textile trade, the town now makes its living from tourists. Only 15km (9 miles) from town in Drumballyroney is the Brontë Interpretative Centre (028 4062 3322), where the father of Emily Brontë (author of *Wuthering Heights*) was an educator.

 Essential

Portaferry and Strangford are connected across the Narrows by the Strangford Ferry (028 4488 1637), which sails daily every half-hour from 7:30 A.M. to 10:30 P.M., starting at 9:30 A.M. on Sunday. Once across, continue along the A2 to explore Greyabbey and the eastern half of Strangford Lough.

Strangford and Strangford Lough

Located near Downpatrick, the petite fishing hamlet of Strangford is known for its seafood and as a waterway to the more bustling, yet lovely, Portaferry. It is also on the fringe of the Lecale

Peninsula and Strangford Lough, with its impressive drumlin islands. The lough itself is teeming with animal and bird life. Travelers here should visit the Castle Espie Wildfowl and Wetland Centre (028 9187 4146) off of Ballydrain Road.

Things to See and Do

The outskirts of Belfast and its two southerly neighboring counties of Armagh and Down have much in the way of things to see and do. Belfast is home to one of the United Kingdom's finest zoos and extravagant botanical gardens. Farther out are country parks, interactive museums, mythic monuments, noble mountains, and adventure centers.

If you will be in Belfast for more than a day or two, the outlying areas of the city have all sorts of recreational diversions to keep you moving. The Belfast Zoo (028 9077 6277, *www .belfastzoo.co.uk*), located off of Antrim Road, has splendid views over the Belfast Lough. Home to well over 1,000 animals in their menagerie, the zoo is a great place to bring the kids. Open daily, April–September, 10 A.M.–7 P.M.; October–March, 10 A.M.–4P.M. Admission £3.40/6.70. Seniors and children under four enter free of charge. Note: Get here two hours before closing for admittance.

On a sunny day, head for the Belfast Botanic Gardens (028 9031 4762), located near the renowned Queen's University. The Botanic Gardens are home to the Palm House, which has an impressive iron and glass conservatory, a stately rose garden, children's play area, and the Tropical Ravine with banana trees and orchids. The grounds play host to a variety of musical presentations. Open daily, 7:30 A.M. until sundown. Admission free.

Last but not least, the Belfast Castle (028 9077 6925, *www .belfastcastle.co.uk*) is a worthwhile stop en route to the Cave Hill Country Park (028 9077 6925), which has recently revamped many of its trails. Castle open year-round, Monday–Saturday,

9:00 A.M.–10:00 P.M.; Sunday, 9:00 A.M.–5:30 P.M. Cave Hill Park open year-round, daily, 7:30 A.M. until sundown. Admission free to both.

Ulster Folk and Transport Museum

Located across the street from one another, the Ulster Folk and Transport Museum (028 9042 8428, *www.uftm.org.uk*) are two fascinating exhibition areas off of Bangor Road. The Ulster Folk Museum is a step back in time with its original mill, farmhouses, schools, print shop, and bank, among other nineteenth-century structures. The nearby Transport Museum is Europe's finest and includes a history of ship and aircraft building in Northern Ireland, along with a permanent exhibit on the *Titanic*. Open October–February: Tuesday–Friday, 10 A.M.–4 P.M.; Saturday–Sunday, 11 A.M.–4 P.M. March–September: Tuesday–Sunday, 10 A.M.–5 A.M. Admission to both museums £3.90/6.80, family £12.70/18.60. Free entrance to children under five.

 Fact

Arguably, the coolest item on display in the Ulster Folk and Transport Museum is a DeLorean DMN replica. The car is a reproduction of the famed auto that was used as the time machine in the *Back to the Future* trilogy. The stainless-steel car was produced in a factory outside of Belfast.

Navan Fort, County Armagh

Just a few kilometers outside of Armagh city is the most prominent historical site in Northern Ireland, Navan Fort (028 3752 5550). Akin to the Hill of Tara in County Meath, this area is shrouded in alluring mystery. Thought to be the high throne of the primeval kings of Ulster and the Knights of the Red Branch, the place is often referred to as *Emain Macha* (Twins of Macha).

Mythically, it is the setting of the battle between Queen Maeve and Cúchulainn. Site open all year round. Navan Visitor Centre open June–August: Monday–Saturday, 10 A.M.–5 P.M.; Sunday, noon–5 P.M. April–May and September: Saturday, 10 A.M.–5 P.M.; Sunday, noon–5 P.M. Admission £3/5.

 Essential

A lot of events are centered on North Ireland's massive Lough Neagh. Accessible from Antrim Town or Oxford Island is the Lough Shore Trail (*www.loughshoretrail.com*) cycle way. For die-hard athletes, it is also home to the Lough Neagh Triathlon (*www.loughneaghtri.com*) in August each year. The lake also offers nature preserves, walking trails, an artificial ski slope, paintball, and canoeing.

Mount Stewart House, County Down

Northern Ireland's most regal mansion and garden combo, Mount Stewart House (028 4278 8387) has become one of the focal points of interest on the Ards Peninsula. The house itself was constructed in the eighteenth century for the Londonderry family, but the real draw is the eminent gardens with its subtropical plants and tree species. Of special note is the Shamrock Garden, with an ornamental shrub designed in the form of a harp, and the Dodo Terrace representing Lady Londonderry's curious social club known as the Ark Club. The Temple of the Winds pavilion sits ashore the lough and was built by the neoclassical architect James Stuart, who was inspired by the similar house of worship (of the same name) in Athens, Greece. House open daily May–September, excluding Tuesdays in May and September; Easter–October, Saturday–Sunday only, noon–6 P.M. Gardens open daily April–October; March, Saturday–Sunday only. Tour of house and gardens costs £3.50/7.00, family £17.50.

Greyabbey Ruins, County Down

Located a few kilometers from the Mount Stewart House and the old-fashioned town of Greyabbey are the Greyabbey Ruins (028 9181 1491). This Cistercian abbey is a pre-Gothic delight founded originally in 1193 by Affreca, the daughter of Godred, the Norse king of the Isle of Man, and her husband, John de Courcy, a Norman knight. It was settled by monks thereafter. Two thirteenth-century effigies mark separate domains; one in the chapel resembles a knight, while the other in the chancel is thought to depict Affreca herself. Guided tours available. Open April–September, Tuesday–Saturday, 9 A.M.–6 P.M., Sunday, 2 P.M.–6 P.M.; October–March, Sunday only, 10 A.M.–4 P.M. Admission free.

Tollymore and Castlewellan Forest Park

Outside of Newcastle and Bryansford off of the B180 is Tollymore Forest Park (028 4372 2428). There are three main trails— Blue, Red, and Black—each with its own highlights. The Blue trail is .7km (.4 miles), the Red is 5.2km (3.2 miles), and the Black is 8.8km (5.5 miles). The red and black offer more in the way of scenery, passing burbling brooks and the foothills of the spectacular Mourne Mountains. A wonderful picnic spot, parking for cars, and camping for recreational vehicles is offered. Park open daily, 10 A.M. until sundown. The visitor centre is located in the central Clanbrassil barn. Open June–August, daily, noon–5 P.M.; September–May, Saturday–Sunday only, noon–5 P.M. Parking is £5.

Nearby Castlewellan Forest Park (028 4377 8664) is centered on the castle grounds. Not nearly as worthwhile as Tollymore for walking or picturesque ruggedness, this parkland does have a lake with trout fishing available. Be sure to investigate the Peace Maze planted in 2000 to symbolize a path to peace for Northern Ireland. Open daily, 10 A.M.–sundown. Admission £2/4.

Tollymore Mountain Centre

Great for the young and old, the Tollymore Mountain Centre (028 4372 2158, *www.tollymore.com*) is west of Bryansford. The indoor activity space claims the wondrous "Hotrock" climbing wall. They promote activities and classes throughout the year, including mountaineering and rock climbing, canoeing, and wilderness first-aid. Dorm-style facilities on site are available. Costs vary.

Mourne Mountains

With walks explained in greater detail in Chapter 19, the Mourne Mountains are the backdrop to the coastal town of New-castle. Overshadowed and undervisited by those speeding north to the Glens of Antrim and the Giant's Causeway, these granite hills are one of North Ireland's best-kept secrets. An area of profound beauty, locals in the area are attempting to ensure the eternal exis-tence of their jewel through the formation of a national park.

Accommodations

Lodges, cottages, and guesthouses abound around Belfast and in its neighboring counties. If flying into the International Belfast Airport, various accommodations are only a bus ride away. If you have a car, consider sleeping in nearby Bangor. Both County Down and Armagh take advantage of their pristine environments to bring you eco-lodges and country houses.

Killead Lodge

25 Killead Rd., Aldergrove, Crumlin, Co. Antrim (Belfast)
028 9445 9896
www.killeadlodge.com
£45–70 per room, S/D/T; Family £75–85

Only five minutes from the airport and about thirty from the center of Belfast, the tranquility and décor of the inside of the Killead Lodge make it a spectacular and restful place to stay. The eastern-Asian motif for the twin-bed rooms are great for the kids, while the Africa suite might work well for the parents. For those flying into Belfast or just passing through, it's the crème de la crème in the area. Breakfasts are taken seriously—seasonal fruit, a full Irish breakfast, cereal, and even peanut butter.

Tara Lodge

36 Cromwell Rd., Belfast
028 9059 0900
www.taralodge.com
£70–85 per room; S/D/T/F. MC/V

This four-star lodge is located within walking distance of excellent restaurants and area pubs. Besides the handsomely decorated rooms, the real draw is the amazing hospitality one receives; the place feels more like a B&B than a small hotel.

Tory Bush Cottages (Eco-Friendly)

79 Tullyree Rd., Bryansford, Newcastle,
Co. Down
028 4372 4348
www.torybush.com
£112+ per two nights; S/D/T/F. MC/V

The proprietor, David Maginn, is paving the way for how tourism in the area will be structured for the next millennium. His luxurious eco-lofts and apartments are just one example of how green building methods and sustainable products can be used to construct, maintain, and power our livelihoods. The walls are insulated using sheep's wool, water is heated with solar panels, central heating is provided via wood pellet boiler, and rainwater takes care of the laundry. They also run Mourne Cycle Tours (*www.mournecycletours.com*) for biking enthusiasts.

Ballydugan Cottages

Ballydugan, Co. Down
028 4461 4151
www.ballydugan.com
£130–310+ per two nights; sleeps 2–7 persons

With good weekly rates, the Ballydugan Cottages are inspired by local dairy farmers Jim and Jeanie Morrison. With obvious artistic talent, the couple has converted the once-derelict cottages into tasteful modern holiday dwellings. Their location could not be better near Downpatrick, with golfing, fishing, horseback riding, and Saint Patrick's burial place.

Dundrum House

116 Dundrum Rd., Tassagh, Co. Armagh
028 3753 1257
www.dundrumhouse.com
£28 per person; S/D/T/F. MC/V

The Dundrum House is an impressive eighteenth-century manor amidst calming, pristine farmland. With rooms and a self-catering cottage available, it is the best-situated lodging in Armagh. Due to its popularity, excellent prices, and wonderful breakfasts, reserve ahead. Children five to eleven are half price, and those four and under are only £5.

Newforge House

58 Newforge Rd., Magheralin, Craigavon, Co., Armagh

028 9261 1255

www.newforgehouse.com

£75–165+ per room; S/D/F

A deserved winner of the Northern Ireland Tourism Award, the Newforge House is a Georgian country house built in the latter 1700s. With six lavish rooms that mix antique charm with magnificent comfort and amenities, they are close to area golf courses, lakes, and various castles. They are unable to accommodate children under ten years old.

Other Accommodations

Here are some other accommodations you might consider while in and around Belfast. (In the listings that follow, £ = around 25 pounds per person.)

- **££ Crescent Townhouse. 13 Lower Crescent, Belfast**
  028 9032 3340
  www.crescenttownhouse.com
- **££ Premier Inn. City Centre, Alfred St., Belfast**
  087 0850 6316
  www.premierinn.com
- **£ Belfast International Hostel. 22-32 Donegall Rd., Belfast**
  028 9031 5435
  www.hihostels.com
- **££ No. "108". Seacliff Road. Bangor, Co. Down (near Belfast).**
  028 9146 1077
  www.bandb-bangor.co.uk

- **££££ Cobbler's Yard. 135 Main St., Dundrum, Co. Down.**
  077 7764 2090
  www.holidaydundrum.com
- **££ Hilltop Lodge B&B. 44 Barrack Hill, Banbridge, Co. Down.**
  028 4062 7240
  www.barrackhill.co.uk
- **££ Fortwilliam Country House. 210 Ballynahinch Rd., Hillsborough, Co. Down.**
  028 9268 2255
  www.fortwilliamcountryhouse.com
- **££ Hillview Lodge. 33 Newtownhamilton Rd., Armagh.**
  028 3752 2000
  www.hillviewlodge.com
- **£ Armagh City Hostel. 39 Abbey St., Armagh**
  028 3751 1800

Restaurants and Pubs

The creative names match the creative dishes in the selection of top-notch restaurants described in Belfast and Counties Armagh and Down. Listings include the world's most-renowned bars and the best restaurants that even keep the locals coming back for more.

Crown Bar Liquor Saloon
46 Great Victoria Street, Belfast
028 9024 3187
www.crownbar.com
£

Looked after by the National Trust, the Crown Bar Liquor Saloon claims to be the most beautiful bar in the world.

Undoubtedly true, the bar's décor is over-the-top Victorian with a hint of Italian, aligned with glass, gold, and mosaic tiling. A well-priced place to grab a pint and pub food, it's open Monday–Saturday, 11:30 A.M.–11:00 P.M., and Sunday, 11:30 A.M.–10 P.M.

The Barking Dog
33-35 Malone Road, Belfast
028 9066 1885
http://barkingdogbelfast.com
££

The Barking Dog restaurant is a recently established gem gaining in local popularity. With exemplary service and inspired cuisine, you will want to reserve on the weekend. And, do not fill up on the scrumptious starters; the main-course servings are a mighty undertaking even for the proficient gourmand.

Shu
253 Lisburn Rd., Belfast
028 9038 1655
www.shu-restaurant.com
££

This world-class restaurant parlor and bar is setting a new precedent for fusion in Belfast. Guests can order à la carte or partake in one of two nightly menu offerings. Savory soups, dressings, and especially the locally renowned Lough Neagh smoked eel are worth every cent.

Seasalt Delicatessen and Bistro

51 Central Promenade, Newcastle, Co. Down
028 4372 5027
www.seasaltnewcastle.co.uk
££

The Seasalt Delicatessen and Bistro is a great lunch stop or makes for a wonderful weekend dinner (served Thurday–Saturday, 7 P.M.–9 P.M.). The menus are oftentimes thematic; reservations necessary.

The Stage Bar-Bistro

Market Place Theatre & Arts Centre, Armagh City
028 3752 1828
www.stonebridgerestaurant.co.uk
££

The Stage is associated with the Stone Bridge Group of restaurants, known for their high quality and stellar customer satisfaction. They carry a light lunch menu from 12:30 P.M. to 2:30 P.M. and à la carte specials after 3:00 P.M. until late evening. Book ahead for weekend meals.

Traveler's Tidbits

Here you will find the necessary information for Belfast and Counties Down and Armagh. The best websites to check out information are *www.belfastcity.gov.uk*, *www.belfast.net*, *www.gotobelfast.com*, *www.ni-environment.gov.uk*, and *www.discovernorthernireland.com*.

In the following Tourist Office chart, "Seasonal" identifies tourist offices generally open May through September. Tourist offices are open during regular business hours.

BELFAST, DOWN, AND ARMAGH TOURIST OFFICES

Town	Address	Phone Number	In Operation
Belfast Welcome Centre	47 Donegall Pl.	028 9024 6609	All year
Belfast Tourist Information	53 Castle St.	028 9026 5500	All year
Armagh Tourist Office	40 English St.	028 3752 1800	All year
Newcastle Tourist Office	10-14 Central Promenade, Co. Down	028 4372 2222	All year

Following is other pertinent travel information. In the case of an emergency, dial 112 or 999 anywhere in Northern Ireland. For the police, request the Police Service of Northern Ireland (PSNI).

TRAVEL INFORMATION

Name	Address	Phone Number
Belfast City Hospital	Lisburn Rd.	028 9032 9241
Armagh Community Hospital	Tower Hill, Armagh City	028 3752 2281
Mourne Hospital	Newry St., Kilkeel, Newry, Co. Down	028 4176 2626
Belfast Post Office	Castle Place	
GoodNews24 Internet	25 Central Frames Shop, Newcastle, Co. Down	028 4372 6886
Northern Ireland Genealogy Resources	*www.n-ireland.co.uk/ pages/Genealogy*	

CHAPTER 18

Playing Golf
in Ireland

G olfers the world over would trade a pot of gold for the chance to play the Emerald Isle's world-renowned courses. Golf and Ireland are synonymous with verdant rolling greens, exquisitely manicured grounds, and impassioning vistas. Ireland boasts over 400 courses, many of which are outstanding. While most fairways are accessible from main cities, others are more off the beaten track. Included here are the most noteworthy links in location and affordability. Only a handful will require a pot of gold for the green fees!

Ireland Golf Tips

Besides the unparalleled scenery and changeable weather, the rules and etiquette of playing golf in Ireland are similar to those in the United States or Canada. While green fees tend to be high across the globe, Ireland attracts golfers of various levels because, in comparison, it is still affordable. Additionally, it is easy to arrange games on various courses as long as it is reserved ahead of time, especially during the peak seasons.

When putting together your vacation plans to Ireland, it is best to first decide what part golf will play in your overall itinerary. Some avid players will base their entire trip on the game, while others will be delighted to tee off anywhere.

As with any itinerary, your route will be affected by budget and the amount of time you have to travel. Oftentimes, a regionally focused golf itinerary proves the best choice, giving you a greater amount of time to enjoy an area rather than hauling your clubs (and perhaps family) around the entire island.

 Fact

When e-mailing or calling up a golf course in Ireland, ask if there are any special considerations. Some require certain attire above the norm, have handicap minimums, or do not allow carts. The less-expensive courses tend to have less-stringent regulations. Moreover, reserving your round midweek will save you the most money.

Keeping your luggage to a minimum (as discussed in Chapter 5) and bringing along a set of golf clubs might seem oxymoronic. On the contrary, while all of the necessary golf items are available in Ireland, if you own them, bring them along. Forgetting any of the essentials (aside from a few items) will be slightly expensive to replace.

Golfers should not forget:

- ✓ Golf clubs
- ✓ Golf bag
- ✓ Protective travel bag cover
- ✓ Golf glove
- ✓ Golf balls and tees
- ✓ Golf shoes
- ✓ Sunglasses
- ✓ Sports rain jacket
- ✓ Sports towel

A protective travel cover will ensure your clubs are securely fastened, protected, and airline compliant. Quality cases enclose the club set in padding and make the case more manageable to carry. Hybrid cases, usually composed of hard plastic, conceal only the top portion of the golf bag; the bottom half of your container will be exposed to the elements of travel.

 Alert

When considering a travel case for your clubs, opt for a fully enclosed carry case if possible. Baggage handlers and conveyor belts are not fabric friendly (even with today's strong nylons), so having a protective layer between equipment and the elements is important. If you travel with secondary clubs, then a hybrid case is the more-affordable option.

For enthusiasts who do not want to bother with bringing their own clubs, renting is an easy alternative. When inquiring about reservations, ask about the rental fee. It might prove cheaper and less burdensome than paying for and carrying the extra weight. You can still bring along certain items such as gloves, glasses, and balls. Rental clubs generally range from €25 to 50 per day.

Weather for Golf

Unless you are lucky enough to have only sunshine on your trip, expect some rain if you will be playing a lot of golf. The Irish will keep on playing through drizzle and even bouts of light fog. During more severe periods, such as summertime thunderstorms, take cover until the inclement weather passes.

Ladies Golf in Ireland

The Irish Ladies Golf Union (*www.ilgu.ie*) lists news, information, and golf events geared for women players. For those interested in watching a game, attend the yearly AIB Ladies Irish Open (*www.aibladiesirishopen.ie*), which is hoping to draw enough crowds and sponsorship to host the prestigious Solheim Cup.

Left-Handed Golfers

Left-handed golfers are well represented in Ireland thanks to the formation of the National Association of Left Handed Golfers (*www.left-handed-golfers.com*). Formed in 1986, the club has been fostering and encouraging left-handed players from both Ireland and abroad. The association hosts a number of tournaments, the most prestigious is the WALG (World Left Handed Golf Championships), among others throughout the year.

Affordable Games Near Dublin

Those wanting to golf Ireland's top courses should expect to pay for the honor. Elite courses offer resort-style, five-star service, rooms, and dining. You will find a majority of Irish locals, however, at the less-expensive venues where the minimum requirement is splendid greens and a good pint to follow. Similarly, with careful planning, tourists can enjoy a round without breaking the bank.

 Alert

As with courses around the world, certain attire is preferred in Ireland. Most male golfers wear polo shirts and trousers, although in the summer tailored golf shorts are sometimes worn. In the latter parts of the year, such as October through April, golfers generally bring along warm sweaters that allow for easy movement.

Some of Ireland's better courses are overshadowed by the big names. A plethora of courses are playable in the range of €40 to 150 per round, while the truly affordable are in the €20–30 range. A fine example is the Deer Park Hotel (*www.deerpark-hotel.ie*) near Dublin in Howth, which advertises similar midweek and weekend rates.

Similarly, in North Dublin, the Corrstown Golf Club (*www.corrstowngolfclub.com*) in Kilsallaghan is an esteemed twenty-seven-hole course with equally appealing prices.

Another affordable course is quite close to the Dublin airport. The Island Golf Club (*www.theislandgolfclub.com*) beats out many in its league. While more expensive than the aforementioned, its greens fees range from €70 in winter to over €135 in the peak months. Its claim to fame is that it was once ranked in *Golf World's* top "must play" courses in the world. An additional course near the airport is the outstanding St. Margaret's Golf and Country Club (*www.stmargaretsgolf.com*), which has well-priced midweek fees starting at €60. Early birds can cut this charge in half Monday through Thursday.

Preeminent Links Around Dublin

Possible to incorporate during your time in Dublin, the areas surrounding the city host some of Ireland's most renowned golf courses. One of those is the famous K Club (*www.kclub.com*) in County Kildare, which has hosted major European competitions including the Ryder Cup and numerous European Opens on its Palmer Ryder Cup Course and the Smurfit European Open Course. The luxury hotel and spa promotes its best package deals online; low-season specials include a one-night stay and rounds on both courses for €235.

Located in County Cavan, the prestigious Slieve Russell Golf and Country Club (*www.slieverussellcavanhotel.com*) is one of Ireland's finest championship courses. Heralded by scores of golfers as the number one golf course in Ireland, the greens shine in the surrounding valley; the spa is a true delight after a round.

The Portmarnock Golf Club (*www.portmarnockgolfclub.ie*) is another of Ireland's most regarded courses, located just 15km (10 miles) north of Dublin's center. Hosting several tournaments and competitions throughout the year, this crème de la crème club has various times and prices dependent upon the number of golfers in a group.

Welcoming visitors all year long, the Druid's Glen (*www .druidsglen.ie*) is no longer one of Dublin's best-kept secrets. The resort-style complex is owned and operated by Marriott Hotel and those staying on the grounds can enjoy green fees starting at €95 for a full round. Visitor's rates start at €150 in the summer months. On hand is the second course, Druid's Heath. A round costs €90 here in the high season and €60 in the low. Check their website for decent bargains.

Gems in Wicklow

Not far from Dublin in County Wicklow is the Woodenbridge Golf Club (*www.woodenbridgegolfclub.com*). Described by many as one of Ireland's premier hidden gems, the course sits huddled in the Vale of Avoca. With a history of great names and players visiting its lulling hills, this course is worth a couple of days' play.

Farther along is the Powerscourt Golf Club (*www.powerscourt .ie/golfclub*) boasting two ultra-pristine golf courses, named the West Course and East Course. Having hosted PGA tournaments and rated in the top parkland courses in the country, a few rounds here is very much worthwhile. Winter specials include lunch or dinner along with a round of golf for as little as €80. Early-bird specials in summer are also well priced.

What was once the playground of England's nobility is now the Coollattin Golf Club (*www.coollattingolfclub.com*) set in the picturesque Wicklow Mountains. With greens fees at €35 midweek and weekend play starting at €45, this humbly alluring course should top anyone's list visiting the southeast.

A club in which Tiger Woods set the record on his first visit is the European Club (*www.theeuropeanclub.com*), a wonderful venue set on the unique sand dunes along the coast of the Irish Sea set near Mizen Head. Winter rates start at €100 and summer rates begin at €180 for one round, or €250 for two. Currently, no caddies are available at this course.

Tour Operators and Itineraries

Using a tour operator to help plan a golf itinerary is advantageous for various reasons. Not only will you save time and possibly money, but also an agency will be able to help accommodate nongolfers by recommending areas that will appeal to the varied interests of the group.

In-country tour operators are generally associated with the Ireland Golf Tour Operators' Association (IGTOA). Those with offices inside or outside of Ireland might belong to any number of other travel conglomerates as well, including the American Society of Travel Agents (ASTA; *www.asta.org*) or the National Tour Association (NTA; *www.ntaonline.com*). The International Association of Golf Tour Operators (IAGTO; *www.iagto.com*) represents agencies around the globe in print and online via their Golf Holiday Search Engine.

Some of the best golf tour operators to Ireland include:

- **Eire Golf Tours** (*www.eiregolftours.com*) promotes trips through both Ireland and Scotland. With their tailored packages, they can take the hassle out of arranging your own trip and get you excellent rates on golf and accommodations all around the country.
- **Ireland Golf** (*www.irelandgolf.com*) offers custom tours of some of Ireland's most renowned courses. They have a

variety of well-priced regional itineraries outlined on their website. Packages include hotels and transfers.

- **Golf Vacations Ireland** (*www.golfvacationsireland.com*) is another in-country quality agency with an online "Plan your Tour" feature that gives you accurate quotes on customized itineraries.

- **JD Golf Tours** (*www.jdgolf.ie*) is a premier inbound tour agency located in the Shannon region that helps set up tee times for individuals, couples, and larger groups. They can help you take care of accommodations, transport, and help you select the best courses that fit your desires.

- **Irish Links Tours and Travel** (*www.irish-links.com*) is unsurpassed for their personal and professional services, promoting various travel incentives online. They do a nice job of gearing tours for golfers traveling with companions who do not play the game.

- **The Wide World of Golf** (*www.wideworldofgolf.com*) offers trips throughout the globe and has a variety of options available on the Emerald Isle.

Ireland's Fore!-most Golf Courses

For those of you with less time to browse all the courses in Ireland, focus on the ones that come highly recommended here. Separated by region, each course has a small description with midweek summer green fees listed. Some of the courses described are reasonably famous, while others are less known.

According to golf enthusiasts and various polls, Ireland's top ten courses are:

1. Old Head Golf Links
2. Mount Juliet Golf Course
3. Ballyliffin's Glashedy Course
4. Lahinch Golf Club

5. The Island Golf Club
6. Killarney Golf and Fishing Club
7. Druids Glen
8. The K Club
9. Royal County Down Golf Club
10. Slieve Russell Golf and Country Club

If you are heading up into Northern Ireland, play some of the wonderful, yet slightly more expensive, courses there. (Remember, Northern Ireland uses the pound sterling.) One great choice is the Royal County Down (*www.royalcountydown.org*) near Newcastle. Perched on the sea with a backdrop of the Mourne Mountain's Slieve Donard, the championship course will set you back £75 in the low season and a whopping £160 midweek in the peak season. The place has a noteworthy history, but it is overpriced for the average golfer. The club also offers a more-affordable option at the Annesley Links with fees ranging £30–40.

Moving up along the Antrim Coast, the Royal Portrush Golf Club (*www.royalportrushgolfclub.com*) hosts the prestigious Dunluce Links and Valley Links courses. Dunluce will set you back £125 midweek, while Valley Links begins at £35. In County Derry, the Portstewart Golf Club (*www.portstewartgc.co.uk*) is of equal stature, offering three full-length courses. The most extraordinary of these is the Strand, which is a par-72 with low-season rates starting at £40 and summer midweek rates starting at £80. County Armagh's Portadown Golf Club (*www.portadowngolfclub.co.uk*) sits among orchards and is a good value starting at £30.

The Sunny Southeast

The southeast is Ireland's sunniest location. In the winter months, the splendid courses here will mean less chance of rain. In the summer, the area offers amazing beaches and sightseeing to appeal to golfers and nongolfers alike. In County Wexford, St. Helen's Bay Golf Club (*www.sthelensbay.com*) appears at the top of any avid golfers to-hit list. Midweek peak-season rates start at €45. Purchasing a Wexford Coastal Golf Pass for €125 will allow you to play three panoramic greens, including Rosslare Golf Club (*www.rosslaregolf.com*) and Seafield Golf Club (*www.seafieldgolf.com*).

In County Waterford, the Dunmore East Golf Club (*www.dunmoreeastgolfclub.ie*) is the region's premier parkland and golf arena, with impressive seaside vistas overlooking Hook Peninsula and the harbor. Not far away is the Mount Juliet Golf Course (*www.mountjuliet.ie/golf*) in Kilkenny. A premier getaway and golfer's haven, the fantastic layout was envisioned by none other than Jack Nicklaus. The course has won various awards and was named the best parkland golf course by *Backspin Golf Magazine*. Fees start at €100 midweek.

Courses in Cork and Kerry

For removed splendor and unparalled scenery, Counties Cork and Kerry offer some of Ireland's premier ranges. The region is renowned for its courses designed purposely to inspire with a backdrop of mountains and seascapes. With nearly fifty courses, the southwest is Ireland's most popular and premier golf destination.

County Cork has an amazing array of venues. Close to the city is the Cork Golf Club (*www.corkgolfclub.ie*). Fees start at €85 midweek with early-bird fees as low as €50. Weekends can get crowded, so book ahead. The fine clubhouse has a strict dress code, so if you want to enjoy the course's full amenities, bring pristinely pressed smart-casual attire.

In Clash, Little Island, outside of town is the formidable Harbour Point Golf Club (021 435 3094) with excellent midweek green fees starting at €37. For those profiting from time in the country's prettiest harbor town of Kinsale, the wildlife-friendly Old Head Golf Links (*www.oldhead.com*) is said to be Tiger Woods's favorite spot to play in all of Ireland. Bring your pot of gold to play; fees start at €295. The caddies are arguably some of the best in Europe.

Made ever popular as a practice range by visiting superstar Tiger Woods, the Waterville Golf Links (*www.watervillegolflinks.ie*) is one of Ireland's premier championship courses and deserves its ranking as one of the most-coveted courses to play in the world. Green fees start at €180 and they offer accommodations at the Waterville House; guests (and Tiger) receive preferential tee times.

The aptly titled Blarney Golf Resort (*www.blarneygolfresort.com*) in the Shournagh Valley offers a lovely eighteen-hole, par-71 course that was codesigned by John Daly. An on-site health spa, fairly priced luxury accommodations, and Lion's Den Bar are highlights best enjoyed after an enthralling day at the links. Contact the resort for various specials throughout the year.

County Kerry's Highlights

The otherworldly Dingle Peninsula is home to the equally alluring Dingle Golf Links (Ceann Sibéal; *www.dinglelinks.com*), which is an outstanding course overlooking the Blasket Islands and Atlantic Ocean. This often uncrowded golf course's noteworthy claim is its location; it is Europe's most westerly point to play the game!

Also in County Kerry, the Ballybunion Golf Club (*www.ballbuniongolfclub.ie*) hosts two courses, the famous Old Course and the rising star, the Cashen Course. Hosting various tourneys, this club has an interesting history with visitors such as Jack Nicklaus, Nick Faldo, Pat Bradley, and Cindy Rarick. The Cashen Course starts at €110, but combined tickets for the "Two-Course Experience" start at €265.

Golf legends the world over have gone into raptures about the Killarney Golf and Fishing Club (*www.killarney-golf.com*), which boasts three championship golf courses designated Mahony's Point, Lackabane, and Killeen. Each of the three offers its own crowning moments; the most challenging course is Killeen, with tight fairways and obstacles at every swing.

Fact

The Kerry Shamrock Golf Pass allows players to purchase three games on three of Kerry's most stunning courses. The ever-popular Killarney Golf and Fishing Club, Dingle Golf Links, and Dooks Golf Links in Glenbeigh are all a part of this promotion. Ask about the Shamrock Golf Pass when you call or frequent the pro shop at any of these participating courses.

Located on the edge of Kerry's central city, the Tralee Golf Club (*www.traleegolfclub.com*) is another of Arnold Palmer's gems. Fees start out at €180 per round; often two-for-one and husband-wife deals are promoted on their website. Also in northern Kerry, the Listowel Golf Club (068 21 592) was christened in the mid-1990s. The course is adorned with a forest and river running through its middle. This parkland course has excellent green fees starting at €20 per round.

One golf pass that continues to be on offer for €125 is the Cork Kerry International Golf Challenge Pass, which allows tee times at three grand courses. This pass is available at the Ring of Kerry Golf and Country Club (*www.ringofkerrygolf.com*), the Kenmare Golf Club (*www.kenmaregolfclub.com*), and the Lee Valley Golf and Country Club (*www.leevalleygcc.ie*).

The West and Northwest

The starkly beautiful Shannon and northwest sections of Ireland offer stupendous links situated among undulating hills, sublime sea cliffs, and Gaeltacht charm. This rather large region will truly appeal to golfers searching for distinctive play with unrivaled beauty.

One of the most popular names and courses in the region is the Lahinch Golf Club (*www.lahinchgolf.com*), which has two sets of links in the Old Course and the Castle Course. Located less than one hour from the Shannon Airport and positioned along the Atlantic coastline; the most favored shot is the fifth, which calls for strategic play over a sand dune. Old Course rates start at €165, while the Caste Course starts at €55.

The Adare Golf Resort (*www.adaregolfclub.com*) in County Limerick is the area's premier championship golf destination. Owned and operated by the adorned Adare Manor (*www.adaremanor.com*), the course is a stretch of the Shannon region's most pristine scenery. Inviting packages include a round of golf and a night's accommodations starting at €190.

A more affordable option in Shannon is the Woodstock Golf and Country Club (*www.woodstockgolfclub.com*), situated outside of Ennis. This parkland course has midweek rates around €50 and a friendly atmosphere to boot. Another parkland course of equal caliber is the Ennis Golf Club (*www.ennisgolfclub.com*), with superbly priced green fees set at €35 through the week and €40 on weekends.

Travelers spending time in Galway will want to check out the Galway Bay Golf and Country Club (*www.galwaybaygolfresort .com*). Exposed to the sweeping winds from the Atlantic, this PGA championship course is playable for €100 midweek and offers some of the west's most challenging barriers this far from Dublin! Another is the nearby Galway Golf Club (*www.galwaygolf.com*), located along the bayside it offers ocean views and is only a few minutes drive outside the city center in the burb of Salthill. Green fees start at €50.

The Connemara Championship Links (095 23 502) has exceptional midweek rates starting at €65. Designed by Eddie Hackett and Tom Craddock, the breathtaking course is superimposed with the sepia backdrop of the Twelve Ben peaks.

A Historical Gem: County Sligo Golf Club

Moving north, one of the region's most splendid courses is the County Sligo Golf Club (*www.countysligogolfclub.ie*). Positioned on the inspirational Rosses Point, this course might be Ireland's most historically significant for its connection to Yeats Country; the original land was rented by the uncle of Jack and W. B. Yeats. Originally their uncle did not want to renew the one-year lease but succumbed to one persistent member named James Campbell who offered a ten-year plan and made the uncle an honorary associate. With the prominent Benbulben in the foreground and mount Knocknarea just behind, the regular green fee of €75 is not too much to ask.

 Fact

While searching for golf courses in the west and northwest of Ireland, one handy resource is the North and West Coast Links (*www .northandwestcoastlinks.com*) association. They promote and offer a varied selection of golf passes, packages, and reasonable rates on accommodations. With twelve championship links represented, bargains and up-to-date information are their forte.

Golfer's Retreat: County Donegal

Any traveler heading off the beaten path will do well here; golfers will revel in the unvarnished allure of this truly removed corner of Ireland. The Rosapenna Golf Resort (*www.rosapenna .ie*) is one fine example of two adjacent courses that beckon play. The first is the legendary Old Tom Morris Club. Sitting next to it is the Sandy Hill Links, designed and detailed by the acclaimed Pat Ruddy. A bargain for those staying at the resort, a round is fixed at €30.

For the truly removed, a visit to the twin courses at the Ballyliffin Golf Club (*www.ballyliffingolfclub.com*) on the Inishowen Peninsula and overlooking the Pollan Bay is a delight not found elsewhere. Green fees to the Old Links course and the Glashedy Links are similar, commencing with peak midweek rates at €75. Play-and-stay packages are worthwhile; the clubhouse holds true to Irish hospitality with wonderful *craic* and a great pint!

CHAPTER 19

Walking in
Ireland

Walking has only recently become Ireland's national pastime. In the late 1970s and throughout the 1980s, word spread about the verdurous thoroughfares and coastal walks awaiting discovery. Once the Celtic Tiger roared, the citizenry of Dublin began looking for a way to escape the busy pace of their new lifestyles. The result was the first of many national trails, the 130km (80-mile) Wicklow Way. Taking time to walk this or any of the other marked paths takes you into the Emerald Isle's true soul.

Essentials of Walking in Ireland

As the popularity in walking increased, so did the network of "National Waymarked Way" paths throughout the Republic. Over thirty-two of these trails are currently registered with the National Waymarked Ways Advisory Committee (NWWAC; 01 860 8823, *www.walkireland.ie*). This and Mountain Views (*www.mountainviews.ie*) are great resources to discover all that is available.

As a warning, even with their popularity, numerous national trails are inadequately signposted. Markers are often far apart and may not appear in some of the more crucial areas. Maps are necessary for trails outside of the smaller parks (such as Lough Key Forest Park in Roscommon or Tollymore Forest Park in County Down).

Even longer coastal jaunts, which one would assume easier to navigate, should be walked with a map in hand.

Walking and Hiking Maps

The most readily available maps for sale in tourist offices are Discovery Series Ordnance Survey Ireland 1:50,000 (1¼ inch = 1 mile) maps. The Ordnance Survey Service (01 802 5300, *www.osi.ie*) is located in Phoenix Park, Dublin 8.

 Essential

The Irish do not use the word *hiking* in their everyday language. They are more apt to call it *walking*. A *walk* in Ireland is actually what we would call a light or moderate hike. They will also use the word *ramble*, which could be described as an off-trail trek.

These maps are referred to by different acronyms. For this guide's purposes, they are "OS Map," plus a number. For example, OS Map #10 covers the western coastal edge of Donegal Bay. A total of eighty-nine maps costing €8–15 each cover Ireland's entirety.

Maps are also available for the Republic from East West Mapping (053 937 7835, *www.eastwestmapping.ie*). The Ordnance Survey of Northern Ireland (028 9025 5755, *www.ordnancesurvey.co.uk*) provides maps for all of their six counties, located at Colby House in Belfast.

Being Prepared to Walk

Because much of Ireland is readily exposed to the elements, inclement weather can move in quickly. A sunny day can become rainy or foggy within minutes, so be prepared. Hiking with a buddy is best to ensure safety, even on one-day outings. Before you head out, leave a folded note with your name and a contact phone number in your car describing your planned route. Also, make sure to tell your hotel staff what path you will be taking.

Here is a list of suggested items to bring along:

✓ OS Map
✓ Regular compass
✓ GPS (optional)
✓ Rain/wind gear
✓ Comfortable, waterproof hiking boots
✓ Fully charged mobile phone
✓ Whistle
✓ Hiking poles (optional)
✓ Suitable sleeping bag
✓ Waterproof matches and fire-starting cubes
✓ Water purifier tablets and backup food

For active travelers seeking daylong excursions, consider purchasing *Best Irish Walks*, edited by Joss Lynam, available in various tourist offices and from online book vendors.

 Alert

Do not expect tourist offices in each area to have all the maps available. Popular ones sell out fast. Attempt to purchase OS maps before leaving Dublin, or the nearest big city, which will offer the widest selection at the best price. Outdoor and bookshops often sell them. Occasionally, waterproof versions are available.

Walking and Trekking
Tour Operators

Each year a slew of companies offer walking excursions through-out Ireland. For trekkers seeking multiday trips, or the lone traveler wanting to meet up with others, a guided hiking holiday might make sense. Booking a hiking holiday often means that several facets of travel planning are taken care of, including accommodations, some meals, transportation, certain gear, and a guide.

Tour operators offer both set-date and/or customizable itineraries that are flexible to your needs and dates. The tours may or may not be guided. Self-guided trips mean that in-country transport, accommodations, and even a map with itinerary might be arranged, but that you will have your own adventure navigating the terrain.

Some excellent walking and adventure tour operators in Ireland include:

- **Go Visit Ireland** (066 976 2094, 1 800 721 4672 U.S., *www .govisitireland.com*) offers a range of walking and cycling tours, among other cultural adventures. Impressive are their helpful staff, informative website, and value.
- **Boundless Journeys** (1 800 941 8010 U.S., *www .boundlessjourneys.com*) offers set-date tours in the Shannon region, including Killarney National Park and the Burren. Accommodations are reserved in first-rate hotels and inns.
- **South West Walks Ireland** (066 712 8733, *www.southwest walksireland.com*) is a local Irish team putting together stellar walks all over Ireland. They offer customizable packages for guided or self-guided excursions.
- **Hidden Trails** (1 888 987 2457 U.S., *www.hiddentrails.com*) offer numerous well-priced walking excursions with fully

detailed itineraries. Guided and self-guided journeys are offered.

- **Wanderlust** (027 63 609, *www.wanderlust.ie*) offers regular and Nordic walking excursions in Glengarriff and in the Beara, Sheep's Head, and Mizen peninsulas of County Cork.

- **Hidden Ireland Tours** (087 221 4002 or 1 251 478 7519, *www .hiddenirelandtours.com*) promote several alluring walking tours throughout Kerry, Cork, Connemara, and Donegal, among other regions. This friendly bunch will help you personalize a perfect itinerary.

- **Tailormade Tours Ltd**. (066 976 6007, *www.tailor-madetours. com*) is located in the Dingle Peninsula and offers long-distance walks following Ireland's National Waymarked Ways. They provide a wide variety of well-established itineraries with attention to detail.

The Best Hikes near Dublin

Getting out into the great outdoors from Dublin is not all that difficult. While having your own car facilitates traveling from one spot to the next, nearby counties such as Wicklow are easily accessible on local buses. County Wicklow is home to the Wicklow National Park, iconic Glendalough, Powerscourt Waterfall, and other mesmerizing sights. The best hikes near Dublin in County Wicklow are:

Glendalough Valley

The Glendalough Valley (see Chapter 8) contains some of the best easy walking in East Ireland. The trails are well marked in color and do not require a compass. Maps can be purchased from the on-site visitor center and the views afforded from the Lugduff Mountain overlooking the An Spinc are worth the sweat.

Wicklow Way

Not only was the Wicklow Way (*www.wicklowway.com*) Ireland's first National Waymarked Way, it is also one of Ireland's top-rated routes. Typically walked north to south, the 130km (80-mile) path departs from south Dublin at Marlay Park and ends at Clonegal in County Carlow. The hardest part of the journey takes place through the Wicklow Mountains, while the easiest section is from Tinahely to Shillelagh and into Clonegal.

Numerous hikers opt to hike small sections of the Wicklow Way. The entire route can last eight to twelve nights. Staying in B&Bs throughout the journey is the best option. The average hiking time per day is five to eight hours, covering 12km (7.5 miles) to 22km (13.6 miles), with a total ascent of 3200 meters (10,500 feet). More information, maps, and reference material is available at the Dublin Tourist Offices.

 Essential

On the Wicklow Way, going to Glenmacnass and to the top of the popular 925-meter (3,035-feet) peak of Lugnaquilla, commonly called Lug, is an optional side trip. Other worthwhile sights in Wicklow include Devil's Glenn, which has a Sculpture Trail, the steep Djouce Mountain, and Luggala, known as "Fancy Mountain," with views of the white and sandy beach of Lough Tay.

St. Kevin's Way

An easier and shorter route than the full Wicklow Way, St. Kevin's Way (*www.visitwicklow.ie*) is a pilgrimage route from Hollywood to Glendalough. Not impossible to do in one summer's day, the 30km (18-mile) route traverses forests, mountains, and back roads. OS Map #56 details the area in full.

Waymarked Ways
in the Southwest

With several Waymarked Ways throughout Ireland, a handful are a cut above the rest for their scenery, time off the beaten path, and accessibility. For East Ireland, the Wicklow Way is unbeatable. For the coastal midwest, the 35km (22-mile) Burren Way is a gem for its moonlike terrain and surprising amount of flora and fauna.

The best national routes in Southwest Ireland are in County Cork and Kerry.

 Alert

> Thorough research will ensure that you have a place to stay and a hot plate of food each night. Physically preparing for your journey is important, as none of the trails are for complete amateur walkers. For mountain rescue, trekkers should dial 999 and state their position as accurately as possible. Additionally, check the weather forecast before each day out.

Planning a walk on one of these national routes should be done carefully. Camping along the routes is discouraged unless absolutely necessary and doing so in national forests is illegal. If you and your walking partner find yourself in a predicament, assess the situation and attempt to find a local resident who can point you in the right direction or give you permission to camp. Bring a light tarp with ropes or tent, along with the supplies mentioned in the packing list.

Ireland's countryside is fairly open to walkers, especially on marked or national trails. If you encounter an issue with a farmer, another local, or a sign or other physical barrier on a trail, contact the local tourist office to find out the best way to continue. If rambling about, seek the permission of a local or farmer if you believe you are walking on private land. Never leave trash on the trails or surrounding lands. Always leave farm gates the way you found them (usually closed). Ireland's best southwest Waymarked Ways are:

Sheep's Head Way, County Clare

While County Kerry might overshadow others in the southwest for various outdoor pursuits, County Cork beats Kerry in regards to its hidden hiking and trail walking opportunities. The 90km (55-mile) Sheep's Head Way is a great introduction into southwestern Ireland's diverse landscapes. The trail offers astonishing cliffs and onerous terrain overlooking the Dunmanus Bay to the south and Bantry Bay to the north.

Beara Way, Counties Cork and Kerry

The Beara Way (*www.bearatourism.com*) is one of Ireland's easier (and less crowded) national trails. The 196km (122-mile) path circumnavigates the wondrous Beara Peninsula. It is not a wooded or hill walk, per se, but does cross over back roads and decently marked paths through fields and hills of not more than 300 meters (985 feet). Recommended is the inclusion of the Bere Island (*www.bereisland.net*) and Dursey Islands, but this will add on an extra day or two to the total itinerary. Most walkers plan for five to seven days to complete the full path from Castletownbere to Kenmare.

Dingle Way, County Kerry

Surpassing the grandeur of the Ring of Kerry, the Dingle Way (*www.dingleway.net*) is Kerry's most astounding walk. Passing beaches, back roads, mountains, and moorland, the 168km (104-mile) loop is an eight- to ten-day journey, officially starting and ending in the city of Tralee. The tourist office and local guides, however, recommend starting the journey in the town of Camp, which is more scenic and can be accessed on a bus from Tralee. This shortens the hike by one to two days.

Donegal:
Hidden Walking Country

The endless hiking opportunities available in Donegal warrant their own book, but an overview will at least highlight some of the county's best possibilities. Whether the remote allure of the Blue Stack Mountains beckons, cliff ridge walks of Slieve League, or the readily marked paths of Glenveagh National Park, Donegal has one-way routes, various combined circuits, and loops to please even the most active and outdoorsy. Some of Donegal's more challenging hikes are:

The Blue Stack Way
Requiring some preplanning, the 20km (12-mile) Blue Stack Way is a hill walker's dream. The serpentine loop is a six- to eight-hour journey through Donegal's most pristine, yet jagged, countryside. Only prepared and fit hikers with maps should attempt the several 625-meter (2050-feet) mountain peaks that comprise this trail. The starting point of the trail is Edergole, accessible on the roads to Lough Eske from Donegal Town.

Bealach na Gaeltachta
Hard to pronounce and difficult to do, this trail is actually a combination of four trails found around Donegal. Totaling 290km (180 miles) of rural landscapes, small towns, and peninsulas, these routes were established by the National Waymarked Way of the Donegal County Council. The walks are Slí an Earagail near Bunbeg, Slí na Finne near Fintown, Slí na Rossan close to Crohy Head, and Slí Cholmcille intersecting Glencolmcille, Carrick, Killybegs, and Ardara. Topographical maps and walking

Ireland guides are sold at the Discover Ireland Centre in Donegal Town.

Derryveagh Mountains

Accessible from Glenveagh National Park, the Derryveagh Mountains provide both hikers and onlookers an impressive view of Donegal's highest peak, the quartzite (and therefore reflective) Mount Errigal (Aireagal). The mountain beckons trekkers who yearn for the prize of a view over the entire Rosses country. The easiest route starts off the R251 at the car park. Obtain topographical OS Map #1, which details the area. The preferred route for walkers is outlined on a map at the car park. Longer routes are available that include starting out by climbing Mackoght, known erroneously as "Little Errigal," which sits beside its bigger brother.

OTHER DONEGAL HIKES

Route	Starting Point	Distance	Grade
Tower Loop	St. Columba's Church, Glencolmcille	4.6 miles	Moderate
Tory Island Loop	Tory Island	5 miles	Easy
Inishowen Head Loop	R241, Greencastle	5 miles	Moderate
Creevy Shore Walk	Rossnowlagh	6 miles	Easy/Moderate

Slieve League Mountains to One Man's Pass

The Slieve League (Sliabh Liag) cliffs easily compete with the more-popular Giant's Causeway in Northern Ireland in both sublimity and grandeur. Located on the southwest coast of Donegal (OS Map #10, available in Killybegs or Kilcar), a clear day walking here is divine. With views of the Atlantic Ocean, the not-so-distant mountains of Sligo, and the calming Donegal Bay, it's a purely placid picture.

You do not have to hike the area to enjoy the Slieve League's serenity. You can park at one of the two parking lots available at the cliff top. Heed caution if driving to the second car park, as a one-lane path and hills make it difficult to see oncoming traffic and walkers. A light honk will let others know you are coming.

Hiking one-way from the Slieve League parking lot through Eagles Nest and onward to One Man's Pass will take roughly two to three hours. One Man's Pass refers to a section of the Slieve League cliffside where the terrain slopes down on both sides. From here, the pinnacle point of the 595-meter (1952-feet) Slieve League Mountain is not far off.

 Alert

Walking over One Man's Pass is not as dangerous as it sounds. Strong winds are eternally present, but the path itself is well over 1 meter (1 yard) wide. If inclement weather inhibits your view of the other side of the pass, it is advisable to turn around and go back from the ridge trail where you started.

Walks in Northern Ireland

The most spectacular routes in Northern Ireland are along its northern and southeastern coasts. The most dramatic and visited landscape in the north is that surrounding the Giant's Causeway in County Antrim. Farther south and west of Newcastle, the Mourne Mountains are a trove yet undiscovered by swarms of hikers.

The best hiking in Northern Ireland is found in the Glens of Antrim and along the Giant's Causeway coastline. For a full list of various walks and excursions in the region, visit the superb Walk North Ireland (*www.walkni.com*) site that labels "Quality Walks" throughout all the counties.

Walking the Giant's Causeway, County Antrim

For those who want to explore the most stunning coast of Northern Ireland, this walk is startlingly diverse and offers great solitude during off-peak seasons. The walk itself can start or end at the Giant's Causeway, a UNESCO Heritage Site, or farther down the road at one of the parking lots en route.

 Fact

> The longest trail in Ireland, which actually begins in Donegal and connects all the six counties of Northern Ireland is the 870km (540-mile) Ulsterway. For the long-term adventurer, the total trail takes five to six weeks. The trail was totally revamped with new signage in 2009; certain signs had supposedly led trekkers into some boggy areas before the overhaul.

A clear morning is an advantageous time to start walking. If, however, you begin in the afternoon, start at the Visitor Centre (028 2073 1855, *www.giantscausewaycentre.com*) in order to have the best light hitting the cliffs.

The full Giant's Causeway walking route is 53km (33 miles) and connects Portstewart to Ballycastle. The most-inspiring portion, however, is the 17km (11-mile) path between Carrick-a-Rede and the Giant's Causeway, which can be completed in one day in five to seven hours. The trek is best begun at Carrick-a-Rede, where a car park is available. It can also be completed in reverse, starting at the Giant's Causeway Visitor Centre. Bring plenty of sterling to pay for the pricey £8–10 cost of parking.

The top of the cliff in Carrick-a-Rede intersects the trail and heads to Ballintoy Church. From here, turn right to the harbor where you will carefully walk over the limestone precipice until reaching White Park Bay beach. Here the trail subsides and walking on the beach is best at low tide. Toward the end of the beach, the White Park Bay Youth Hostel (028 2073 1745, *www.hini.org.uk/hostels/whitepark.cfm*) sits atop the hill with the best sea view around. Starting a hike from here is also possible, but parking is reserved for guests only. If it happens to be high tide, walk the road from the hostel to the next destination, Portbradden.

Bedazzling Portbradden sits tucked against its own impressive cliffs. With only a few residents, the place is a real gem and worth a stop. The subsequent path continues around the outer, lower edge of the harbor along sheltered bays before connecting to a road, followed by marked stair steps giving way to grassland and later a bridge over a cascade. This approach proceeds to the ruins of Dunseverick Castle; its pillars and scant remains sit near the B146 road and a bathroom is on site, as well as free car park—another good starting point to cut this entire route in half. Walking west from here takes three hours to reach the Giant's Causeway.

 Fact

The church next to the first house in Portbradden is the smallest in North Ireland (and possibly the world). The little chapel welcomes visitors and is filled with religious accoutrements—a real photo opportunity. If the door is ajar, feel free to enter and snap a couple of shots.

From Dunseverick Castle, the path continues along the cliff path, affording wonderful views at the peak of Benbane Head and of the entire coastline. The path is clearly marked here and stiles indicate where walkers should pass through.

For independent adventurers wanting the perfect stroll, park your car for free at Dunseverick Castle and walk 50 meters (50 yards) down the road and wait near the bus sign (on the correct side of the road). Flag down the bus as it approaches and let the driver know you want to stop at Giant's Causeway. You can then walk from Giant's Causeway to Dunseverick Castle, meeting up with your parked car in about three hours. In the summer, buses run often; less in the off-season.

At the Giant's Causeway Visitor Centre, take the path going up toward the cliffs for the long walk, or take the lower road down to the water if you want to simply snap some photos. A minibus is available. End your day-hike with a meal at the Nook Pub and Restaurant (028 2073 2993, daily, 10:30 A.M.–8:30 P.M.) near the Giant's Causeway parking lot. Refuel with Guinness pie or baked bluecheese pasta served with a pint.

Hiking the Mourne Mountains, County Down

The 100km (60-mile) Mourne Trail connecting Newry to Strangford is unmatched. It takes trekkers through granite knolls and some of the steepest hills in the region. The area is home to twelve peaks over 610 meters (2,000 feet) including the 810-meter (2789-feet) Slieve Donard, the highest mountain in Northern Ireland.

 Essential

Guides to the Mourne Mountains are available from the tourist office in Newcastle, County Down. The best one for day hikes and combination routes is the packet called *Mourne Mountain Walks: Ten Walks on Full Colour Maps* published by the Mourne Heritage Trust (*www.mournelive.com*), a well-done site with a handy interactive map.

For day-hiking and biking trips, the Mourne Mountain chain lends itself to various excursions from the surrounding towns or villages. The medium-sized seaside town of Newcastle or quaint Bryansford puts travelers at the entry points to both the mountains and delightful Tollymore Forest Park. For cycling the Mourne Mountains, contact Mourne Cycle (028 4372 4348, *www* *.mournecycletours.com*) for daily or weekly bike rentals.

One of the easiest, quickest, and most historical walks is the out-and-back "Hare's Gap." Outlined as Map #10 in the *Mourne Mountain Walks* packet, this route is a three- to four-hour roundtrip that begins 4km (2 miles) west of Bryansford on the Trassey Road. Here, a small parking lot is available and the actual trailhead is 50 meters (50 yards) up the road through a turnstile and gate. The route is easy enough to follow, as it is a clear gravel route giving way to a smaller path working its way along the Trassey River, which is more like a stream in drier times.

To keep your bearings heading southeast up the rocky terrain toward the Mourne Wall, a stone wall runs along most of the area peaks. The crossing point at the wall is the actual "Hare's Gap," which gives way to the Brandy Pad trail continuing east, passing under the Diamond Rocks. A path to the right leads up to the 739-meter (2,425-feet) Slieve Bearnagh.

For hikers wanting a longer, more strenuous and rocky route, the Slieve Meelmore (Map #9, *Mourne Mountain Walks* packet) is a great circuit forming a loop around along the Ulster Way, Trassey River, and a good portion of the Mourne Wall.

CHAPTER 20

The Wilds
of Ireland

O scar Wilde once penned in his essay "The Broken Resolution," "Nature . . . will have clefts in the rocks where I may hide, and secret valleys in whose silence I may weep undisturbed." The Irish affinity for the great outdoors is closely linked to their art, history, and sublime natural wonders. In a land filled with hidden places and formidable landscapes, it is also a mecca of outdoor activity and adventure.

Outside in Ireland

Excursions into the wilder places of the country will give travelers a greater appreciation of the verdurous marvels around them. While an entire itinerary need not focus on one place or activity, oftentimes certain regions are more suitable to particular diversions.

Adventure in Dublin

Some fun adventures within Dublin can be had with Viking Splash Tours (01 707 6000, *www.vikingsplash.ie*), which uses replica WWII amphibious vehicles to take passengers back to bygone days when Vikings roamed and ruled.

Biking around Dublin is another way to explore the city. Travelers wanting to rent should contact Neill's Wheels (085 153 0648, *www.rentabikedublin.com*) for daily and weekly packages.

In the summer, take the DART or the local city bus to one of the various beaches within reach from Dublin. The exurb of Dún Laoghaire has a notable walking beach at Sandycove, while Dollymount and Sutton are closer to the city center. Fishing is also an option along Dublin's east coast. Peruse the Fisheries Board (*www.fishingireland.net*) site for more information and read on to learn about the best fishing spots in the country.

Ireland's National Parks

The Emerald Isle abounds in protected habitats and boasts six national parks. While walking is one of the best ways to negotiate the terrain, other activities are available within or around these wilderness areas. Especially in summer, operators advertise fishing, cycling, canoeing, and horseback riding. To find out more about each protected wilderness area, browse through the county-specific chapters in this guide.

The six national parks of Ireland include:

- **The Wicklow Mountains National Park** (*www.wicklow mountainsnationalpark.ie*) is the only national park near Dublin (besides Northern Ireland's Mourne Mountains). The heart of the park is Glendalough, where various monastic ruins can be explored, as well as an assortment of trails for day walks. The area is home to heath, peat plots, along with scenic lakes and streams.
- **The Killarney National Park** (*www.killarneynationalpark.ie*) in County Kerry is best described as rugged, mountainous, and dotted with pristine loughs. The central focal point of the park is the Muckross House and Gardens. Biking around the park, taking a boat ride to Inisfallen Island, or a jaunting

car around the nature reserve are some of the best ways to explore the park.

- **The Burren National Park** (*www.burrennationalpark.ie*) in County Clare is an unfathomable moonlike landscape holding Ireland's (and some of Europe's) most diverse plant species. Walking around the extensive limestone is the best way to get around, while cycling various backgrounds to explore the environs is also possible.

- **The Connemara National Park** (*www.connemaranationalpark.ie*) in County Galway is a fascinatingly remote and expansive conservation area filled with all the mountains, grassland, and bog that one could hope to encounter. The estate of Kylemore Abbey is a worthwhile trip after a walk around the trails. Biking around the Connemara countryside is an especially invigorating endeavor.

- **The Ballycroy National Park** (*www.ballycroynationalpark.ie*) in County Mayo is the Republic's newest, currently least visited, and one of its largest parks. Set amidst the Nephin Beg Mountains, its not all bog land. The grassy knolls are home to abounding flora in summer; bird watching and fishing day trips are available for the outdoor enthusiast.

- **The Glenveagh National Park** (*www.glenveaghnationalpark.ie*) in County Donegal is one of Ireland's most removed and spectacular wilderness preservations. Mountains, lakes, and an abundance of wildlife make it especially attractive to those exploring Ireland's northwest. Walking the well-marked trails is one way to access the remote areas where you will increase your chances of spotting red deer, golden eagles, and hare. Guided ranger walks are available from the tourist office.

Outdoor and Adventure Tour Operators

Ireland has several well-established outdoor and adventure tour operators. Most agencies offer numerous types of activities lasting one or more days. Traveling with an adventure operator is appealing for various reasons. Most often trips are accompanied by certified guides and drivers, and are geared for small groups.

Some excellent outdoor and adventure tour operators in Ireland include:

- Hidden Ireland Adventures (087 221 4002, *www.hidden irelandadventures.com*), a part of Hidden Ireland Tours, offers adventure challenges, fishing, cycling, climbing, and golfing. Interestingly, they also offer spiritual pilgrimages and genealogy tours.
- Ireland Adventures (091 443934, *www.irelandadventures .com*) has an inviting and informative website, and their superb staff offer tailor-made and customized tours mixing and matching Ireland's best outdoor activities. Whether golfing, cycling, walking, or sea angling, they seem to have it all.
- With an array of suitable adventure itineraries, Extreme Ireland (01 825 5167, *www.extremeireland.ie*) offers one- and multiday excursions throughout the Emerald Isle. The Full Moon Walks in Wicklow are quite appealing, as are their one-day mountain-biking trip from Dublin.
- If an all-inclusive and small-group adventure is what you are after, then Vagabond Tours of Ireland (1 660 7399, *www .vagabondtoursofireland.ie*) should be your pick. With top-notch guides, Vagabond will truly take you to Ireland's most hidden and remote corners.

- Offering budget and adventure tours, Shamrocker Irish Adventures (01 672 7651, *www.shamrockeradventures.com*) offers multiday excursions of various regions throughout Ireland. Check their site for last-minute specials.
- Another first-rate operator offering small group trips is Wolfhound Adventure Tours (0876 665 049, *www.wolfhoundtours.com*). The team at Wolfhound offers private trips all throughout Ireland and caters well to adventurous families. Of note are their heritage hikes and wilderness cycles.

Adventure Centers in Ireland

Certain companies operate adventure activities from their respective home bases. The Delphi Adventure Centre, operated by the Delphi Mountain Resort (095 42208, *www.delphimountainresort.com*) in Connemara, County Galway, offers inclusive adventure packages ranging from kayaking and surfing to high ropes courses and zip lines. Also in Connemara is the Killary Adventure Company (095 43 411, *www.killary.com*) offering similar adventure packages, including cycling and skiing holidays.

Closer to Dublin, the Dunmore East Adventure Centre (051 383783, *www.dunmoreadventure.com*) in County Waterford offers team-building events, as well as rock climbing, kayaking, archery, sailing, and power boating.

 Fact

Skydiving over the Emerald Isle gives you a thrilling view of Ireland's awe-inspiring landscape. For the truly adventurous, Skydive Ireland (01 414 7778, *www.skydiveireland.ie*) at the Erinagh Airfield in County Tipperary offers several packages, including tandem jumps, solo jump courses, and charity skydives.

In the north, the Donegal Adventure Centre (07198 42418, *www.donegaladventurecentre.net*) is a great place for surf lessons and to take instructor courses throughout the year. The company also has a high ropes course, cliff jump, canoeing, zip line, and trapeze. Special-priced packages are available. During the summer period, it is best to book ahead.

Horseback Riding in Ireland

As close to Dublin as Kildare or as remote as Dingle, horseback riding is an enjoyable pastime for locals and travelers alike. The equestrian pursuits available in Ireland include beach runs, cross-country and trail riding, along with beginner and intermediate lessons and camps.

 Fact

Pony riding is quite popular in Ireland. The Connemara ponies in County Galway, for example, are a world-famous breed known for their tolerance and good nature. Locals avow that the ponies once bred with Spanish horses that swam to shore from an aground galleon, giving them an uncanny strength and sturdy frame. Kids and adults alike enjoy riding these little beauties, which is easily arranged in Clifden.

Many riding centers offer inclusive package deals that can include accommodations and meals. One great resource is Equestrian Holidays Ireland (*www.ehi.ie*), which lists various operators that can tailor trips based on your experience level or regional interests. They have an informational pamphlet in most large tourist offices. Additionally, Riding Tours (*www.ridingtours.com*) has a plethora of riding trips throughout Ireland and other countries.

Their main regions of expertise are Wicklow, Dingle, Connemara, and Donegal.

Best Places to Horse Around

Ireland's horseback riding centers are based all over the country. A great concentration of riding facilities can be found around Dublin, in the central south, and in the northwest. Most establishments offer various packages depending upon experience level. Several operators are reluctant to accept children under the age of twelve for multiday trail riding.

 Alert

Accredited horseback riding companies in Ireland will be a member of the Association of Irish Riding Establishments (AIRE; 045 850 800, www.aire.ie). The website details a listing of certified businesses by county. Additionally, horseback riders are required to have proof of full accidental insurance coverage before beginning any riding exercises or excursions.

Inside Dublin, the Ashtown Riding Stables (01 838 3807) operates trots through Phoenix Park. And, near Dublin in County Wicklow, the Bel Air Hotel and Equestrian Centre (04 044 0109, www.belairhotelequestrian.com), with its luxury four-star "holiday village," is the most established riding center in Ireland.

Just west of Kinsale in County Cork, the small area of Ballinadee offers both guided pony trekking and horse riding in some of the county's most picturesque hills. Contact Ballinadee Pony Trekking and Horse Riding Farm (021 477 8152), owned and operated by Philomena and Denis O'Donoghue. They cater to both beginners and experienced riders. For race fans, the Mallow Race Track (022 50 207, www.corkracecourse.ie) off the Killarney Road has year-round competitions.

A mesmerizing ride through the Dingle Peninsula in County Kerry is an unforgettable experience. Dingle Horse Riding (066 915 2199, *www.dinglehorseriding.com*) offers one-day and six-day journeys around Dingle. Nearby, the Killarney Riding Stables (064 31 686, *www.killarney-trail-riding.com*) are situated next to the National Park and offer daily ventures to Ross Castle and Ross Island and multiday excursions along the ever-popular 160km (100-mile) Killarney Reeks Trail.

Equestrian pursuits are hugely popular in Ireland's west and northwest. In Galway, contact the Aille Cross Equestrian Center (091 841216, *www.aille-cross.com*) for a myriad of riding options. In Donegal, the friendly folks at Donegal Equestrian Holidays (071 982 9357, *www.donegalequestrianholidays.com*) in Bundoran, the Five Oaks Ranch (071 985 1030, *fiveoaksranch@eircom.net*), and Long's Horse Riding and Trekking Centre (066 915 97 23, *www.longsriding.com*) all cater to travelers of all ages searching for horseback riding holidays.

Cycling and Mountain Biking in Ireland

Cycling is a fascinating way to explore the Irish countryside. Biking entire counties is not an uncommon way to see the best of Ireland. For the less ambitious, taking a day to pedal around the sights is a sure-fire way to fully enjoy the scenery. Bike rental shops are located throughout each county, especially in the more touristy areas. Bike rental fees range from €15 to 25 per day and €80 to 100 per week.

Hiring a bike before you arrive in the country is paramount if cycling is a central component of your travel plans. This will ensure you the type, style, model, and size desired. Certain agencies, such as Eurotrek Raleigh (01 465 9659, *www.raleigh.ie*) in Dublin and Emerald Cycles (061 416983, *www.irelandrentabike.com*) in Limerick allow one-way rentals.

Undeniably, planning and arranging your own bike trip helps build the enthusiasm and knowledge necessary to carry through with such an adventure. However, various bike tour operators run professionally arranged trips that take the inconvenience out of preplanning. Easy Rider Tours (1 800 488 8332 U.S., *www .easyridertours.com*) runs affordable and fun biking adventures in the southwest, west, and northwestern counties. Bike Riders Tours (1 800 473 7040 U.S., *www.bikeriderstours.com*) offers more upscale biking adventures in Ireland and throughout the world. Finally, Biking in Ireland (1 800 257 2226 U.S., *www.bikeireland .com*) has high-quality, bargain trips run by the amiable folks at Bike Vermont.

 Essential

For cycling trips, cyclers should bring along some of their own equipment. Such accoutrements include a helmet, waterproof panniers, pedals, and cycle shoes. This will ensure a certain level of comfort to make your trip all the more enjoyable. Additionally, bring wind and rain gear, as changeable weather is a guarantee.

Best Places to Cycle and Mountain Bike

Although more hilly than other parts of Ireland, Counties Cork and Kerry offer unspoiled splendor with on- and off-road cycling potential. One- or two-day trips can be had on the 80km (50-mile) Sheep's Head Cycle Route (087 232 4984, *Bernietobin7@eircom .net*) southwest of Bantry. Or, consider the 94km (59-mile) Cork-Beara-Gúgán Barra Route, offering spectacular views of the Cork countryside. The Gougane Barra Hotel (026 47 069, *www .gouganebarrahotel.com*) in Macroom, an epicenter for great back-road cycling, has bikes for rent.

In County Kerry, contact Irish Cycle Tours (066 712 8733, *www.irishcycletours.com*) in Tralee to put together guided and self-guided excursions in the Iveragh and Dingle peninsulas, among other spots in Ireland.

If on your own in Dingle, rent bikes from Mountain Man (066 915 2400) off of Strand Street and head out 45km (28 miles) to Slea Head to view the wondrous Blasket Islands. For a leg-burner, ride from Dingle over Conor Pass to Castlegregory, a village between the Brandon and Tralee bays.

The north Cork and east Limerick area called Ballyhoura (*www.ballyhouracountry.com*) is an outdoor paradise with trail walking, paragliding, hunting excursions, and best of all, mountain biking. Contact Chris O'Callaghan at XCT1 Bike Rental (087 131 4577 or 087 203 3060, *www.xct1.com*) based in Kilfinane Village, County Limerick, to put together an amazing trail-riding adventure. If you have your own suspension bike, head to the Ballyhoura MTB Trails (063 91 300), which has light-to-demanding loops, some pressing on for over 50km (30 miles).

The northwest of Ireland, with its varied terrain and remarkable vistas, has some equally splendid biking opportunities for the resilient two-wheeled tourist. The Northwest Trail (*www .northwest-trail.com*) is a 326km (202-mile) circular route linking Counties Donegal, Sligo, and Northern Ireland. A family-friendly section of this route includes the short 55km (32-mile) route known as the Inis Eoghain Cycleway (*www.iniseoghaincycleway .com*).

 Fact

Northern Ireland has a well-developed and extensive network of outdoor pursuits and adventure available to the active traveler. One of the best places to search is on the Outdoor Northern Ireland (*www.outdoorni.com*) website. Preplan your adventure and save a tree by downloading a specific activity brochure online (*www .activitybrochuresni.com*).

Northern Ireland has a highly developed cycling infrastructure with its Sustrans and National Cycle Network (*www.sustrans.org.uk*) movement. The Faughan Valley Cycleway in Derry (*www.derryvisitor.com*), County Londonderry, is a popular network of three circular routes, each slightly over 32km (20 miles).

Additionally, the Sperrin Mountains in County Tyrone is comprised of twelve circuitous routes designed for the average cycler. Each trail is clearly marked and signposted. The 50km (31-mile) Gold Cycle Route and remote 66km (41-mile) Lough Fea Cycle Route top the rest. Information and maps are available at the Cookstown Centre Tourist Office (028 8676 6727) off of Molesworth Street. It is open during regular business hours. For more about cycling in Northern Ireland, visit Cycle NI (*www.cycleni.com*).

Watersports in Ireland

With a seaboard nearly 5,000km (3,000-miles) long, not to mention an abundance of loughs and river systems, Ireland is a natural pick for watersport enthusiasts. Watersports in Ireland include, but are not limited to, kayaking, canoeing, waterskiing, diving, surfing, windsurfing, kite boarding, and sailing.

Near Dublin, the Surfdock Centre (01 668 3945, *www.surfdock.ie*) sells gear and has a watersports school where they teach surfing and windsurfing. Their highly qualified and relaxed style of coaching is great for both beginner and intermediate aqua athletes. Courses run from June until September. Located in the Grand Canal Dockyard, their shop is open all year long, Monday–Friday, 10 A.M.–6 P.M.; until 5 P.M. on Saturday.

True to its namesake, County Waterford is a happening splish-splash spot. And, the best point to catch some sun (and wind) is Dunmore East. Composed of wonderful inlets and coves coaxing investigation, the best beach venues near Waterford Town are Counsellor's Cove and Ladies Cove. The Dunmore East Adventure

Centre (see "Adventure Centers" above) has excellent sailing, sea kayaking, and windsurfing packages.

Water-Lover's Paradise: Counties Cork and Kerry

Boasting one of Europe's best cruising grounds, blue-flag beaches, a multitude of watersports, sheer cliffs, and hundreds of bays and coves, Counties Cork and Kerry are Ireland's watersports meccas. Beach lovers should head to the littorals of Mizen Head's Barleyclove Beach and Inchydoney Beach on Clonakilty Bay, while a visit to Galley Head, Sherkin Island, and Streek Head offer enticing remoteness. The windy, yet strangely calm waters of Kinsale are a sailor's dream, while the views from Bray Head are a painter's reverie.

Various companies operating from Kinsale include:

- Oysterhaven Centre (021 477 0738, *www.oysterhaven.com*) offers windsurfing courses and adventure sailing on their 21-meter (70-foot) schooner.
- The Kinsale Outdoor Education Centre (021 477 2896, *www .kinsaleoutdoors.com*) is well respected for its sailing courses and cruises.
- Sail Ireland Charters (*www.sailireland.com/sichome.htm*) offers luxury yacht charters.
- Shearwater Cruises (023 49 610) and Sovereign Sailing (021 477 4145, *www.sovereignsailing.com*) are great for small groups interested in half- and full-day cruises.
- Sea kayaking operators include Sea Kayaking West Cork (086 309 8654, *www.seakayakingwestcork.com*), which leads guided trips in the cloistered Bantry Bay, and the attentive team at Atlantic Sea Kayaking (028 21 058, *www .atlanticseakayaking.com*), offering trips throughout Ireland.

For team building, kayaking, and canoeing, among other adventures on hand, Nathan Kingerlee Outdoor Training (086 860 4563, *www.outdoorsireland.com*) in Killorglin, County Kerry, is revered for its quality and flexible approach with affordable rates. Check the blog for specials, rates, and dates.

Scuba diving enthusiasts should contact Aquaventures (028 20 511, *www.aquaventures.ie*), which also runs whale-watching trips. The Baltimore Diving Centre (028 20 300, *www.baltimore diving.com*) is a specialist in the area. The handy Tempo Web (*www.tempoweb.com/diveireland/centres.htm*) resource is helpful to locate diving spots all over the Republic.

Surfing in Ireland

Shubees, newbies, and pros alike can find bodacious barrels along Ireland's vast shores. Ireland's best surfing spots are in Sligo and Donegal with their year-round surf spots at Easky, Strandhill, and Bundorvan. Notwithstanding, Tramore Beach in County Waterford and Rosslare Strand in County Wexford claim stellar sets and decent windsurfing. Wind- and kite-surfing aficionados, however, should head to Achill Island in County Mayo and Portnablagh in the northwest.

Contact the West Cork Surf School (086 869 5396, *www .westcorksurfing.com*), located on the Blue Flag beach of Inchydoney, near Clonakilty, for fairly priced lessons. In Donegal, Bundoran and Rossnowlagh boast the best surfing in Ireland. Contact the Bundoran Surf School (071 984 1968, *www .bundoransurfco.com*). The ambitious should head to the Turf and Surf Lodge (071 984 1091, *www.turfnsurf.ie*), which has rooms with ample amenities. Closer to Dublin, contact the Tramore Bay Surf School (051 391 297, *www.surftbay.com*), which caters to all levels and ages.

Fishing in Ireland

A popular pastime and renowned with some of the most-pristine waters in Europe, Ireland is a fisherman's delight. Freshwater lakes are filled with pike, bream, and perch. Rivers teem with salmon. Mullet, flounder, and bass abound in coastal waters, while deep-sea fishing proffers shark, skate, and dogfish.

The Shannon and Erne rivers are two of the country's most-popular fishing grounds. Bountiful loughs, such as Corrib and Maske, also have a plethora of angling operators taking tourists out daily.

Sea angling is a popular pastime in County Cork. Finding an operator who specializes in various forms of fishing, from seining to trawling, is not overly difficult. The most popular tourist towns such as Kinsale, Glengarriff, and Bantry all have angling companies with modern equipment. Deep-sea fishermen can contact Ireland Seafishing (027 70 979) in Castletownbere or the Baltimore Sea Angling Center (028 36 450, *www.wreckfish.com*).

 Fact

Fishermen should read over the Fisheries Board (*www.nrfb.ie*) and Central Fisheries Board *(www.cfb.ie)* sites that list up-to-date regulations. Explained briefly are the major rules one should adhere to: no using live fish as bait, no more than two poles, and no foul-hooked catches (a fish not caught with a hook in the mouth). Catch a big fish and they might feature your photo!

The tucked-away lakes of Lough Derg, Kilgory Lough, Doon Lough, and the 80-hectare (200-acre) Lough Graney in east County Clare offer some splendid scenery and amazing pike, trout, and coarse fishing. On site, Treacy's Service Station has a Fishing Tackle Shop (061 921 1014) on hand.

Another fisherman's mecca is Donegal, where salmon on the Owenea River near the Lough Ea are superb. The Eske Fishery in the summer months, near the Blue Stack and Tawnawully Mountains, has an excellent sea trout run. If fishing is a top-listed item on your vacation list, then contact Donegal Angling Holidays (*www.donegalanglingholidays.com*) or charter a boat with Ireland Angling Charters (*www.irishanglingcharters.ie*).

Fishing in Northern Ireland can be especially rewarding, although once enjoying the catch, prying yourself from the paradise of the Fermanagh Lakelands might prove a difficult task.

Note that fishing licenses distributed in Ireland will not suffice in Northern Ireland. Anglers should contact the Department of Culture, Arts, and Leisure (*www.dcalni.gov.uk*) for the latest information.

APPENDIX A

Film and Reading Checklist

Following are the ten must-see films and must-read books that relate to Ireland. They appear in no particular order.

Ten Must-See Films

THE WIND THAT SHAKES THE BARLEY (2006)

A film about Ireland being occupied by the British during the Irish War for Independence and two brothers joining the IRA.

ONCE (2007)

A wonderful film debut, this flick is about a busker (street musician) in Dublin who meets an immigrant flower seller. They record music together, one of which is entitled "Falling Slowly." The song won an Oscar for Best Original Song.

THE QUIET MAN (1952)

A drama starring John Wayne based on a short story from the *Saturday Evening Post*. Parts of the film were shot in Cong, County Mayo.

BLOODY SUNDAY (2002)

A made-for-TV movie that premiered at the Sundance Festival and made its way to the big screen. The film is based on the Bloody Sunday shootings in Derry, Northern Ireland.

IN BRUGES (2008)

A Golden Globe winner, *In Bruges* was written by Martin McDonagh and stars Colin Farrell and Brendan Gleeson, who play hit men sent to hide out in Bruges, Belgium. One hates the city while the other enjoys it; the two are criminals dealing with their past, the present, and each other.

IN THE NAME OF THE FATHER (1993)

Based on a true story, this film follows the life of a wrongly convicted Irishman thought to have bombed a pub in England.

THE SNAPPER (1993)

A TV movie based on the novel (1990) by Roddy Doyle of the same name, *The Snapper* is a look at the Curley family and how they become the talk of the town when their twenty-year-old daughter gets pregnant and refuses to name the father.

THE MAGDALENE SISTERS (2002)

Based on events that took place in the Magdalene Asylums, which housed "fallen women," the story follows the lives of teenage girls forced to work as inmates under oppressive conditions.

THE MOLLY MAGUIRES (1970)

This Irish-American film set in Pennsylvania depicts the true story of Irish Americans working the mines and fighting for social justice.

THE DEPARTED (2006)

The winner of four Oscars (2007), *The Departed* is another Irish-American film noted as a violent crime thriller focusing on police officers attempting to work as double agents under an Irish mob boss.

Ten Must-Read Books

AMONGST WOMEN (1990),
JOHN MCGAHERN

Considered for the Booker Prize, *Amongst Women* is a novel about a farm family domineered by a veteran of the IRA. The character of Michael Moran is feared, but he is cared for by his daughters and wife, who attempt to re-create his happiest days.

PADDY CLARKE HA HA HA (1993),
RODDY DOYLE

Following the life of a ten-year-old boy, this lovely piece of fiction won the Booker Prize in 1993. Noted for its scattered plot line, the book is still cohesive in that the events are described as a young boy might outline them.

THE LAST SEPTEMBER (1929),
ELIZABETH BOWEN

This novel depicts life at a country mansion in County Cork. The story focuses on the privileged English who enjoy their time denying that their world will soon collapse. A film based on the book was released in 1999.

ANGELA'S ASHES (1996),
FRANK MCCOURT

This memoir won a Pulitzer Prize and focuses on the story of McCourt's life as his family leaves New York for Limerick, Ireland. Following the death of his siblings, Frank's father cannot hold a job, partially due to his alcoholism, and the family must live in a decrepit house in dire straits.

TROUBLES (1970),
J. G. FARRELL

An English novelist, J. G. Farrell writes of Major Brendan Archer, who seeks the hand of the daughter of the owner of the Majestic Hotel in County Wexford. The tale focuses on the unionist's family's slow breakdown, corresponding to the state of the hotel around them.

DUBLINERS (1914),
JAMES JOYCE

A collection of short stories by the famed Joyce, *Dubliners* depicts the lives of those living in Dublin in the early part of the century. Narrators of the tales include children, adolescents, and adults. Interestingly, some of the characters later appear in the gargantuan masterpiece *Ulysses*.

STAR OF THE SEA (2004),
JOSEPH O'CONNOR

Recently published and recognized with a plethora of awards, O'Connor's novel is part historical and part mystery. Focusing on several main characters, the plot deals with a murder and the hardships that occurred on an Irish famine ship on its way to New York.

THE THIRD POLICEMAN (1967),
FLANN O'BRIEN

This book by writer Brian O'Nolan, written under the pseudonym of Flann O'Brien, was published posthumously. A nameless narrator who becomes obsessed with the works of De Selby, a regarded, yet fictitious, philosopher, tells the story. The work progresses to reveal the narrator, Divney, and Mathers and the breakdown of their relationship due to a murderous scenario and unfolding of events.

THY TEARS MIGHT CEASE (1963),
MICHAEL FARRELL

The author's only masterpiece, a life-long work, *Thy Tears Might Cease* is thought to be an autobiographical piece published under the safety net of fiction. The tale depicts the life and times of the protagonist, who grows up during Ireland's roughest political years throughout the early twentieth century.

ALL SUMMER (2003),
CLAIRE KILROY

A revealing thriller involving character Anna Hunt, the story begins with the main character waking up in a barn, holding a suitcase of cash, and having no memory of her life, but only events leading up to the robbery of a prized piece of art.

APPENDIX B

Additional Web Resources

DISCOVER IRELAND
This is the Republic of Ireland's official tourist office website, chock-full of descriptive information on things to see and do.
www.discoverireland.ie

HERITAGE IRELAND
This resource is dedicated to the historic and significant sites around the country.
www.heritageireland.ie

IRELAND HOTELS FEDERATION
Search this site to look through accommodation choices in each region of Ireland.
www.irelandhotels.com

IRELAND BLUE BOOK
This is a good reference for luxury accommodation and the finest dining.
www.irelands-blue-book.ie

GOOD FOOD IRELAND
Living up to its name, this website lists the
best eats in the entire country.
www.goodfoodireland.ie

GEORGINA CAMPBELL'S IRELAND
This fine website delves into Ireland's best dining venues
and gives thorough insight into renowned places to stay.
www.ireland-guide.com

VISIT DUBLIN
Visit Dublin is *the* resource for those spending any time in Ireland's bustling capital.
www.visitdublin.ie

DISCOVER DUBLIN
For everyone visiting the city and looking for the
best parties, pub-crawls, and all sorts of activities, peruse the various channels here.
www.discoverdublin.ie

VISIT WICKLOW
If traveling south of Dublin, this resource does a nice job in
outlining all that is going on in the "Garden of Ireland."
www.visitwicklow.ie

GLEN OF AHERLOW
Promoted in this guidebook as an off-the-beaten path
gem, the website gives an overview of all there is to do
in this special, often overlooked region of the country.
www.aherlow.com

CORK GUIDE
This site compiles a listing of events, accommodations, and sites in Ireland's most-happening southwestern city.
www.cork-guide.com

DINGLE PENINSULA
This resource is a compilation of all the up-to-the-minute activities going on in Dingle.
www.dingle-peninsula.ie

VISIT LIMERICK
This is a good portal to find out all that is going on in what is becoming a popular place to visit, especially thanks to the memoir *Angela's Ashes*.
www.visitlimerick.com

THE CONNEMARA LOOP
This resource is dedicated to helping travelers plan their trip around Ireland's most stark, beautiful regions.
www.goconnemara.com

DISCOVER NORTHERN IRELAND
This is Northern Ireland Tourist Board's official tourist resource.
www.discovernorthernireland.com

INDEX

A

B